Planets in Composite

Other books by Robert Hand

Horoscope Symbols

Planets in Transit: Life Cycles for Living

Planets in Youth: Patterns of Early Development

Robert Hand

Planets in Composite

*Analyzing
Human Relationships*

4880 Lower Valley Road, Atglen, Pennsylvania 19310

We are always looking for people to write books on new and related subjects.
If you have an idea for a book, please contact us at the address below.

Published by Schiffer Publishing Ltd.
4880 Lower Valley Road
Atglen, PA 19310
Phone: (610) 593-1777
FAX: (610) 593-2002
E-mail: Info@schifferbooks.com.
Visit our web site at: **www.schifferbooks.com**
Please write for a free catalog.
This book may be purchased from the publisher.
Please include $5.00 postage.
Try your bookstore first.

In Europe, Schiffer books are distributed by:
Bushwood Books
6 Marksbury Ave.
Kew Gardens, Surrey TW9 4JF
England
Phone: 44 (0)20 8392-8585
FAX: 44 (0)20 8392-9876
E-mail: info@bushwoodbooks.co.uk
www.bushwoodbooks.co.uk

Planets in Composite
by Robert Hand

Designed by Bob Boeberitz
Edited by Margaret E. Anderson

Printed in China.
ISBN: 978-0-914918-22-6

To create anything like this requires opportunity, encouragement, and incentive from others. I therefore dedicate this book to Frank Molinski who provided all these.

Contents

Foreword

Foreword

The origin of the composite chart is shrouded in obscurity. According to the noted German astrologer Edith Wangemann, two researchers were working on it in Germany in the 1920s. But the technique predates that time and, like a good folk song, it must be considered traditional in origin. More recently, astrologers on both sides of the Atlantic claim to have invented and/or developed the composite chart, and there is probably some truth to their claims. When the right time for an idea has come, it tends to pop up independently in various places.

Whatever its origin, the composite chart was unknown to most astrologers in England and the United States until 1974, when Samuel Weiser published my work, *The Composite Chart*, outlining basic composite structure. In the comparatively brief span of time since then, I have watched skeptical or uninterested astrologers become enthusiastic about the technique.

Just a few years earlier there was a similar growth of enthusiasm for midpoints. In the late 1960s, few American astrologers knew what midpoints were, much less used them. Now every astrology student studies them as a necessary part of their education, and most professionals are well-versed in their use. It is very likely, therefore, that composite charts will come to be as widely used as midpoints, because the composite is really a midpoint chart.

But in order for any technique to gain wide acceptance and use, there must be a definitive work on the subject, so that each astrologer will not have to do extensive research on the technique. In the case of midpoints, Reinhold Ebertin's *The Combination of Stellar Influences* was the definitive work. Now Robert Hand has produced the much-needed definitive volume on composite charts. This broad and thorough work on the subject will aid both the astrologer and the student in the delineation of an important technique.

As I leafed through the manuscript of this book, I was delighted to find that the interpretations of the various aspects and house positions reconfirmed my own experience with composites. Also there are many subtle interpretations here that had never occurred to me. I was particularly pleased to see Mr. Hand's more realistic and fruitful approach to multiple composites.

Of special interest are the example cases, which use the composite technique to unravel details of relationships that would otherwise remain hidden. Since much of astrology is concerned with personal relationships, the composite technique is necessarily an important tool. The most sophisticated synastry (chart comparison) does give the range of potentials in a relationship between two people, but the composite chart paints a clearer picture of the actual relationship. In addition, the transits and progressions to the composite chart point out the ups and downs of the relationship for as long as it lasts. Thus the composite chart is essential to any astrologer trying to understand his own personal relationships or those of his client.

I am happy that of all the astrologers I know, Robert Hand has written this book. Not just because he is a friend, but because he has a more practical and realistic understanding of astrology than almost anyone else in the field. He has brought both sense and humor to the subject, as well as the critical eye of a mathematician and statistical researcher.

Robert Hand has an enviable talent for writing with depth and expansiveness, and the result is a work that is both large and complete. I expect it will be many years before another book will add significantly to what he has written. *Planets in Composite* should prove to be an invaluable tool to the working astrologer and a classic text for the student of astrology.

John Townley

Introduction

I have found the technique of composite charts, as described in this book, to be the most reliable and descriptive new astrological technique that I have ever encountered. New astrological methods are constantly being devised and promoted by their discoverers, but no other method has given me so much new material for analysis. Many times I have taken the charts of utter strangers, and by using the composite chart, described the most intimate details of their relationship with each other. I have been able to describe not only how they get along on a day-to-day level, but also details about major events in their relationship.

In reading composite charts I have found little or none of the ambiguity that occurs with conventional techniques of synastry. Creative and positive relationships are recognized clearly and unambiguously, and so are difficult and relatively unrewarding ones. The composite allows me to see the precise nature of the difficulties in a problematic relationship and enables me to give the persons involved insightful and useful advice about possible solutions to the problems they face with each other.

To be sure, much of this material would be accessible by traditional methods, but it could not be seen with such ease and clarity. And many relationships that made little or no sense in terms of synastry have become completely clear with the composite chart. An example of such an instance is given in the case study of Fred and Mary.

The composite chart deals with relationships in a new way. The technique takes into account the fact that a relationship of any kind is not simply two (or more) people together; it is also an entity in its own right. If two people are involved with each other in some way, there are three entities—the two people and their relationship. Often in everyday experience we know of people whose being together makes no sense but who have an excellent and fulfilling relationship. Somehow, being together calls up parts of themselves that were not apparent before. These new parts really belong to the third entity, the relationship.

When I first encountered composite charts in 1972 I was not impressed. It struck me as a formal mathematical device based on a gimmick that did not reflect any kind of astrological reality. Needless to say, this was an *a priori* opinion not based on experience, which illustrates the danger of such judgments in astrology. Later I became convinced that the technique was valid and recently have been working on a theory of astrological influence which also accounts for the composite chart. This theory has suggested some of the changes I have introduced in the technique of creating multiple composites, changes that have been verified in practice. The entire theory is rather complex, but I will present it here in somewhat simplified form.

Each planet can be regarded as a directed stress or pull in the heavens. That is to say, each planet produces upon the earth a pull in the direction of the planet's zodiacal longitude. Each planet has its own kind of pull, which differs from the others in quality rather than quantity. Here I must stress that although the planets do pull on the earth literally through gravitational attraction, that is not what I am referring to. I am using "pull" as a metaphorical term here; the important point is that there is something like a pull and that it has direction.

People who are familiar with mathematics or physics will recognize that what I am describing has some resemblance to a vector. A vector is a quantity that also has a direction. The sentence, "He traveled at 60 miles per hour," is a statement of quantity alone. But "He traveled east at 60 miles per hour," introduces the factor of direction and makes the quantity a vector. Similarly, if one states that there was a pull of 90 pounds to the right, 90° from the direction of travel, that is a description of a force vector. Any quantity that acts in a certain direction is a vector. Like ordinary numbers, vectors can be added, subtracted, multiplied, or divided by each other, although the rules are rather complex. I refer the reader to any college math text for more information.

The planets act like vectors in that they set up stress patterns in the zodiac. And when the planets are in certain significant angles to each other (the aspects), which are derived by dividing the full 360° circle by small whole numbers, they set up vibrations or wave patterns in the zodiac. These vibrations establish the influence of the planets.

One can object that planets not in aspect to each other must still have influence, to which I would agree. However, it can be shown that in fact every planet is in aspect to every other planet, if we do not limit ourselves to the traditional basic aspects. It is not necessary to divide the circle just by 1, conjunction; 2, opposition; 3, trine; 4, square; 5, quintile; 6, sextile; and so forth. One can also divide the circle by 13, 23, and any other number. We do not understand how to use these aspects, yet they do exist and have significance almost certainly. All pairs of planets set up these wave patterns determined by their angular separation and influence the chart accordingly. A full description of how the waves work would be beyond the scope of this book. For our purposes, we need only establish some simple points.

The planets, like vectors, have a quantitative stress, and more important, a qualitative stress, in a certain direction. Eventually we may find the quantitative basis for these qualitative differences, but that is not important for this discussion. We can consider all planets approximately equal quantitatively, except possibly the Sun and Moon may be stronger. At any rate, we assign all the planets a value of one unit. Such vectors are called "unit vectors."

The important point here is that using the rules given in this book, the angular positions of the planets in a composite chart are the same as they would be if the planets were treated as unit vectors and added according to the rules of vector addition. This is true of multiple composites as well as two-way composites. The sum of vectors is often called a resultant. The positions of the planets in the composite chart are resultants of their positions in the natal charts. The natal chart shows how the stress factors (planets) relate to each other and produce wave patterns, which I believe are the ultimate key to understanding astrological influence. And the composite chart shows the resultants of these stresses when two (or more) people come together in a relationship.

In this discussion I have not touched on the quantitative aspects of vectors, because at this time I have no idea what their effect is. But I am certain that eventually the quantitative factor will be found to be very important.

The main point I am trying to stress is that the composite chart is not just a mathematical abstraction. It is based on principles that have important parallels in physics. I was originally taught to do multiple composites by a method that did not fit this model at all, and it did not seem to work very well. One day this older method indicated that I could not get along very well with two old friends because the twelfth house was very strongly emphasized. When I investigated, I found that the technique I had been using produced an erroneous Midheaven! From that time I began to work out the principles that I have employed in this book.

Of course, no argument from principles as employed here can be decisive in astrology, and this argument is not intended to "prove" composite charts.

We are simply not secure enough in our basic principles to do that. The only test is to try out a technique and then if necessary try to figure out why it works. I urge you to do this with composite charts.

The purpose of this book is twofold. First of all, it is a complete description of the technical aspects of creating a composite horoscope. In using this book, you should not have to consult any other source, except for ephemerides, tables of houses, and the like.

The second purpose of the book is to acquaint the reader with the methods of reading the composite horoscope. This is done in three ways. First of all, there is a complete chapter on how to read composite charts, which gives a useful order of priorities to follow in reading. Here also some technical problems are dealt with that arise only in composite charts.

Second, several case studies are given, which take the reader through the process of reading actual composite horoscopes. Each case has been selected because it exemplifies some important fact about reading composites. Various techniques that can be used with composite horoscopes, such as progressions and transits, the vertex point, and solar returns, are also discussed. Extensive descriptions are not given in all cases, because the techniques differ little from those used in natal horoscopes.

Third, the main text of the book gives extensive delineations of planets in houses and in aspect with each other. As I have stated elsewhere in this book, the meanings of the planets in aspect and in the houses are not radically different from their meanings in ordinary charts. Usually the same principles are applied to composites, although some peculiarities are worth noting. But some readers may find it difficult to make the mental leap from reading a person to reading a relationship. This is particularly likely to be a problem for students of astrology, to whom this section is especially addressed.

More experienced astrologers will find it relatively easy to follow the reasoning used in these delineations and to apply their own methods of reasoning. I encourage this, for I do not mean this book to be a gospel in any way. The delineations are only sample possibilities and cannot take into account all the individual issues that arise in every chart. The student is asked to use this book as a guide, not as a crutch. Everyone must develop techniques of analysis based on their individual experience, and no one should use my experience or anyone else's as a substitute for his or her own. In the delineations, particular stress has been laid on personal relationships such as friendships, love affairs, marriage, and the like, but with very little stretching of the imagination they can be applied to almost any kind of human relationship, profession, family, or whatever.

For reasons of simplicity in language, all of the delineations are written for relationships between two people. In fact, composites can be cast for more than two people. There is a complete section on the casting of such composites.

This technique has not been in use long enough for all possible questions about it to be answered. Even in this book are several new practices that have never been described elsewhere. Other new developments will emerge, and this process of discovery will continue. I ask that readers share their observations and discoveries with me by getting in touch with me through the publisher.

Subsequent to the first printing of this book, I found that the horoscopes for Hickman and Parker, Case Five, were based on inaccurate data. Securing accurate birth data is a problem that astrologers constantly face, and incorrect data can obviously cause confusion and discrepancies. In this edition, therefore, I have deleted the above-mentioned case study and substituted an examination of a different relationship: that between Sigmund Freud and Carl Jung.* I feel quite confident that the data used to compile their charts are accurate and come from valid sources.

Good luck with composites.

For a different treatment of the same relationship, see Michael Meyer, The Astrology of Relationship (Garden City, New York: Anchor Books, 1976), pp. 191–210.

Chapter One

Casting the Chart

The composite horoscope is created by finding the midpoint between pairs of planets and other sensitive points of the two natal horoscopes, that is, the Sun of one and the Sun of the other, the Moon of one and the Moon of the other, and so forth. The composite Sun is the midpoint of the two Suns; the composite Moon is the midpoint of the two Moons; the composite Mercury is the midpoint of the two Mercuries, and so on for all the other planets. The houses, however, are calculated in a different manner. But before discussing the construction of the chart, it is important to understand some things about midpoints.

A midpoint is a point in the zodiac equidistant from two other points, usually planets. It is believed, and extensive practice bears this out, that the midpoint combines the qualities of the two planets from which it is derived. Whole systems of astrology have been created around these points, most notably the Uranian system and Cosmobiology. Many traditionalists use them also. They have been discussed by Dane Rudhyar and Charles Jayne, to mention but two of the many who have used midpoints as well as traditional techniques with great effect. Midpoints are not new, and nothing about this technique of working with them departs radically from traditional practice.

However, the use of midpoints in the composite chart raises a problem. On a straight line there is only one midpoint between any pair of points. But on a circle, any pair of points will yield two midpoints. This is because each pair of points divides the circle into two arcs, both of which can be divided by midpoints into two equal halves. In the illustration (see Figure 1) we have a circle with two points, A and B, which gives us two arcs, AB and BA, of which AB is the shorter. Arc AB is bisected by the point P, while arc BA is bisected by the point P'. If A and B were planets, P and P' would be the two midpoints. Fortunately, P and P' are always exactly 180° from each other.

The working hypothesis upon which the composite chart is based is that P , the midpoint of the shorter arc AB, is the more powerful of the two and

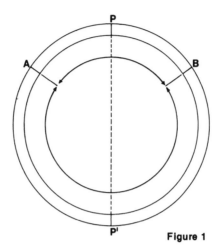

Figure 1

therefore the one used in the chart. We call the midpoint of the shorter arc the "nearer midpoint," and the other midpoint, P', the "farther midpoint." An exception to the use of the nearer midpoint occurs when the planets being combined are more than 150° apart in their shorter arc. In this case the two midpoints are nearly equal in strength, and both should be taken into consideration.

The rule that all pairs of planets have two midpoints is important in understanding the houses of the composite horoscope, which differ somewhat from the houses of an ordinary birthchart. These differences will be discussed in Chapter Four. But another phenomenon that arises from this same fact should be mentioned.

In all horoscopes, the Sun and the planets Venus and Mercury travel around together as a unit and are always in approximately the same part of the zodiac. In the composite chart, however, the combining technique that will be described here can yield such curiosities as a Sun-Mercury opposition or a Venus-Mercury opposition, which are clearly impossible in an ordinary chart. This can only happen when the Sun-Mercury-Venus clusters are nearly opposite each other in the two natal charts. In such cases I believe in using the rule formulated above for planets in near opposition; that is, use both sets of midpoints. Alternatively, one could also use only the nearer midpoint of the two Suns and then use the Mercury and Venus midpoints that are on the same side of the zodiac as the nearer Sun. At any rate, a Sun-Venus, Sun-Mercury, or Mercury-Venus opposition should be treated like a conjunction, not a true opposition. Instances of this will be referred to in the case studies.

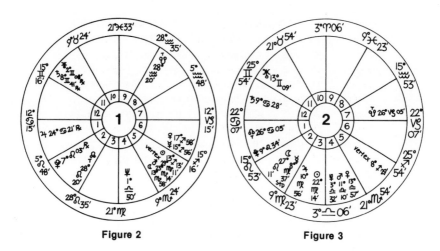

Figure 2   **Figure 3**

In Figures 2 and 3 are the charts of a man and a woman who will be discussed later on in the case studies. For the present, we will use their charts to illustrate the construction of a composite chart. Their data are not given in order to help preserve their anonymity. Proceeding step by step:

1. Take both charts and change the longitude of each chart element from the usual notation in terms of signs to notation in terms of a 360° circle; that is, count all chart positions from 0° Aries instead of from 0° of their sign. For each sign, add the number of degrees given in the table below.

Aries	0°
Taurus	30°
Gemini	60°
Cancer	90°
Leo	120°
Virgo	150°
Libra	180°
Scorpio	210°
Sagittarius	240°
Capricorn	270°
Aquarius	300°
Pisces	330°

For example, if the longitude is 22° Ⅱ 07′, we add 60° for Gemini, according to the table, which gives 82° 07′ in 360° notation. Below, tabulated in full, are the conversions of both sample charts from sign notation to 360° notation.

13

	Person 1	Person 2
Sun	13° ♐ 13' + 240° = 253°13'	22° ♍ 14' + 150° = 172°14'
Moon	13° ♏ 58' + 210° = 223°58'	27° ♌ 11' + 120° = 147°11'
Mercury	15° ♐ 56' + 240° = 255°56'	8° ♍ 37' + 150° = 158°37'
Venus	17° ♐ 58' + 240° = 257°58'	13° ♎ 57' + 180° = 193°57'
Mars	23° ♏ 14' + 210° = 233°14'	11° ♎ 10' + 180° = 191°10'
Jupiter	24° ♋ 21' + 90° = 114°21'	10° ♍ 56' + 150° = 160°56'
Saturn	8° ♊ 41' + 60° = 68°41'	9° ♋ 28' + 90° = 99°28'
Uranus	2° ♊ 08' + 60° = 62°08'	13° ♊ 09' + 60° = 73°09'
Neptune	1° ♎ 50' + 180° = 181°50'	3° ♎ 32' + 180° = 183°32'
Pluto	7° ♌ 03' + 120° = 127°03'	9° ♌ 34' + 120° = 129°34'
Nodes	28° ♌ 20' + 120° = 148°20'	26° ♋ 05' + 90° = 116°05'
M.C.	21° ♓ 33' + 330° = 351°33'	3° ♈ 06' + 0° = 3°06'
Asc.	12° ♋ 15' + 90° = 102°15'	22° ♋ 07' + 90° = 112°07'
Vertex	29° ♏ 10' + 210° = 239°11'	8° ♐ 29' + 240° = 248°29'

2. Take the longitudes for each pair of chart elements—the two Suns, the two Moons, the two Mercuries, etc.—add together, and divide by two. (Remember that you always find the midpoint of a pair of same planets, not two different ones.) Using the two Suns, we get the following:

> a. 172°14' + 253°13' = 425°27'
> b. 425°27' ÷ 2　　　= 212°43.5', rounded to 212°44'

3. Convert back to sign notation.

> 212°44' = 2° ♏ 44'

4. Check to see whether steps 2 and 3 have given you the nearer or the farther midpoint. If the result is the farther midpoint, replace the sign in step 3 with the opposite sign. In this example, dividing by two gives the correct side of the zodiac. Below is the computation for all the elements of the two charts:

	Person 1　Person 2	Composite
Sun	253°13' + 172°14' = 425°27' ÷ 2 = 212°44'	2° ♏ 44'
Moon	223°58' + 147°11' = 371°09' ÷ 2 = 185°35'	5° ♎ 35'
Mercury	255°56' + 158°37' = 414°33' ÷ 2 = 207°17'	27° ♎ 17'
Venus	257°58' + 193°57' = 451°55' ÷ 2 = 225°58'	15° ♏ 58'
Mars	233°14' + 191°10' = 424°24' ÷ 2 = 212°12'	2° ♏ 12'
Jupiter	114°21' + 160°56' = 275°17' ÷ 2 = 137°39'	17° ♌ 39'
Saturn	68°41' + 99°28' = 168°09' ÷ 2 = 84°05'	24° ♊ 05'
Uranus	62°08' + 73°09' = 135°17' ÷ 2 = 67°39'	7° ♊ 39'

Neptune	183°32' + 181°50' = 365°22' ÷ 2 = 182°41'	2° ♎ 41'
Pluto	129°34' + 127°03' = 256°37' ÷ 2 = 128°19'	8° ♌ 19'
Nodes	116°05' + 148°20' = 264°25' ÷ 2 = 132°13'	12° ♌ 13'
M.C.	3°06' + 351°33' = 354°39' ÷ 2 = 177°20'	27° ♓ 20'
Asc.	112°07' + 102°15' = 214°22' ÷ 2 = 107°11'	17° ♋ 11'
Vertex	248°29' + 239°10' = 487°39' ÷ 2 = 243°50'	3° ♐ 50'

Only the composite M.C., see table above, comes out on the wrong side of the zodiac, because the combining technique produces the farther midpoint. Its sign is reversed when converted to sign notation.

The houses are not calculated by this technique. Only the M.C. is calculated in the same manner as the planets. Although we have calculated a composite Ascendant and vertex* using this technique, we will not use it as the cusp of the first house. The midpoint of the two Ascendants, the "composite Ascendant," is entered in the final chart as an important sensitive point, but the cusp of the first house is calculated as follows:

Take the composite M.C. as the cusp of the tenth house and erect a new set of house cusps for that M.C., using the latitude of the residence where the two people live or where their relationship is taking place. You may use any house system you prefer, but the examples in this book are calculated according to the Birthplace House System of Walter Koch of Germany. The calculations were done on a Wang 500 desk calculator directly through trigonometry.

Below is an example of the method for calculating house cusps from the table of houses. The method is very similar to that used in an ordinary chart, except that we start with the longitude of the M.C., which means that the sidereal time is dispensed with altogether. If you are unused to the method, this example should help.

Our example couple took up residence at geographic latitude 41°N47' geocentric latitude 41°N36'. (I use geocentric latitude instead of geographic latitude. This distinction is described in several textbooks, and I refer the reader to them for more information.) The longitude of residence is not needed because we already have the M.C., which is 27° ♓ 20', which lies between 27° and 28° ♓ in the tables. (As mentioned above, the Koch Tables were used for these calculations.) For our example we will calculate in full

---

* *This is called the "composite vertex" as opposed to the "derived vertex." See page 24 for a discussion of the difference between the two as well as a discussion about the vertex in general.*

the first-house cusp, but the same procedure is used for the other house cusps. Remember that the composite first-house cusp is not the same as the composite Ascendant, which was derived by taking the nearer midpoint of the two natal Ascendants.

Our latitude for this calculation is geocentric 41°N36′, which lies between 41°N and 42°N in the tables. For a M.C. of 27°♓ , we have a first-house cusp of 16° ♋ 49′ at 41°N and 17° ♋ 28′ at 42°N. For the M.C. of 28° ♓ we have a first-house cusp of 17° ♋ 35′ at 41°N, and 18° ♋ 13′ at 42°N. I recommend that you arrange the work in the following manner:

M.C.	27° ♓ 00′	27° ♓ 20′	28° ♓ 00′
First House 41°N	16° ♋ 49′	?	17° ♋ 35′
First House 41°N36′		?	
First House 42°N	17° ♋ 28′	?	18° ♋ 13′

Now we must fill in the middle column by interpolation. We start by finding the first-house cusp corresponding to 27°♓20′ at 41°N. The composite M.C. 27°♓20′ is 20/60ths, or 1/3, of the way between 27°♓ and 28°♓ . In this case it would be easier to do the interpolation by means of the fraction 1/3 than by logarithms, but the logarithm calculation is shown here in case some readers are not familiar with the process. Since the composite M.C. is 20/60ths of the way between the two M.C.'s in the table, the Ascendant at 41°N will be 20/60ths of the way between 16° ♋ 49′ and 17° ♋ 35′, the separation between these two Ascendants being 46′. Using any table of diurnal logs, the set-up looks like this:

$$
\begin{array}{ll}
\log 20' = 1.85733 \\
+ \log 46' = 1.49561 \\
- \log 60' = \underline{1.38021} \\
\text{sum} \quad\ \ 1.97273
\end{array}
$$

The sum is the antilog of 15′ rounded off to the nearest minute. Therefore we add 15′ to 16° ♋ 49′ to get 17° ♋ 04′. Repeat the above procedure to get the first-house cusp corresponding to our composite M.C. for 42°N. We find that the two first-house cusps for 27°♓ and 28°♓ at 42°N are 17° ♋ 28′ and 18° ♋ 13′, which are separated by 45′ of arc. The set-up looks like this:

$$\begin{array}{rl} \log 20' = & 1.85733 \\ + \log 45' = & 1.50515 \\ - \log 60' = & \underline{1.38021} \\ \text{sum} & 1.98227 \end{array}$$

In this case the result is exactly the antilog of 15' again. We add the 15' to 17° ♋ 28' to get 17° ♋ 43'. Our worksheet should now look like this:

M.C.	27° ♓ 00'	27° ♓ 20'	28° ♓ 00'
First House 41°N	16° ♋ 49'	17° ♋ 04'	17° ♋ 35'
First House 41°N36'		?	
First House 42°N	17° ♋ 28'	17° ♋ 43'	18° ♋ 13'

We now have the first-house cusps for 27° ♓ 20' at 41°N and at 42°N, but we want the cusp for 41°N36', so we must find the Ascendant that is 36/60ths of the way between 17° ♋ 04' and 17° ♋ 43', which is an arc of 39'. The set-up will look like this:

$$\begin{array}{rl} \log 36' = & 1.60206 \\ + \log 39' = & 1.56730 \\ - \log 60' = & \underline{1.38021} \\ & 1.78915 \end{array}$$

This is the antilog of 23' to the nearest minute. We add 23' to 17° ♋ 04' to get 17° ♋ 27'. The completed worksheet should look like this:

M.C.	27° ♓ 00'	27° ♓ 20'	28° ♓ 00'
First House 41°N	16° ♋ 49'	17° ♋ 04'	17° ♋ 35'
First House 41°N36'		17° ♋ 27'	
First House 42°N	17° ♋ 28'	17° ♋ 43'	18° ♋ 13'

The final answer, 17° ♋ 27'.

The other houses may be calculated in the same manner if desired. However, the inaccuracy of most birth data makes it unnecessary to be this precise. Usually you can estimate by eye to the nearest degree on the intermediate cusps. Actually, you can get away with this for the first-house cusp also. I have outlined the complete method here for the occasions when the need for accuracy justifies the extra work. The full set of house cusps is given below so that you may check out your work. These cusps were calculated directly on a calculator, using the direct trigonometric method. Assuming that you use the Koch Tables, yours should agree within plus or minus 3' of arc. Placidus and other systems will, of course yield different results.

10.	27° ♓ 20'
11.	16° ♉ 02'
12.	20° ♊ 58'
1.	17° ♋ 27'
2.	11° ♌ 00'
3.	4° ♍ 03'
Derived vertex	3° ♐ 59'

We are now ready to enter the planets, Sun, Moon, and composite Ascendant in the chart, as shown in the illustration of the completed chart (see Figure 4). Although it did not happen in this sample chart, remember that if any of the natal pairs are more than 150° apart in their shorter arc, take both midpoints into consideration. A reading of the chart we have just cast is given in Chapter Three.

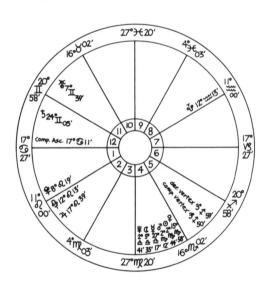

Figure 4

Multiple Composites

Although the delineations in this text are written for relationships between two people, composites can be done for more than two. This is one exceptional feature of this technique that distinguishes it from conventional techniques of chart comparison, which are limited to two persons. However, with multiple composites some problems arise that require explanation here. Incidentally, these problems, which are extremely important, have never before been written about. Although other astrologers may be aware of them, I discovered them independently while doing research on composite charts. If these problems are not taken into account, they can completely distort the reading of a multiple composite.

The problem is that in many cases, the technique for multiple composites taught by earlier authorities is incorrect and can give rise to spurious and ineffective composite points. This technique can also result in the house cusps being completely wrong, which negates all attempts at interpretation.

Previous writers and older authorities on this subject have taught the following step-by-step method:

1.   Change all longitudes to 360° measure, as described on pages 13 and 14.

2.   Add together all Suns, all Moons, all Mercuries, and so on, as for a double composite, except that here you have more than two, of course.

3.   Divide each sum by the number of charts being combined.

4.   Convert back to sign notation.

You may recall that the last step in making a double composite was to see whether you obtained the nearer or farther midpoint when you divided by two, and then to change the sign of the composite midpoint to that of the nearer midpoint. I explained that the nearer midpoint was the stronger of the two unless the two planets being combined were near opposition, in which case you use both midpoints. The figure chosen for this purpose was 150°; that is, if the planets were beyond 150°, both midpoints would be used.

You will note that in the older rules for multiple composites there is no step that is analogous to this one, and that is the source of the problem. On page 11 I mentioned that the issue of two midpoints arises because the zodiac is a circle. On a circle any two points will yield two midpoints, and these

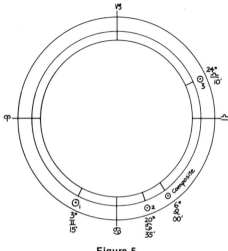

Figure 5

two midpoints are always opposite each other. This also applies to multiple composites. The older technique given above would work if the zodiac were a straight line, but since the zodiac is a circle, it is not adequate. I have chosen three hypothetical three-person composites in order to point out what the problems are and how to deal with them.

Case One (see Figure 5) is a fairly simple situation in which all three Suns are in an arc less than 180°, and 0° Aries does not lie among them. (The importance of these two conditions will become clear as we go on.) If we handle these Suns according to the old rules given above, the chart will work out fairly well. Below is the calculation:

$$3° \text{ II } 15' + 60° = 63°15'$$
$$20° \text{ ♋ } 35' + 90° = 110°35'$$
$$24° \text{ ♎ } 10' + 180° = 204°10'$$

The sum of these is 378°00', which when divided by three, the number of Suns, gives 126°00', or 6° ♌ 00'. If you examine the representation of Case One you can see that this result looks plausible. The composite Sun is contained in the same arc that encompasses the three Suns.

Now let us turn to Case Two (see Figure 6). Here we have three Suns at 27° ♈ 10', 5° II 36' and 2° ♓ 50'. If you examine the illustration of this case, a curious discrepancy emerges. The position marked "First Composite Sun" is the longitude that you would get by following the same procedure as in

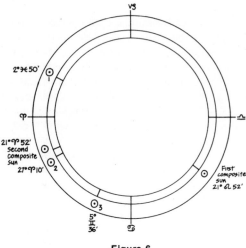

Figure 6

Case One. As you can see, it does not fall within the arc that encompasses the three natal Suns. One would expect it to fall somewhere between 2° ⅹ 50′ and 5° ♊ 36′, but instead it falls at 21° ♌ 52′.

If the zodiac were a straight line with a beginning and an end, the result would be quite plausible. But a circle does not have a beginning or an end, and calling 0° Aries the beginning of the zodiac and counting all positions from that point is just a mathematical convention. The beginning of Aries is a convenient reference point, but the zodiac actually is continuous. We must take this fact into consideration when we do a multiple composite, and this is how it is done.

Instead of taking 0° Aries for our starting point, we have to find a new point that does not fall within the arc containing the three Suns (or whatever other planets are being combined). The following steps must be taken:

1.   Examine the three natal positions and find the shortest arc in the zodiac that contains all three.
2.   Find the natal planet that comes first in that arc, and start your measurements from 0° of that sign rather than 0° Aries. In other words, express all longitudes in 360° measure from the beginning of that sign, just as if it were the beginning of the zodiac. It may help to give a rigorous formula for this process:
   a.   Convert all longitudes to 360° measure from 0° Aries in the normal manner.
   b.   Subtract the longitude of the beginning of the sign (0° for Aires, 30°

21

for Taurus, 60° for Gemini and so on) containing the first planet in the arc from all the above longitudes, adding 360° to each longitude if necessary to avoid negative angles. This gives the longitude as measured from the beginning of the sign containing the first planet.

3. Add together the longitudes that result from Step 2 and divide the result by the number of planets being combined—in this case, three.
4. Now add back the longitude of the beginning of the sign from which you have been measuring and subtract 360° if the result of the addition is more than 360°.
5. Convert back to sign notation in the normal manner.

This may seem like a complex procedure, and it is. There are other, simpler ways of doing it, but they all incorporate the same principle, that is, measuring from the sign of the first planet in the shortest arc encompassing all three (or however many) planets. I have described the method in this manner because it is the only rigorous statement of rules that works in all cases. Other methods work only in special cases and have to be worked out each time you do a multiple composite chart. The method presented here would work even for a two-person composite, although it would be needlessly complicated in that instance.

Now we will go through a calculation to demonstrate the technique. In Case Two, we examine the three Suns, at 27° ♈ 10′, 5° ♊ 36′, and 2° ♓ 50′. We find that the arc from 2° ♓ 50′ to 5° ♊ 36′ is the shortest arc that includes all three Suns. (It may help to plot out the three positions with a protractor, as was done in the illustration, but if you are experienced in visualizing the zodiac, this will not be necessary.) Therefore we will calculate all our positions from 0° Pisces instead of 0° Aries, Pisces being the first sign in the arc. Following Step 2 for each of the three positions, we get the following calculations:

$$2° ♓ 50' + 330° - 330° \quad = 2°50'$$
$$27° ♈ 10' + \ 00° + 360° - 330° = 57°10'$$
$$5° ♊ 36' + \ 60° + 360° - 330° = 95°36'$$

The sum of these comes to 155°36′, which we divide by three to obtain 51°52′. Now, following Step 4, we add 330° to obtain 381°52′ and then subtract 360°, because 381°52′ is above 360°. The result is 21° ♈ 52′. This point lies in the arc and is the true composite Sun.

Note that this point is in trine to the Sun obtained by the older method. On the drawing it is marked "Second Composite Sun." In a three-way chart, the actual composite always trines (or conjoins in some cases) the composite

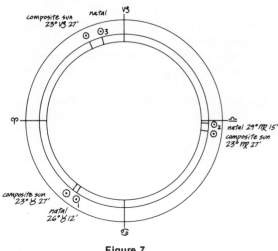

composite sun
23° ♑ 27'

natal ♑

⊙ ⊙♄

♈

⊙♃ ♎ natal 29° ♍ 15'
⊙ composite sun
23° ♍ 27'

composite sun
23° ♉ 27'

⊙ ⊙

natal
26° ♉ 12'

♋

Figure 7

position obtained by the older method, just as in a two-way chart the farther midpoint of two planets is opposite the nearer. By the same token, in a four-way chart the correct composite point will be in square, opposition, or conjunction to the one created by the old technique; in a five-way chart it will be in quintile, biquintile, or conjunction; and so forth.

This gives rise to another problem, which is illustrated by Case Three (see Figure 7). Here we have three natal Suns at 26° ♉ 12', 29° ♍ 15', and 14° ♑ 55'. In Case Two, the shortest arc that contains all three planets is obvious. But in Case Three, while one of the three possible arcs is shorter than the other two, it is not much shorter. This presents a problem much like that in the two-way composite in which two planets are in near opposition. Here, instead of an opposition, we have a wide grand trine among the three Suns. The solution is similar.

Applying the rigorous rules given above, we find that the composite Sun is at 23° ♍ 27'. (Actually, in this case the older technique would have worked also. It is only when the vernal equinox lies in the shortest arc that there is trouble with the old technique.) However, since the arcs separating the three Suns are so close to being a grand trine, the other points in the trine must also be taken into consideration. Thus, just as in some two-person composites we get two Suns (or whatever), in a three-person composite we can get three Suns in grand trine. If this were to happen with a Midheaven, you could conceivably get three sets of cusps. Experience shows, however, that the point that lies in the shortest arc is the strongest, even though the others should be considered.

Fortunately, as the number of points being combined in a composite chart goes up, the probability of encountering this problem goes down. In a four-person composite, the four points would have to be in a grand cross; in a five-person composite, in grand quintile; and so forth.

This problem does, however, put a practical upper limit on the number of people that can be combined in a single composite, totally aside from the complexity of the mathematics involved. I would estimate this number to be about ten, but that is only an estimate. As more people are combined in a composite chart, it becomes increasingly difficult to determine the shortest arc, so the rules given above become harder and harder to apply. This is not likely to be a severe problem in practical use. Ninety percent of all composite charts are two-way, and most of the rest are three-way.

The Vertex and the Composite Chart

In the charts covered in the case studies you will notice a sensitive point called the vertex. While the delineations in the text do not describe this point, I have nevertheless found it to be significant in the study of composite charts and wish to mention it here.

Although the vertex is obviously important, I do not yet have enough experience with it to give extensive delineations for its aspects in the way I have for the other points of the horoscope. However, the position of the vertex is given in the case studies in this book, and references are made to it whenever it is important to the discussion.

The vertex, originally discovered by the late L. Edward Johndro, one of America's leading technical astrologers, has been very strongly advocated by Charles Jayne of New York. I first encountered it through several of his students. According to Jayne and others, the vertex means "fateful" or "karmic" encounters. By this is meant encounters with either persons or circumstances over which the native seems to have no conscious control, encounters that seem to be fated. Usually such encounters have the effect of changing the native's life and altering its course. Relationships that have strong vertex ties have the strongest effect on the lives of those involved.

The encounters indicated by the vertex are not necessarily negative. They are simply important and have a quality of portentousness. I have found that the house occupied by the vertex, usually the fifth through eighth, identifies the sphere of experience that will be most significant for the native in terms of his or her overall destiny. Planets aspecting the vertex, most powerfully by the conjunction or opposition, indicate the kinds of energies that will influence the native's destiny. In my own chart, Uranus opposes my vertex, and I am an astrologer, astrology being ruled by Uranus.

John Townley, the author of another work on composite charts, strongly advocates the use of the vertex in composite charts, and I have to concur.

As with the composite first-house cusp and the composite Ascendant, there are two possible vertices in a composite chart. The first of these is the actual nearer midpoint (or meanpoint in the case of multiple composites) of the two natal vertices. This I call the "composite vertex" by analogy with the composite Ascendant. The second vertex is derived from the composite M.C. for the latitude at which the couple resides. This I call the "derived vertex" to denote that it is derived from the composite M.C. Both of these points are given in the case studies.

But what is the vertex, astronomically speaking, and how is it calculated? The vertex is the degree of the zodiac that is exactly due west of the native at the time and place of birth. Technically it is the intersection of the great circles of the ecliptic and the prime vertical in the west at the time and place of birth. There is also a point called the "anti-vertex" in the east, which is exactly opposite the vertex in the zodiac.

Here are the rules for calculating the vertex. If you can calculate an Ascendant, you can calculate a vertex.

1.   Subtract the geocentric latitude of the birthplace from 90°. This gives the co-latitude of the birthplace.
2.   Enter a table of houses or Ascendants, using the fourth-house cusp exactly as if it were a M.C., and calculate the Ascendant that corresponds to it for the co-latitude as if it were an ordinary latitude. The resulting "Ascendant" is the vertex. In other words, the vertex is calculated as if it were the Ascendant of the fourth-house cusp at the co-latitude of birth.

That is all there is to it. I think you will find that the extra work is more than justified by the results, especially when you discover that it will help you trace your way through the intricacies of a person's relationships.

Additional Techniques

A composite chart is not limited to the analysis of initial potentials in a relationship. The most common use of a composite chart is as a kind of natal chart, that is, a static chart describing the beginning of the relationship. But one can do almost everything with a composite chart that one can do with a conventional chart. It can be progressed and transited, and there is even a technique for doing solar returns based on the composite chart.

Transits can be made to the composite chart by the same method as is used for a conventional chart. The only limitation, which I suspect but do not know for sure, is that one should not do very much midpoint work with a composite chart because the planets in the composite chart are already midpoints. In other words, it would be taking transits to midpoints of midpoints. However, in the work of the Uranian school of Alfred Witte, there is precedent for using midpoints of midpoints, and they do so quite often. In my own work there is also some indication that you can take transits to midpoints in the composite chart, but I have not yet reached a firm conclusion on this point.

Progressions or secondary directions to a composite chart are done simply by calculating the progressed chart of each person involved in the relationship and then making a composite chart of the two progressed charts. The technique is the same as that for doing a composite of natal charts. Preliminary research suggests that this works quite well, and an example is given in the case study of Will and Sylvia in Chapter Three.

By the same token, one can also use solar arc directions in a composite chart simply by subtracting the natal composite Sun from the progressed composite Sun and adding that arc to all the natal composite planets in the usual manner. I have not yet had much experience with this technique, but everything suggests that it ought to work.

For those who use tertiary directions, I would suggest that you try composites of tertiary charts as well. Again, the technique would not differ from that for combining natal charts.

I have had extensive experience with solar and lunar returns in natal charts, but I have not yet arrived at any firm conclusions about them. I have not found any return charts to be very reliable, whether cast in the sidereal or the tropical zodiac. However, for those who wish to experiment, the technique is simply to cast a chart for the return of the Sun or Moon to its position in the natal composite chart. One can do this either in the tropical or sidereal zodiac. But it is necessary to calculate the composite Sun to the nearest second of arc. Because of my current uncertainty about return charts, I have not given any examples in the case studies.

Other techniques have occurred to those of us who use composite charts, but none of us has had much experience with them. More research is in order. Here is an example:

In checking out the significance of an event in a person's life, make a composite of the transit chart and the natal chart. This chart should give a very good idea of the person's relationship to the event. I have not done this extensively because conventional transit techniques are quite satisfactory in my work, but it may be worthwhile to check this out.

Actually, two or more charts of any kind may be combined by this technique if one wishes to examine the relationship between the entities signified by the charts. John Townley, in his book on composite charts, gives an example of combining the chart of John Lindsay with the chart of New York City. I have done very little with such charts because of the dubious nature of most mundane horoscopes.

The composite chart provides an almost unlimited field of research. I invite anyone who is interested to try out these techniques and share their results with the rest of the astrological community.

Text and Calculations by Computer

The original impetus for writing this book came from the need to produce a superior text dealing with relationships for use in a computer horoscope. I felt that the composite technique was superior to the traditional techniques of synastry and therefore recommended that this be the basis of the computer chart. The delineations in this book of the house positions of the planets and their aspects are also used in Para Research's computer text, the *Astral Composite*.

The *Astral Composite* offers you complete calculations for any two-person composite—that is, both natal charts and the composite chart. It also lists all the house positions of the planets and their aspects to each other. In addition there is a complete print-out of all the text in the book that pertains to your composite chart. This will be of considerable help if you are uncertain about the mechanics of casting and reading a horoscope. You are also assured of complete mathematical accuracy.

Having everything that pertains to your own chart in a separate booklet enables you to easily make notes and mark significant passages. And the *Astral Composite* is also good for people who want to know what astrology can tell them about their relationships, but who are not currently interested in learning the technique of casting charts.

All computer horoscopes, including the *Astral Composite,* as well as textbooks of delineations such as this one, have the limitations of not being able to synthesize the chart as a whole. They give you a good idea of the usefulness of astrology, but they should not be employed in an extremely critical situation. In such cases the personal insight and experience of an astrologer will prove more effective.

I recommend the *Astral Composite* as a good text for encountering astrology. However, if you have a serious relationship problem, you should consult a competent astrologer or other counselor.

Below is a sample coupon for ordering the *Astral Composite.* You can also order the computer calculations without the text, if you wish. There are additional coupons in the back of the book.

Para Research, Inc., Department PC, 85 Eastern Ave. Gloucester, MA 01930

☐ I enclose $23.50 for the composite horoscope
   offered in *Planets in Composite.*
☐ I enclose $6.50 for the computer calculations alone.

Sent to: _____

Address _____

City _____ State _____ Zip _____

My Birth Data   Birth Data # 2

Date: Mo.____Day____Yr.____   Date: Mo.____Day____Yr.____

Place: _____   Place: _____

Time: _____AM/PM   Time: _____AM/PM

Chapter Two

Reading the Chart

Reading a composite horoscope will not be very difficult for anyone who has mastered the art of reading a conventional natal chart. The only real difference you may have to adjust to is that you are working with a relationship rather than an individual. Also, composite charts have technical peculiarities that have to be dealt with in reading the chart. We will handle these first and then set down some rules for reading these charts.

In reading this book you may be struck by the fact that there are no references to the signs of the zodiac. In this book there are no delineations of the rising sign in the composite chart or the planets in the signs, and no use is made of the signs to indicate house rulerships. This is not an oversight. Earlier astrologers using this technique have felt that in the composite chart the signs were not real signs, that the zodiac in this case is an abstraction that serves only to measure the positions of the planets. In truth, this matter has not really been settled. The signs may have the same importance in composites as they do in other charts. But I have not arrived at a firm conclusion through my own experience, and neither has anyone else. Therefore I leave this matter to you to decide from your own experience.

It would be rather unwise to give delineations of a component in the chart, namely the signs of the zodiac, whose effect on the reading is unknown.* In any case, it can be stated that readings of the composite chart without the signs are reasonably complete for psychological delineation. In forecasting events, however, it may be necessary to restore the signs to their normal place. One result of not using the signs for this technique is that everything in this book can be applied in either the tropical or sidereal zodiac without any difficulty. But in conclusion I must repeat that I do not yet have a firm opinion on the use of signs in composite charts.

Many recent experiences suggest that the signs upon the Ascendant and containing the Sun and Moon are important. The signs have exactly the influence one would expect. The use of signs in the composite chart seems to be identical with their use in the natal chart.

With regard to the outer planets some facts should be noted. The house positions of the outer planets—Saturn, Uranus, Neptune, and Pluto—are as important as those of the inner planets in determining the nature of a personal relationship. However, it is questionable whether the aspects of the outer planets have much effect in an individual chart, because they are the same for all combinations of certain age groups. Probably the outer planet aspects signify the way in which whole generations interact.

It is my opinion that these aspects should be taken as important only if one of the pair of planets is within orb of a conjunction to the Ascendant, midheaven, Descendant, or imum coeli, the four angles of the composite chart. The delineations are written with the understanding that at least one of the pair of planets involved is so placed.

You will also notice that the lists of aspects between Uranus, Neptune, and Pluto are not complete. There are no delineations for the Uranus-Neptune conjunction; for the Uranus-Pluto conjunction, trine, or opposition, or for any of the aspects of Neptune and Pluto. Either the aspect will never occur in the composite chart of any living person, or, like the sextile of Neptune and Pluto, it is found in the composite charts of almost all persons now living, except the elderly. In the first case we have no data on the effects, and in the second, it has been impossible to sort out the effects of the particular aspect from the effects of the other aspects, because it is always there.

Another peculiarity of composite charts arises from the 150⁰ rule, which states that if planets in the two natal charts are more than 150⁰ apart, you should use both midpoints. This rule creates a perpetual opposition between a pair of Suns or Saturns or whatever. In the case of Moon's nodes in a natal chart, of course, this kind of perpetual opposition has a precedent. And as with the nodes, three different aspect situations can arise whenever both midpoints are used. Here is what we suggest in each case:

1. If a planet is conjunct a nearer or farther midpoint, simply treat the aspect as a conjunction.
2. If a planet is trine one midpoint and sextile the other, blend the interpretations of the trine and the sextile, which are not that different.
3. If a planet is square both midpoints, treat it like an ordinary square. Nothing else need be done.

Because of the 150⁰ rule, you can also have two complete sets of house cusps for the composite chart, if the two natal M.C.'s are more than 150⁰ apart. In this case, the nearer M.C. cusps seem to take precedence, while the farther

M.C. cusps are used for supplementary information. The case study of William Hickman and Marion Parker illustrates this situation.

The other principal peculiarity of composite charts is that they always refer to more than one person. In this book I have tried to aid the student in making the mental changeover from individual to relationship by giving sample delineations for all the house positions and aspects of the planets. As in any text, none of these delineations is a complete exploration of the possibilities inherent in any planetary placement. It is impossible in a single text to take into account all contingencies that may modify the reading of an aspect or house placement. For this reason, as I stated earlier, I encourage you to check these readings with your own experience.

One final note before taking on the problem of reading a composite chart. You may wonder about the role of the minor aspects in a composite chart. The answer seems to be that they have the same importance as in a conventional natal chart. But at this time I do not understand them well enough to write much about them. Hopefully, future editions of this work will have additional chapters on the quincunx, semisquare, sesquiquadrate, and quintile aspects. I feel that the quintile is especially important in sexual relationships, but it is not yet understood well enough to write about. Again, share your discoveries with me.

I have found that the following order is useful for reading the composite chart. This procedure is followed, more or less, in the sample readings, but since each reading highlights certain facets of the composite chart, only the first case study of Will and Sylvia follows all the steps completely. To do this in each case would have been too tedious. Nevertheless, I strongly recommend that you follow these steps at least initially, until the patterns inherent in the chart become clear to you upon first inspection. The steps are as follows:

1. Before you examine the composite chart, evaluate the two natal charts for their inherent capacity to have relationships. See what the individual seems to want in a relationship and the kind of person he or she is attracted to.
2. Check the composite chart for any strong house emphasis, that is, a house with four or more planets in it.
3. Check the houses of composite Sun and Moon.
4. Check the aspects to composite Sun and Moon.
5. Check the house positions and aspects to Venus and Mars.
6. Check the aspects involving planets near the four angular house cusps.
7. See what is happening in the first, fifth, seventh, and eleventh houses,

the principal houses of relationships.

8. Check the house position and aspects of Saturn.

9. Check whatever is left over.

Now we will go through each step thoroughly.

Step 1. Examine the natal charts. Relationships are very strange entities, and the real reasons for a particular relationship may be quite different from what you would expect. The desire for love and happiness may be completely superseded by the desire for security, wealth, or status. And some relationships exist solely because two people fulfill a need in each other that is quite separate from love or happiness. It is safe to say that even the best relationships are held together in part by something of this kind. You must recognize that every relationship fills some need at the time and in the circumstances when it happens, however perverse or destructive it may seem to others. At times, people even seem to need painful relationships, and at such times they will pass up an opportunity for a really beautiful and loving relationship, simply because it does not fill their need at the moment.

The needs of the moment as well as both individuals' general needs throughout life can be determined only by checking the structure of the natal charts and examining the transits and progressions to them. Therefore, in order to make the best use of composite charts, you must have a thorough understanding of natal charts. As a technique for evaluating relationships, the composite chart stands alone quite well. But you will encounter many relationships that don't seem to make sense in terms of this or any other technique unless you check the natal charts. This is the most difficult part of examining a relationship and could very well be the subject of a book in itself. All I can do here is suggest ways to use the natal charts to see if a relationship is appropriate to the people involved at the time.

First, you must find out from the couple what type of relationship they have. That will determine which houses in the natal chart must be examined most closely. For love and/or marital relationships, check the signs on the cusps of the fifth and seventh houses as well as the aspects, the rulers of those houses, and the planets contained in them. These all help to describe the kind of person whom the native is likely to be attracted to and the kind of relationship they will have.

In sexual relationships, another very important factor is the condition of the planets that are opposite in sex from the native. For men, these are Moon, Venus, and Neptune; for women, Sun and Mars in particular, and there is some evidence that Uranus may be important in forming a woman's mental image of men.

Some readers may be surprised to see Neptune included as a feminine planet. I believe that Neptune is completely misnamed; everything about its symbolism is feminine rather than masculine—darkness, moistness, the association with unconsciousness, subjectivity, and vagueness. (In this regard I would prefer to classify planets as *yin* and *yang*, according to the old Taoist view of the two world principles, rather than male and female, which are only aspects of *yin* and *yang*, not the totality. In this classification Neptune is one of the *yin* planets, along with Moon and Venus.)

The planets of opposite polarity from the person's sex signify the ideal mental image of the opposite sex that one forms. This image, in turn, determines the kind of person that the native seeks for sexual relationships. Sometimes men with Moon-Pluto aspects, for example, will form relationships with women who have Sun-Pluto aspects, or men with Venus-Saturn afflictions will be attracted to women with Mars-Saturn afflictions, and so forth. Also sometimes the polarity will reverse and, for example, Mars-Saturn men will attract Venus-Saturn women. This is true regardless of the aspects that are formed when one chart is superimposed on the other, as in synastry. Unfortunately, the details of this approach are too complex to go into in this text, but it is covered in other books that deal with relationships from a more traditional point of view.

The houses and rulerships to check for other types of relationships are as follows. Business relationships are described by planets in and ruling the seventh, second, sixth, and tenth houses. Friendships are described by planets in and ruling the eleventh and fifth houses. Although the eleventh is traditionally the house of friendships, the fifth house describes the native's needs for self-expression and his or her ability to express love. It should not be overlooked in friendships any more than in love affairs.

Step 2. Examine the composite chart for strong house emphasis. Very often a composite chart will have four or more planets in one house. This tells you that the issues associated with the house are very important in this relationship. To get some idea of these issues, read the general house delineations in the text, which describe the overall significance of each house independently of the planets. In determining the basic thrust of a relationship, a house that has many planets in it usually takes precedence over the houses containing Sun and Moon.

Step 3. Examine the houses of composite Sun and Moon. If there are no houses emphasized by clusters of planets, the houses of Sun and Moon, in that order of significance, describe the most important issues that will arise in the relationship. In a personal relationship, the best houses to be emphasized by the Sun, Moon, or strong planetary clusterings are the first, fifth, seventh, and eleventh. After these come the third and ninth houses, which are not specifically related to the formation of relationships, but help to keep vital communication alive. It is good to have the fourth house emphasized in a relationship such as marriage, in which a couple must share their most intimate personal lives and perhaps property. The second house is not especially significant for personal relationships, but it has meaning for professional associations, as does the tenth house. The eighth house is not necessarily difficult, but it often signifies a very fateful relationship. The least desirable houses for a personal relationship are the sixth and the twelfth, but even these can have quite positive effects if the aspects involved with them are good.

Step 4. Check the aspects of composite Sun and Moon. The house emphasis given by the placement of Sun, Moon, or largest cluster of planets describes only the most important issues of the relationship. The aspects to Sun and Moon begin to describe how the couple will deal with those issues. Very often these aspects can make or break a relationship. However, I must repeat that if they choose to, a couple can deal with any energy that is appropriate to their relationship needs as described by their natal charts.

Step 5. Check the house positions of and aspects to Venus and Mars. The energies of Venus and Mars are most relevant to sexual relationships, but the success of any kind of relationship depends on the partners' ability to complement each other, so Venus and Mars are always important. In a sexual relationship, aspects between Venus and Mars, Sun and Venus, or Moon and Venus are ideal.

Step 6. Check planets near the four angles of the chart and their aspects. These can be extremely important in determining the quality of a relationship as well as finding whether or not the relationship will fulfill the couple's expectations. Although this is the sixth step, it is still very important; each of the first six steps is very critical.

Step 7. Check the first, fifth, seventh, and eleventh houses. In ordinary charts the first house is not a house of relationship, but in a composite it is very important to understanding the relationship. Even if these houses have not been emphasized by Sun, Moon, or a cluster of planets, they are always important in a relationship. If there are severe afflictions involving planets in any of these houses, this can signify serious problems in a relationship.

Step 8. Check the house position and aspects of Saturn. This planet is particularly critical because it can tell so much about the strengths and weaknesses of a relationship.

Step 9. Deal with whatever is left over. That may be quite a bit, so this is not a trivial step. But it is impossible to reduce the rest of the reading to a step-by-step procedure, which raises a point about this whole description. An experienced astrologer knows that there is no set pattern to reading a chart, that each chart requires a special approach. Nevertheless, some kind of schema is very helpful to the student, and that is why I have given one. But do not hesitate to abandon this order of procedure if the chart seems to require a different approach. Astrology is an art that requires tremendous flexibility, so do not become a slave to this or any other routine. Strive to develop flexibility in your readings as soon as possible, whether they are composite charts or any other kind.

Chapter Three
Case Studies

Case One: Will and Sylvia

This is a case study of two people whose names have been changed for the sake of privacy. For the same reason, although there are full charts, no data are given. In this study we will go through all the steps outlined in Chapter Two so that the student will get a better idea of how this process works. This case study is the most thorough. The others emphasize particular aspects of chart reading.

Will and Sylvia were acquainted from childhood, having grown up within a few blocks of each other. But their relationship did not begin until they both were in college. They were married and had one child, a girl. After six years of marriage, they separated and one year later obtained a divorce. While no longer intimate in any way, they remain good friends, having completely gotten over any resentments that might have resulted from the divorce. Their charts were presented as examples in the section on calculating composite charts for two people. Their charts and the composite are given again here for convenient reference.

First, let us look at the natal charts (Step 1) and see what they suggest for marriage. Taking Will's chart first, we find that he has Saturn as the ruler of an empty seventh house. Saturn ruling the seventh house indicates that in marriage he sought either someone to act as a parent to him or someone to whom he could act as a parent. This tendency usually results in a marriage to someone older, a late marriage to someone younger, or marriage to someone with strong Saturn symbolism—such as a strong Capricorn—or with a strong and active Saturn. In itself this is not particularly bad; it is simply a factor to be observed. Actually it is quite common and can have a very stabilizing effect on a relationship.

However, checking further, we find that Saturn is in the eleventh house opposition Sun in the fifth. Since the fifth is the house of love relationships, this is not a very positive indication of easy success in love and marriage.

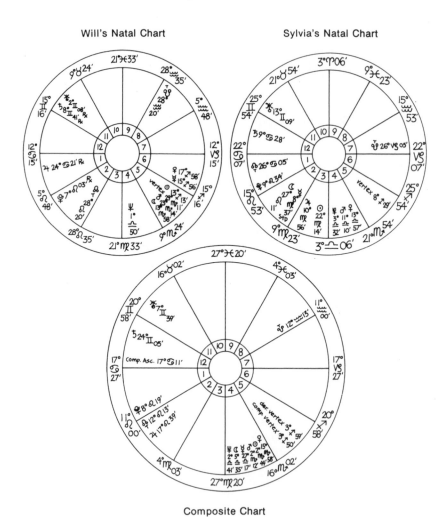

Will's Natal Chart

Sylvia's Natal Chart

Composite Chart

Will has said on a number of occasions that he probably married Sylvia because she was the first woman who paid any attention to him, and he despaired of ever finding another. However, this symbolism also suggests that he is likely to feel, consciously or unconsciously, that an intimate one-to-one relationship (seventh house) would stifle his self-expression (fifth house). Also, he has a Sagittarian Sun and Venus, both of which are likely to produce restlessness in close relationships. Because he has Cancer rising, which denotes a strong domestic streak, he kept his Sagittarian restlessness well hidden.

When we check out the fifth house, we find that it is a very strong house in the chart, containing not only Sun, but also Moon, which is the ruler of his Cancer Ascendant, Mars, and the vertex point. I have already discussed the afflicted Sun, so let us see what these other indications tell us about his relationships.

Moon, the Ascendant ruler, in the fifth house in Scorpio indicates a very strong need for intense self-expression through feelings and emotions. This means that Will's difficulty in forming love relationships, as indicated by the afflicted Sun in the fifth, is especially troublesome to him, because he has a strong need for emotional relationships. Moon here also indicates that he is attracted to women in whom the Cancer symbolism is strong or who have a strong Moon. Mars in this house is trine Jupiter in the first, which will help to minimize the effects of the Sun-Saturn opposition. This combination attracts him to rather strong women who express their strength in a positive, stabilizing, and even protective manner. The trine from Jupiter indicates that he should avoid the Saturnine relationships that activate the opposition and instead move toward Mars-Jupiter relationships, which would have a much better chance of working out. Cancer or Moon should also be strong, either in the composite or in the other person.

Turning to Sylvia's chart, we discover that she too has Saturn ruling an empty seventh house. Her fifth house is also empty except for the vertex point, so we must turn to the rulers of the fifth and seventh for indications about her relationships.

In Sylvia's chart, Saturn, the seventh-house ruler, is in the twelfth house sextile Mercury and Jupiter, but square Venus and Mars. This symbolism is similar to Will's. The sextile to Mercury indicates that she is attracted to intelligent and verbal men as partners or to Geminis and others in whom the Mercury symbolism is strong. The sextile to Jupiter indicates that she might also be attracted to Jupiter types like Will, with his first-house Jupiter and Sun conjunct Mercury, conjunct Venus in Sagittarius.

But the square of Saturn to the Venus-Mars conjunction in the fourth bodes trouble, indicating a strong sexual drive that is repressed by the twelfth-house Saturn. In this house, Saturn often indicates a lack of confidence. With a Venus-Mars conjunction, she could hardly be described as a cold person, but there is likely to be some problem with the free release of sexual energy.

Pluto, the fifth-house ruler, is well aspected, being sextile to the Mars-Venus conjunction. Pluto thus placed denotes a need for emotionally intense relationships, possibly with someone in whom the Pluto or Scorpio symbolism is strong (Will's Scorpio Moon). In fact, both of them have a very strong Scorpio-Pluto symbolism in their relationship picture, which should be a sign of compatibility.

Also notice in Sylvia's chart a close trine of Venus and Uranus enclosing all the planets in the chart. This cannot help but be significant. One might call it her counterpart to his Sagittarian Venus, the restlessness that comes when a relationship becomes routine.

How well does each one fit into the pattern of the other's natal chart? I have already mentioned several ways in which they do. Will is a Jupiter-dominant person with a strong Saturn aspect, and Sylvia has Jupiter sextiling her Saturn ruling the seventh house. With the Pluto-ruled fifth house, she would be attracted to a person with strong Scorpio or Pluto symbolism. Will has a fifth-house Moon in Scorpio. Unfortunately Sylvia has the strong affliction from Saturn, her seventh-house ruler, to the Venus-Mars conjunction. This conjunction is trine Uranus, which suggests that her sexual expression could be more free outside of marriage.

We find that the Saturn symbolism in Will's relationships is not reinforced by Sylvia's chart. Aside from Saturn ruling her relationships, Sylvia is not an especially Saturnine person; several other planets are equally strong. Also she does not reflect completely the symbolism of his Scorpio fifth house. Being a Cancer Ascendant, however, she does fit the symbolism of his fifth-house Moon. Sylvia does not have a great deal of either Mars or Jupiter symbolism. All these planets are active in her chart, but they are about equal in strength, so no single planet stands out.

Was the relationship itself especially Saturnine? Was there an age gap, or did the marriage occur quite late in their lives? The answer is no on both counts. She was twenty and he was twenty-two when they married. Therefore, the Saturn symbolism of their Capricorn seventh houses was not being fulfilled, which indicates that the relationship was not entirely appropriate. This fact is not a very strong indication by itself, but when we add it to the other information from the two natal charts, we can see that it fits into the overall pattern of difficulty.

At this point we have learned two things from the natal charts. First, Sylvia's chart describes Will better than Will's describes Sylvia. Second, the fact that both of them have Saturn as their seventh-house ruler suggests that both were looking for the same kind of partner in a relationship, but not each other. These points, while not final by any means, are a preliminary indication that this relationship could have problems.

What we must keep in mind about this rather sketchy analysis is that it has nothing to do with the way two charts contact each other as in conventional synastry. The initial phases of the description come entirely from deductions made from the two natal charts taken by themselves.

Before we turn to the composite chart, I would like to point out one thing about the chart contacts. Note that Sylvia's Uranus is exactly opposite Will's Sun, and that her Venus is sextile his Sun. Outside of the instability that characterizes any relationship with severe problems, there was almost nothing Uranian about this relationship in and of itself. Nor was it short-lived, unless you call ten years of courtship and marriage a short relationship!

Step 2 tells us to look at the composite chart for any strong house emphasis. In this chart there are five planets solidly in the fourth house, with a sixth, Venus, on the fourth-house side of the fifth-house cusp. Both Sun and Moon are in the fourth house.

A strong fourth house, such as this, denotes two people who have a strong sense of a common past or origin. They are very likely to own property together and to set up housekeeping. All of this is true for Will and Sylvia. They grew up within a half mile of each other and had known each other since he was nine years old and she was seven. He quite literally married the "girl next door," and they promptly settled down in his mother's house, a gigantic, rambling old farmhouse. Later, they built their own house within sight of her parents' home.

Remember that Will is a Sagittarian with Jupiter rising. Even with Cancer on the Ascendant, one would expect him to move around more than that. They moved away from their old neighborhood when he went to graduate school, but immediately afterward they returned to it. Only after their marriage broke up did they move away from their home town. Will now travels thousands of miles a month, true to his Sagittarian nature, and it is likely that he will continue to travel for a long time.

Since we have already dealt with the houses of Sun and Moon (Step 3), let us turn to their aspects (Step 4). Composite Sun is conjunct Mars, an indication that ego conflicts could run high between them. In any relationship, no matter how good, there is anger and resentment, but especially in one with a Sun-Mars conjunction. If Will and Sylvia found it difficult to express these feelings, they would be in trouble. Unfortunately,

Saturn is in the twelfth house, which implies that they would try to keep tension down by not expressing their real feelings. Thus, tension would build up to a dangerous level. In fact, this is what happened in this relationship. Neither person was able to say what was on his or her mind until the internal pressure was unbearable, and then it would come out in a virtual explosion. The Sun-Mars conjunction makes it very likely that they would irritate each other quite a bit. Except for this conjunction, Sun receives no other close aspects.

Composite Moon is a bit more active, having three major aspects—a trine to Uranus, a sextile to Pluto, and a conjunction with Neptune. The trine indicates that this relationship will expose both persons to new and stimulating experiences. Although the trine is not as harsh as the square and opposition, the couple must be flexible with each other in order to derive maximum benefit from its effects. They must avoid trying to force the relationship into set patterns. But Will and Sylvia were not able to do this. Each of them had strong ideas about what a marriage should be, and they tried to make their marriage conform. At that time, neither of them had the confidence to strike out on a marital path of their own.

The sextile of Moon to Pluto suggests the depth of feeling between them. This was a deeply emotional relationship, even though they may not have handled the emotions very well.

Of the three Moon aspects, the Moon-Neptune conjunction is the most serious, for it indicates the danger that this relationship was largely based on illusion rather than reality. Since this conjunction is in the fourth house, it also raises the danger that things would happen to each of them in their home lives that the other would not know about, either through lack of communication or even outright deceit. Clearly it indicates confusion at the root of the relationship, which tends to weaken the whole structure.

Neptune in such a position makes it difficult for two people to withstand periods of crisis in which they have to encounter what they really mean to each other. Also, it made them feel less confident about each other, and consequently the marriage was insecure. Each of them doubted the other's love or suspected that the other loved someone else. This lack of trust is not at all good for a relationship.

Next we check the positions of Venus and Mars and their aspects (Step 5). The chief Mars aspect has already been discussed. By the way, despite its problems, Mars conjunct Sun can be a potent indication of sexual energy in a relationship. But when we look at Venus we see the most positive focus of their love relationship. Venus is very closely conjunct the fifth-house cusp and in a close trine to both the first-house cusp and composite Ascendant. Also it is in square to Jupiter in the second house. All these aspects are solid indications of a love relationship with a great deal of feeling.

It is worth noting with the second-house Jupiter that while they were together, Will and Sylvia had few serious financial problems. It was only after they had separated that they encountered money difficulties.

However, the positive indications of these aspects are not quite enough to make up for the problems that this couple encountered, especially considering what their natal charts have told us about their relationship needs. When the dust cleared after their break-up, they both realized that neither was at fault. It was just that both of them needed something else in a relationship.

In Step 6 we look at the angular houses. But in this case they all are empty, except for the fourth, which we have already discussed.

Step 7 asks us to look at the houses of relationship; one, five, seven, and eleven. Pluto is in the first house, but so near the second-house cusp that I would have to consider it more second-house than first. The seventh house is empty, as is the fifth, except for the vertex point.

But the eleventh house contains Uranus, whose principal aspect to Moon has already been discussed. However, let me say something about the effects of Uranus in this house. Will and Sylvia were fairly conventional people, at least outwardly, but they did have some rather unusual friends. Not that their entire circle of friends was outrageously Uranian, but quite a few of them could be so described. By "Uranian" I mean people who in various ways do not conform to social norms. Even their more conventional-seeming friends were actually quite unusual, certainly not the ordinary citizens of modern suburbia.

In accordance with Step 8, we turn to Saturn. As mentioned previously, Saturn is in the twelfth house, which is not by any means fatal in itself. However, it does indicate a tendency (already noted) to hold in feelings that should be expressed. Also note that Saturn is trine to Mercury in the fourth. This aspect limits rather than kills free communication between two people, but the two aspects together certainly mean that communication was difficult. This was one of the main problems in the relationship.

Now let us look at the marriage itself in order to see how transits and

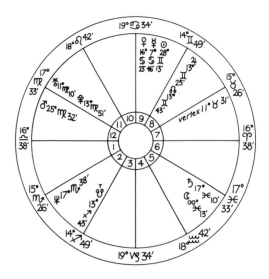

Marriage Chart

progressions work in a composite chart. The wedding chart is given, as well as the individual progressed charts of the marriage and the composite of the two progressed charts. See Chapter One, page 26, for instructions on making a composite progressed chart.

In the chart of the marriage, we see Venus elevated in the ninth house very close to the M.C. in a grand trine with Saturn and Neptune. You will notice that this grand trine falls very tightly onto the trine of Venus and composite Ascendant in the natal composite, as well as contacting the second-house Jupiter. All in all, the marriage chart touches the composite chart more closely than it does the natal charts. The Venus-Neptune-Saturn trine indicates a conflict between illusion and reality, which characterized this relationship from the beginning. Also notice that the fifth-house Moon of the marriage chart is coming to a trine with the Sun-Mars conjunction in the natal composite.

To those who are interested in symbolism, one especially fascinating point is that the theme of the Sun-Mars conjunction in the composite chart is repeated with a square between the transiting Sun and Mars at the time of the wedding. This in turn strongly aspects the M.C.-I.C. axis of the composite chart.

The twelfth-house Mars of the marriage chart squares the twelfth-house

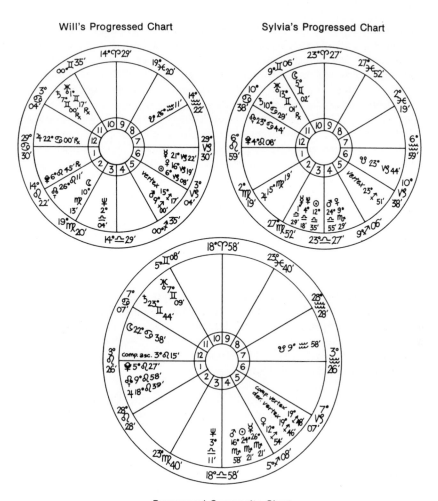

Will's Progressed Chart   Sylvia's Progressed Chart

Progressed Composite Chart

Saturn of the composite chart. Here again we see the theme of repressed anger that is not expressed until the pressure is dangerously high. There are other points here, of course, but I believe these establish how sensitive the composite chart is to transits. Pay special attention to planets that transit the angles of a composite chart. Again and again in these studies we will see the importance of such transits.

Turning to the progressed composite chart, we find a very strong indication of marriage. The progressed composite Moon is coming to a trine with progressed Sun. Another interesting indication is that progressed composite Ascendant and the first-house cusp are both coming to a trine of the fifth-house vertices in the natal composite. The vertex point is the point of "fateful encounters" (see Chapter One, page 24) and it seems to indicate when the most important events occur in a relationship. Also, the progressed composite Ascendant has just left square to the natal composite Sun-Mars conjunction. And progressed Mars is just two years beyond the Venus of the natal composite chart. That corresponds to the time when their relationship began on a physical level. The progressed composite chart is quite a powerful tool in understanding a relationship.

Many other connections can be made among these various charts, and I invite the reader to look for them. From this you can see that the composite chart can receive transits and progressions just as a conventional natal chart does, which helps immensely in timing events in a relationship. Before concluding this study, I would like to say a few things about the transits at the time that this marriage broke up.

Will left Sylvia because he had come to the conclusion that this would never be a happy marriage for him. He felt that it was holding him back in some way from fully expressing his potential (Saturn ruling his seventh opposing Sun in the fifth house). And it does seem to have held both of them back in certain ways. Since their separation, both Will and Sylvia have established different styles of living that suit them better.

However, to return to the transits to their charts on the date of separation. On that day there was a full moon on Will's natal Venus. The most important transit to the composite chart was transiting Pluto on the cusp of the fourth house, indicating the breakdown of their home life. Transiting Pluto was at 26° ♍ 59' stationary direct, while transiting Saturn was trine to Pluto at 28° ♉ 34'. Transiting Venus was conjunct transiting Saturn and trine to transiting Pluto and composite I.C.—the breakdown of the home through love's separation! Transiting Sun was at 17° ♊ 32' (midnight U.T.) trining transiting Mars at 16° ♒ 00', which opposed in turn composite Jupiter, squared composite Venus, and quincunxed composite Ascendant. As you can easily see, the angles of the composite chart were quite busy at this time, which had very important effects.

Case Two: Fred and Mary

The purpose of this case study is to show how the composite chart can greatly aid the interpreter in coming to an accurate conclusion about a relationship. For the sake of privacy, Fred and Mary are fictitious names.

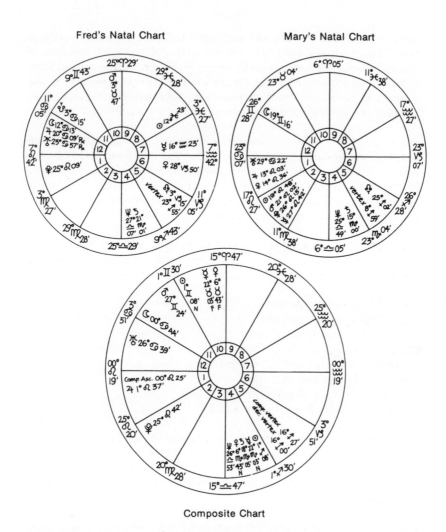

Fred's Natal Chart

Mary's Natal Chart

Composite Chart

The two natal charts are reproduced above. We will look at them first from the standpoint of conventional synastry to see what this technique tells us about their relationship.

The first point that struck me was that Saturn in Fred's chart squares the Sun, Mars, and Pluto in Mary's chart. It has been my experience that a Sun-Saturn square is usually a very bad aspect in synastry between two charts. It indicates that one of the two people makes the other feel insecure, while the other feels trapped by the relationship. Almost always this aspect leads to separation. We also find that Venus in his chart opposes Uranus in hers. This promises a short and unstable relationship at best, with lots of ups and downs. Also notice that Uranus in Fred's chart conjoins Ascendant in Mary's, which indicates much the same thing. At the very least, these two contacts between the charts promise a relationship that will jar both partners out of their normal patterns of life, as it actually did.

Her Neptune opposes his midheaven with great precision, indicating that somehow she would confuse his sense of direction in life and possibly make him feel insecure as well. Her Saturn, meanwhile, squares his seventh-house Mercury, which indicates difficulties in communication and difficulties in achieving an intimate one-to-one relationship. Certainly it does not bode well for a home and family situation.

There are a couple of good aspects, such as the trine of Mary's Sun to Fred's Mercury, but most of the contacts between the two charts are very negative. Let us review the most significant (Ma—Mary, Fr—Fred).

Sun (Ma) square Saturn (Fr).
Mars (Ma) square Saturn (Fr).
Pluto (Ma) square Saturn (Fr).
Uranus (Ma) opposes Venus (Fr).
Ascendant (Ma) conjunct Uranus (Fr).
Neptune (Ma) opposes M.C. (Fr).
Saturn (Ma) square Mercury (Fr).
Moon (Ma) square Sun (Fr) very wide!

There are no significant aspects between Mars and Venus in either direction, and the only contact between Venus and the lights in either direction is a wide Venus (Ma) quincunx Sun (Fr). Obviously there are not too many indications that a relationship between these two people would ever get off the ground.

Now for the facts! Mary and Fred began going together over a year ago and have kept fairly steady company ever since. There has been a little talk of marriage, and they seem to be quite attached to each other. They do have problems, and it would be easy to predict that their relationship will not survive in the long haul except possibly as friendship. In fact, they are gradually becoming friends instead of lovers. They enjoy each other's company, and what they are able to give each other helps both of them to grow. On the emotional level, they seem to be in fairly good harmony with each other. Their main problem is that they have numerous intellectual disagreements.

The question is this: with all the bad contacts between their charts, what is giving this relationship the impetus to survive? In my opinion, this relationship has already done better than the traditional methods of synastry would lead us to expect. When looking at their charts, remember that you now know that this relationship is working out, more or less, but do not read that knowledge into what you see. Ask yourself honestly, "If I knew only their charts, what would I think of the prospects for a valid relationship between these two people?" I think you would consider it very unlikely that they would get together in the first place.

Now we turn to the composite chart, in which we must apply the 150° rule to Sun, Mercury, and Venus. Consequently we have two of each of these, and immediately we find the answer! The composite Suns lie very closely along the 5-11 house-cusp axis and are in a trine-sextile aspect to Jupiter, which lies on the Ascendant. This is a clear indication of a relationship in which two people feel at ease with each other. It suggests that they will grow despite the difficulties and that they will give each other support and comfort.

Also, although there are very few indications of Venus energy in the contacts between the charts, in the composite, Jupiter is square Venus. This is an extremely positive aspect (see also Case One: Will and Sylvia), which emerges only in the composite chart.

At the same time, the problems of this relationship are clearly indicated. Mercury is conjunct Saturn, a clear sign of intellectual conflicts, and the conjunction in turn is square Pluto, which indicates that one of them is not willing to let the other have his or her own opinions. Pluto is conjunct the second-house cusp, indicating that the main conflict is about values. If they had any common financial concerns, these would probably be a source of conflict also. Notice that here the main problem is not emotional harmony but intellectual rapport.

The composite chart shows quickly and accurately the strengths and weaknesses of this relationship in a way that standard chart comparison techniques cannot approach. I would not discard the traditional methods of analyzing relationships, but I would not depend on them alone either.

Case Three: The Duke and Duchess of Windsor

The relationship of the Duke and Duchess of Windsor is a significant one for our analysis. How many relationships have involved a king renouncing his throne for the "woman I love"? The birth data for both persons is from

The Duke's Natal Chart   The Duchess' Natal Chart

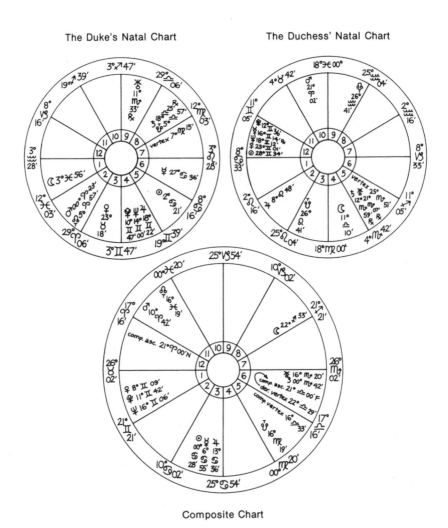

Composite Chart

the Ebertin Press Archive of Germany. The Duke was born at 10:00 PM
G.M.T. at 51°N26', 0°W16' on June 23, 1894. The Duchess was born at 5:30
AM, E.S.T. at 39°N15', 76°W41' on June 19, 1896.

Let us look at the Duke's chart first. Moon, the ruler of the sixth house,
is square to M.C. from the first house, which suggests a conflict in his life
between the duties that were imposed on him (the sixth house) and his
overall sense of life purpose (the M.C.). The ruler of his tenth, Jupiter,
conjunct the fifth-house cusp, however, is trine Saturn in the eighth. This

54

indicates how important love was to him, as does his fifth-house Sun. The trine to Saturn in the eighth suggests that he had to give up his inheritance to fulfill this love, but that he was not as unhappy doing so as another person might have been. Most of the planets in the chart are below the horizon, which is an indication of a person who is not very happy in the public eye. Uranus in the ninth is a sign that the Duke's ideas on how to act, as well as his overall outlook on life, were too eccentric and individualistic to fit in with the demands of a king's life, with its ancient ritual and traditionally prescribed activity.

In general, this chart is not particularly royal; a Cancer with a Pisces Moon is a very sensitive and often very retiring combination. But the trine of the Sun and the Moon, with the Sun ruling the seventh house of marriage, makes a reasonably decent marriage probable, although the square from Mars in the second means that the couple would have some disputes. The same square indicates the Duke was likely to be a big spender, because of the second-house Mars. Fortunately his financial base was solid.

The Duchess does not have the chart of a queen. Notice the large cluster of planets in the twelfth house! Usually a person with such a strongly twelfth-house chart is not terribly fond of living his or her life out in the open. As is well known, both the Duke and the Duchess led very private lives after the Duke abdicated the British throne.

I have no way of knowing whether they ever wanted children, but with Saturn in the Duchess' fifth house it would be unlikely that they ever would have had children, especially since both were in their forties when they married. It is worthwhile to note that the Duchess had no children by either of her two previous marriages.

Turning to their composite chart, we see several interesting details. First there is a rising conjunction of Venus and Pluto in the first house. A Venus-Pluto conjunction often means a sexual relationship that has a particularly urgent force behind it. The relationship must be fulfilled in some way. The sextile from Mars in the eleventh house reinforces this. It would have been very difficult for the powers of society to prevent this relationship from developing. Mars sextile Pluto indicates a strong will in any kind of chart. Here, with Mars in the eleventh, we have the sign that the two of them would pursue their hopes and wishes with unusual firmness, even if it meant that the Duke had to give up his throne.

You will notice that two composite Ascendants are given here. This is because the Ascendants in the natal charts are more than 150° apart. The nearer and farther midpoints are labeled. The nearer composite Ascendant is opposed to the vertex. This is an indication of a "fateful" union. Not only was one of the two people prominent but the relationship, itself, made history.

Moon is in the eighth house, as it often is in a relationship that completely changes the lives of the persons involved. Certainly that was the result in this case. The Moon is also trine the composite Ascendant (the nearer one) and sextile the vertex, which suggests again that the fateful transformation in their lives was not unwelcome.

The transits to this chart are interesting. King George the Fifth, the Duke's father, died on January 20, 1936. On that day, transiting Saturn was at $7°\times45'$ in close square to their composite Venus. This was the event that made it almost impossible for the Duke and Duchess to come together. Neptune was square the composite Neptune from the fifth to the first house. A romantic relationship that was not working on a very practical level? Transiting Jupiter was closely opposed from the composite seventh house to the first-house Pluto of the composite chart. A conflict would be created by this relationship coming into being. Meanwhile, transiting Pluto was beginning its transit over the fourth-house cusp of the relationship. This transit brought about the crisis that finally led to the Duke's abdication the following December 10.

Turning to the transits of the abdication, we find that the Sun had just opposed the Venus-Pluto opposition in the first house from the seventh house of the composite chart. According to history, the Duke made up his mind to abdicate in the days just before he did so. The transiting Sun triggered off the tremendous energies that brought about the relationship and that made his decision almost inevitable.

Transiting Jupiter was opposing the Suns of both natal charts and of the composite chart all through this period, during which high status (Jupiter) was voluntarily given up. Saturn transiting the eleventh house squared the first-house Neptune, a conflict between an ideal and reality. In this case the ideal won, or did it? There are many indications that the Duke would not have made a very good king. Perhaps his choice was quite realistic. Saturn also trined by transit the sixth-house Uranus of the composite chart. In this instance, Uranus in the sixth indicated rebellion against the duties and responsibilities of the royal office. The trine from Saturn signified relinquishing these in favor of what the two of them wanted (eleventh house). Transiting Mercury also conjoined the transiting Jupiter opposing both the two natal and the composite Suns. A Mercury-Jupiter combination is characteristic of a decision-making time. Also, transiting Venus had just gone over the composite M.C. in the previous few days and on the day of abdication was opposed to the transiting Pluto.

The Duke and Duchess of Windsor were married on June 3, 1937. This event, which brought the crisis to a conclusion, was signified by Jupiter being very close to the composite M.C. opposing the transiting Pluto going over the fourth-house cusp. A Jupiter-Pluto combination often signifies attaining an objective, but the opposition aspect means that attainment required challenging society at large. Also, the transit of Pluto over the fourth-house cusp indicates the forces that were opposing the relationship and that brought the couple down from great social prominence to the very quiet and private life that they led from then on. While they got what they wanted, their marriage constituted a "fall from grace" in the eyes of British society. The Duke's family had nothing to do with him for the rest of his life. Yet Jupiter on the tenth at the time of their marriage did enable it to take place.

It is also interesting to note that the transiting Sun was now conjunct the Venus-Pluto conjunction in the composite chart, opposite its position when the Duke abdicated the throne. At the same time, transiting Venus was making a T-square with the Jupiter-Pluto opposition along the M.C.—I.C. axis of the composite chart. Notice that most of the major events of this relationship occurred when the planets were at about 27° of the cardinal signs, about one degree beyond the composite M.C. Probably this is the actual location of the composite M.C., since the birth times given were approximate. Rectification by means of a composite chart may not be the easiest way of doing rectification, but this instance shows that it might be a possible method.

Case Four: Nicholas and Alexandra

Nicholas and Alexandra, the last Czar and Czarina of Russia, have recently been the subject of a book and a movie, and so are well known. The charts given here are recalculated from the data given in Marc Edmund Jones' *Sabian Symbols*. The data are as follows: Czar Nicholas: 12:02 PM, L.M.T., St. Petersburg (now Leningrad) Russia. Czarina Alexandra: 2:15 AM (approximately), Darmstadt, Hesse, Germany. Jones does not give the time. The time given here is derived from the M.C.

Anyone studying Nicholas's chart will immediately become aware that the portrait of him in the book *Nicholas and Alexandra* by Robert K. Massie, is

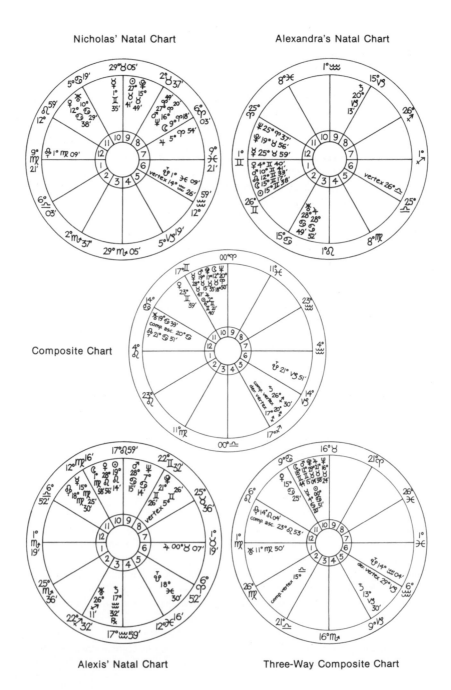

Nicholas' Natal Chart

Alexandra's Natal Chart

Composite Chart

Alexis' Natal Chart

Three-Way Composite Chart

essentially accurate. He was a mild-mannered, decent person who probably could have succeeded as Czar at any other time in history. He was a good man who had the best interest of Russia at heart, but he was not a very capable ruler, for he did not have the ability to understand the tremendous currents that were sweeping Russia during his reign.

The chart shows him as a very good, mild-mannered, romantically inclined person who was not very practical, even though he was a Taurus. Note Venus square Neptune, Moon conjunct Jupiter square Venus. He was obviously fond of beautiful and luxurious things. Mercury in the tenth in Gemini is closely opposed by Saturn in the fourth, which shows very clearly that domestic difficulties, namely his sick son (Saturn ruling the fifth), would work against his career and ultimately cause his downfall. His thinking became so dominated by the problem of his son that he lost the flexibility one normally associates with a Mercury in Gemini, and he could not grasp what was happening around him.

The chief indication of the tragedy that was to befall him is that his Sun and M.C. are both conjunct the Pleiades and opposed by Saturn. The Pleiades are traditionally associated with violent death (see the chart of Marion Parker, who also has a M.C.—Pleiades conjunction). Also, the node axis is square the Mercury-Saturn opposition. This means limited mental connections and difficult communication with other individuals or with groups. Nicholas was unquestionably misunderstood.

Alexandra's chart, if we take the Jones data as correct, is much more impressive. In her own way she was a very strong woman, who poured all her strength, and a good part of Russia's, into caring for her son the Czarevich, who suffered from hemophilia.

Note the strong clustering of planets around the area of the Ascendant, which denotes a person who has a very strong effect on her surroundings. Neptune conjunct the twelfth-house cusp denotes one who spends much time caring for a sick person. That placement can also be read as a tendency toward martyrdom, which she manifested in several ways, both in her behavior toward her son and in her eventual death. But the most extraordinary part of the chart is that it is very close to an annular eclipse of the sun that was visible in the extreme east of Russia. Notice also that the eclipse is conjunct Mars in the first house. This indicates her personal strength as well as the likelihood of violence entering her life at some point. Also, her eighth-house ruler, Jupiter, is conjunct Uranus, the planet of suddenness, square Neptune on the twelfth-house cusp. Saturn in the ninth squares Neptune also, an indication of chronic illness. This aspect again signifies that caring for her son was an important factor in her death.

In the two natal charts, therefore, we see many dramatic indications of what was to happen to this couple. If we turn to the composite chart, we see many of the same indications, even more clearly than in the natal charts. The composite also describes the nature of the relationship very clearly. The most striking element is the preponderance of tenth-house planets—seven, including Sun and Moon! This is truly a tenth-house relationship.

Nicholas and Alexandra came together because the Czar needed a wife to produce an heir. The world knew them as Czar and Czarina, rulers of the largest nation on earth in area, and they always had to be conscious of their role in the world. In fact, to some extent it was the attempt to deny their prominence that afflicted them. They tried to be as private as possible and to deal with their family problems within the family, which cut them off from the Russian people. This lack of consciousness of their responsibility as a couple is signified by the tenth-house Neptune, which is the first planet in the tenth house after the M.C. Notice, by the way, that the composite M.C. is 0° Aries, another indication that Jones's chart of Alexandra is accurate. Many astrologers, especially of the Hamburg school, have noted that a strong emphasis on 0° of the cardinal signs shows that a person will have some significance in the world outside his or her immediate surroundings.

The tenth-house Neptune is closely square the twelfth-house Uranus conjunct node conjunct composite Ascendant. The result of this is to make Neptune more deadly and to ensure that it will affect their relationship with the world (composite Ascendant). The combination of Uranus, the node, and the composite Ascendant signifies disruptive connections with others, and in the twelfth house it signifies that these are likely to be secret. Rasputin? Also, Uranus-Neptune combinations have to do with spiritual matters and altered states of consciousness, such as trances and spiritual states of mind, with which Rasputin was clearly connected.

Venus is in the eleventh house, a good position for a personal relationship, sextile Neptune, indicating that this was a romantic relationship, as was apparently the case. But Venus is also opposed by Saturn in the fifth house of children, which could have more than one effect. For example, it could indicate that this relationship has severe ups and downs because the two people have unrealistic expectations about each other. But in this case, the fifth house is clearly related to children. Saturn in the fifth house of a marriage chart can indicate problems with children such that they become more of a responsibility than normal. Also notice that Venus is in opposition to the composite vertex, indicating a fateful encounter through a child. It is quite evident that although Nicholas and Alexandra were devoted to each other, problems with the Czarevich came between them.

The possibility of violence is shown in the chart by the combination of Uranus conjunct composite Ascendant and the conjunction of Mars and Pluto. A Mars-Pluto conjunction in the tenth can simply signify a tremendous drive to succeed, but even in an excellent chart it is quite likely to produce outbreaks of violence, either from within or from without. Several times during their reign, the royal couple could have averted disaster by compromise. But above all else, Nicholas was the autocrat of all Russia, and Alexandra was his wife. Their inflexibility in this regard did not help the situation and created an atmosphere in which the Bolsheviks concluded that only by destroying the Czar and Czarina could they be safe from counterrevolution. This reaction is typical of the energy that Mars and Pluto generate.

The third player in this drama is the Czarevich, Alexis, whose hemophilia added so much to the problems of the declining Russian Empire. His data are given by Jones as noon L.M.T., St. Petersburg, Russia, August 12, 1904. In the natal chart, one immediately notices that, exactly like his father, he has a Sun-Saturn opposition along the midheaven-fourth house axis. If one were to cast their composite chart, the Sun-Saturn opposition would show up in it also. If an aspect occurs in two charts in the same direction—two sinister trines or two dexter trines, but not a dexter and a sinister trine, for example—it will show up in the composite chart as well.

The three-way composite of Nicholas, Alexandra, and their son, the Czarevich Alexis, is quite remarkable in that it shows so clearly the same patterns as the chart of Nicholas and Alexandra. Once again there are seven planets in the tenth house, and Neptune is not only elevated, it is directly on the M.C. of the composite chart. This is extremely important, for it is a strong sign that this relationship did not have its priorities straight. Although the health of the Czarevich was very important to the future of Russia, Alexandra especially lavished so much attention on the sick boy that all three members of the royal family became withdrawn from the Russian people. And this withdrawal facilitated their overthrow.

Notice Mars in the tenth square the rising Uranus. This is a sign of the violence and disruption that this relationship led to. Also notice in passing that in this chart the Venus-Saturn opposition occurs again in the same houses as in the composite of Nicholas and Alexandra. Again we have the sign of the sick child.

On the day they were assassinated, July 16, 1918, transiting Mars was in trine to composite Mars and formed a T-square with the Venus-Saturn opposition. However, except for this Mars transit, the transits on that day are so mild as to be inappropriate to the violent deaths they suffered. The only chart that shows any hard afflictions of a violent nature, including the three natal charts, is the three-way composite! The lack of heavy close transits to any of the natal charts leads me to wonder if the death date recorded in history books is accurate. There were a number of heavy afflictions to the three natal charts in the period that followed, which suggests that they were assassinated somewhere in this time span. But it does not appear to have been this date.

Case Five: Freud and Jung

In this case study, we shall examine the charts of Sigmund Freud and Carl Jung, two of the most influential intellectual figures of modern times. The purpose of this study is to demonstrate that the composite technique is not limited to sexual relationships, that it can express the subtleties of even the most complex human relationship.

Freud was considerably older than Jung and was already well on the way to establishing his theory of psychoanalysis when Jung first came to work with him. Naturally, Freud regarded Jung as a young protégé, but Jung, even though quite young, was already an established thinker with considerable experience in treating mental illness. In fact, one of the factors that eventually led to the split between the two men was that Jung's experience with psychotics, especially schizophrenics, led him in quite a different direction from Freud, whose original field was neurology. Because of his early experience in treating hysterics, Freud was more concerned with neurotic behavior, while Jung concentrated on the psychotic. Nevertheless, for many years Freud and Jung worked together closely and were intimate friends. Jung was attracted by Freud's innovative method of analyzing the mind according to symbols.

However, Jung had great difficulty with Freud's insistence on infantile sexuality as the cause of all neuroses. Jung began to develop his own ideas on this subject, which he eventually published as *Wandlungen und Symbole der Libido*, the revised edition in English being *Symbols of Transformation*. Publication of the book led to an open split with Freud, although the differences between them had been growing.

We shall use the natal charts of these two men, plus their composite chart, to show what factors brought them together and what drove them apart.

There are several different charts for each of these men in the astrological literature. However, considering that they were born in the nineteenth century, we are on surprisingly solid ground.

The data for Freud, from Ernst Jones's biography, are 6:30 P.M., L.M.T., May 6, 1856, in Freiberg, Moravia, latitude 49°N39', longitude 18°E10'.* According to the *Encyclopaedia Britannica*, that city is now Pribor, Czechoslovakia, but some other charts have used the wrong Freiberg. At that time L.M.T. was used throughout the Austro-Hungarian Empire, to which Freiberg belonged. The L.M.T. of 6:30 P.M. is 17:17:20 U.T.

The data for Jung, which come from his daughter, Gret Baumann-Jung, were originally published in *Spring: An Annual of Archetypal Psychology and Jungian Thought*, 1975, pages 35 to 55, "Some Reflections on the Horoscope of C.G. Jung." The version of the chart presented here is from the *Journal for Geocosmic Research*, Autumn 1975. It has been slightly rectified by Charles Emerson of New York. The time was originally given as 7:32 P.M., L.M.T.; but Doris C. Doane's book, *Time Changes in the World*, indicates that all of Switzerland was on the L.M.T. of the capital, Berne, so the time was probably Berne L.M.T. rather than that of the birthplace. However, as the cusps in these differing versions do not vary by more than a degree or so, I have gone along with Emerson's rectification. In the article for JGR, Emerson made a slight error in converting his U.T. from the rectification to L.M.T.; the data given here are for the U.T. of the corrected chart, not the L.M.T. Carl G. Jung was born July 26, 1875, 18:55:32 U.T. at latitude 47°N36', longitude 9°E19', Kesswil, Switzerland. The chart is internally consistent, because after the rectification, the calculations were redone by Astro Computing Services of Pelham, New York.

Freud's chart shows a seventh-house Sun, which indicates a person who does best in close association with another, either in cooperation or conflict. Also there is a Sun-Uranus conjunction in the seventh house, suggesting a conflict between the Taurean tendency to persist in partnerships and the Uranian desire for freedom. He could be happy in a relationship only if it did not curb his self-expression. Mercury in the seventh indicates the need for intellectual relationships and in sextile with Jupiter in the fifth, it indicates that he enjoyed playing with ideas in close involvement with someone else.

*As I stated in the introduction, this section was written later than the other case studies. Since that time, I have abandoned the use of geocentric latitude in calculating charts. Therefore the charts in this study have been computed for geographic latitude. Because the difference is so small, I have left the data in the other case studies as they were. See Journal for Geocosmic Research, Vol. 2, No. 1.

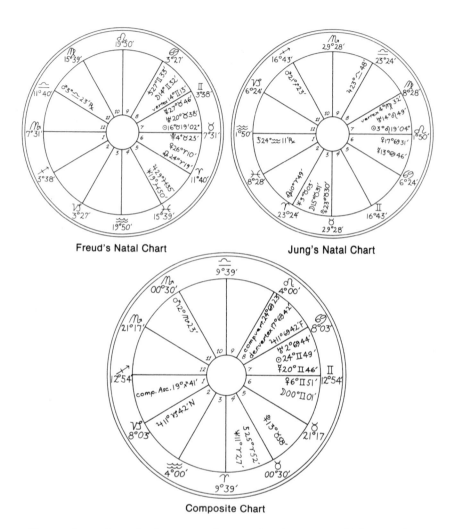

Freud's Natal Chart

Jung's Natal Chart

Composite Chart

Taurus is a sign of pleasure and sensual enjoyment, which are also associated with the fifth house. One of Freud's earliest formulations was the pleasure-pain principle, that is, that behavior is motivated solely by the desire to gain pleasure and avoid pain. Yet Freud was not a sensualist, as his chart shows. The Mercury-Jupiter sextile from seven to five tends to stress the theoretical and intellectual, and with Mercury in Taurus, he could quite easily intellectualize pleasure. Also, the Sun in Taurus in the second is sextile Neptune in Pisces in the fifth. Such a Neptunian Neptune tends to deny expression on a physical plane and promote idealization and

64

abstraction. Freud would be more concerned with abstract ideas of pleasure and sensuality than with the direct experience. His Moon is in Gemini in the eighth house, which is certainly associated with the kind of sexuality that Freud dealt with. In his later work he wrote of the importance of the love-death polarity in human history. Gemini in connection with the Moon again reveals a tendency to intellectualize emotions and the hidden depths of the psyche.

Scorpio is rising in Freud's chart, and Pluto is the planet closest to the angles, and therefore one of the most powerful, which is very appropriate for the father of psychotherapy, especially with his emphasis on infantile sexuality and pleasure-pain. Pluto is also on the west horizon, suggesting power struggles in relationships, which is also shown in Freud's and Jung's composite chart. But his life would grow through the crises brought about by these struggles.

Jupiter in the fifth is also squared by Saturn and opposed by Mars, again indicating that his search for pleasure would be strongly curbed by necessity, personal rigidity or intellectual considerations (Gemini). The opposition to Mars indicates a need to strike out on his own and probable difficulty in dealing with established groups (eleventh house). And Venus sextile Saturn is another indication that he would not exhibit his sensuous Taurean nature on a physical level.

Jung's chart also shows a very strong seventh-house emphasis, with the Sun and Pluto close to the angles. Pluto is near the I.C., which establishes Jung's credentials as a therapist, but it is quite different from Freud's, which is near the west angle, setting. Freud's Pluto suggests his method of personal interaction with his patients. Jung also did this, but he emphasized techniques that would expose the deepest layers of the unconscious mind, which is symbolized by the I.C. area.

Jung's strongly angular Sun in Leo indicates that he wanted to be in control of situations and was not good at taking a subordinate role, which was bound to be a problem in his relationship with Freud. The two men are heavy in fixed signs in square to each other, Leo and Taurus, which is not a good sign. However, Freud's Sun is on Jung's Moon, which is often a sign of strong attraction between two people, although usually one person plays an initiating role, while the other takes a more passive role.

Jung's Sun is in close square to his Neptune, signifying difficulty in asserting his independence as well as concern with mystical and spiritual elements. Freud's desire to be scientific and rigorous reflects his earth signs; Jung was not so strongly earthy. It is easier for fire signs to go off into abstract ideas. Jung's Neptune in the third, squaring the Ascendant, might also indicate difficulty in communicating clearly in a close partnership because he would be misunderstood or simply be hard to follow. In his autobiography, *Memories, Dreams and Reflections,* Jung stated that when he was younger he had several experiences of altered states of consciousness, visions and such. He also paid great attention to his own and later his patients' dreams.

Jung's Uranus in the seventh house, like Freud's, indicates that he would not be easily confined by a close working relationship. With Saturn rising in Aquarius, he would look for someone who could play the father role. However, with Saturn square Pluto near the I.C. in the third, his feelings about a father figure would be very ambivalent. Jung's Aquarius rising and Uranus squaring the Moon indicate a strong need for independence.

In many ways Freud and Jung were too much alike. Both were strong in the fixed signs, both were Uranian and Neptunian, and both would have difficulty in relationships unless each partner gave the other plenty of freedom. Freud triggered this problem by trying to control Jung's thinking, so that Jung had to break away in order to develop his own ideas.

In their composite the seventh and sixth houses are emphasized by the Sun and Moon, respectively. This suggests that their relationship was partly between equals (seventh house) and partly between a superior and a subordinate (sixth house). As their association went on, Jung felt that he should be Freud's colleague rather than merely a protégé, but Freud was unwilling to regard anyone as a true colleague.

That ideas were the dominant issue in their relationship is shown in several ways in the composite. Sagittarius is rising, with both the composite Ascendant and the derived first-house cusp in this sign. Also, Mercury is in close opposition to the composite Ascendant in its own sign, Gemini. It is also conjunct the Sun, putting a strong emphasis on communication of ideas. With Venus and the Moon also in Gemini, the chart has a very strong Gemini cast.

Since writing the earlier case studies, I have determined that individual planets in the chart signify the partner who is most strongly of the symbolism of that planet. In a sexual relationship, the Sun and Mars usually indicate the man's position, while the Moon and Venus indicate the woman's, if they are playing traditional roles. In this case, Saturn indicates the fatherly role, which Freud played quite consciously with Jung. This is shown clearly in the composite by Saturn in the fourth sextiling the Sun, which indicates that fathering was very important in their relationship. But of course difficulties would arise when Jung tired of playing the role of "son," because of Jung's ambivalent feelings toward a father figure. Saturn in the fourth is also square the vertex in the eighth, showing that changes in the relationship would create problems and that the fathering principle would be important in bringing about this fateful relationship.

Also in the fourth house, Neptune, the most angular planet, is very close to the I.C., which indicates that abstract interests brought the two men together. But even more important, misunderstanding and unclear thinking would undermine the relationship. Neptune square the double Jupiter (double because of the quincunx rule, see page 32), suggests possible conflicts of ideals. Jung was more attracted to the mystical and spiritual implications of their work, while Freud insisted on a kind of materialistic orthodoxy as a defense against accusations of occultism, even while he espoused otherwise radical ideas. Note that the nearer Jupiter is in Capricorn in the second house of values.

Jupiter is also trine Pluto in the fifth and sextile Mars in the eleventh. This indicates striving for accomplishment, which would give them both a sense of fulfillment. However, the Mars-Pluto opposition also signifies a power struggle, which is all the more dangerous because the fifth and eleventh are houses of relationship. This composite opposition results from combining the Mars-Pluto inconjuncts in Jung's and Freud's natal charts. Freud's slightly wide inconjunct (2' over the 60' orb) explains his concern with having power over others within the psychoanalytic movement. The history of that movement was one of constant conflict between Freud and others in the group, several of whom split off and founded an independent movement. (An important factor in the intellectual break between Freud and Jung was Freud's insistence that infantile sexuality was the only thing that kept psychoanalysis out of the realm of occultism.)

The Taurus-Scorpio polarity of the composite opposition is especially revealing, because Freud thought Jung unconsciously wished him dead. Jung had had a dream in which he was in an old cellar and found several deeper cellars below that. In the lowest one were heaped bones and other relics. Jung interpreted the dream to mean that he was being shown the layers of the human subconscious. Freud, who was already feeling rather insecure about their relationship, felt that it was a sign that Jung subconsciously wished Freud's death.

The collaboration between the two men came to an end in 1912. During that year Uranus was transiting back and forth across Jung's Ascendant in early Aquarius, an obvious symbol of breaking away to follow his own course. And in the composite chart, Neptune transiting the eighth house indicated changes through dissolution or disappearance, in this case of the relationship itself. With Neptune squaring composite Saturn, the father-son relationship was dissolving. Jung's book, *Symbols of Transformation*, is largely about the will, psychic energy and the symbolism of the hero, but an astrologer can see that it is also about the symbolism of the Sun. Jung, the Leo, was making his break from the father, Freud (Saturn in the fourth).

In 1912, transiting Uranus, in addition to conjoining Jung's Ascendant, also trined the composite Moon from very near the cusp of the third house. The break was signaled by the publication of a book. During the same year Saturn moved from conjunction with Freud's Sun and Jung's Moon to conjunction with the composite Moon in the sixth. This signifies that the two no longer felt that they had anything in common.

Jupiter also transited both direct and retrograde over the derived first-house cusp in Sagittarius and in quincunx to Pluto in the fifth house, signs of a power struggle and breaking away. Jupiter transiting the Ascendant is usually a positive indication because it shows the need for expansion and further growth. But in a rigid relationship that has reached its limits, it can be very difficult, because growth can occur only by ending the relationship. In 1913 Pluto completed this pattern by crossing composite Uranus in the seventh house.

The break-up was bitter, especially on Freud's part, but in many ways the two were better off for it. Freud could carry on his own work without fear of displacement by a more brilliant person, while Jung was free to develop his own more radical theories, which have been so beneficial to those of us who study the symbolism of the human race.

Chapter Four

Houses

The Meaning of the Houses in the Composite Chart

The meaning of the houses in the composite horoscope is clearly very similar to their meaning in the conventional horoscope, except for one major difference, which will be dealt with shortly. The most important point to keep in mind in delineating a composite chart is that you are working with two or more people rather than an individual, so you must adjust the house meaning accordingly. For example, in a conventional natal chart, the tenth house rules one's status in society, one's career, and the overall purpose of one's life. But in the composite chart the tenth house shows the status of the relationship and its overall purpose in existing. It is hard to relate the issue of "career" to a relationship unless it happens to be a business or professional one. In the other houses also, some of the issues are difficult to relate to a composite chart simply because a relationship is not the same kind of entity as an individual.

But aside from this obvious difference, there is another difference, which is much more important in reading a composite chart. At the beginning of Chapter One, it is stated that there are always two midpoints, exactly opposite each other, for any given pair of planets. It is also stated that the nearest midpoint—the midpoint of the shorter of the two arcs into which the planets divide the circle—is the stronger one and therefore used for the composite chart.

However, the farther midpoint also has some effect, and this effect increases as the shorter and longer arcs approach 180°, which happens when the planets from the two birthcharts are in opposition to each other. Therefore, when reading the description of any composite planet in a house, it is a good idea to read it in terms of the opposite house as well. And if the shorter and longer arcs of the two planets are near 180°, it is essential to take both houses into consideration. If you have had any great experience with conventional birthcharts, you know that this is a factor in any kind of horoscope. It is often referred to as "polarity." Every house reflects the qualities of the opposite house to some extent, and in composite charts this is even more important. It is almost as if there were six paired houses in the composite chart rather than twelve separate ones. But since one house in each pair is stronger, we have retained the traditional idea of twelve houses.

One more point. The following are generalized descriptions of the matters that relate to each of the twelve houses, independent of any planet that is in the house. The descriptions are intended to extend the reader's understanding of the significance of the houses, so that you can make judgments beyond those indicated in the delineations in the text. Also, these house delineations become important for an individual chart if there is a large clustering of planets in any one house. That house may very well be more important to an overall understanding of the chart than the Sun and Moon houses, which are usually the most important in a composite chart. In such cases the general descriptions of the houses will be useful.

The Composite First House

The first house of the composite chart is one of the angular houses, which gives greater significance to any planet that is in it. Beyond that, however, the first house is the *persona* of a relationship and indicates the kind of impression it will make on its surroundings and how it will be viewed by others. It tells to what extent a couple will be regarded as a unit in their own right rather than as two separate individuals. The first house resembles the tenth somewhat, but there is an important difference, in that the tenth represents the reality of what the relationship is to the outer world. The first house describes the impression the relationship gives rather than what it really is. A strong first house can be an indication of a relationship that is all show and no substance. The tenth more clearly indicates substance, at least from the standpoint of social significance. Nevertheless, a strong first house is usually a sign of a significant relationship that will have a great impact on the lives of those involved. If one were to cast the composite chart of two people who have just met to see if they would have a significant relationship beyond a chance encounter, one could not say on the basis of house occupancy alone but with a strong first house if the relationship does go beyond the initial meeting, it will be an important one.

The Composite Second House

The second house of the composite chart refers to values—what the two people value, and their relationship to what is valued. This can operate on two different planes. The second house can indicate the role that value-systems play in forming the relationship, that is, to what extent two people come together because they value similar things or ideas. If the second house contains difficult aspects, particularly ones involving Pluto and Mars, disagreements over values may be a major source of conflict within the relationship. Similarly, positive aspects indicate that the couple has compatible values, which helps to bind the relationship together.

On another plane, clearly related to the first, the composite second house refers to whatever finances and property there may be in the relationship. In reading the second house, remember that not all relationships involve common property and finances. In that case only the first manifestation will have any relevance.

Needless to say, a badly afflicted composite second house can mean exactly what it means in a natal chart—difficulties with property and finance. This may result from value conflicts in which the two people cannot agree on what to do with money and property. Or it may result from neither partner having any idea about what to do with money. In such a case, the individuals' natal charts should be consulted.

One final note: in a composite chart all finances are joint finances, because you cannot clearly distinguish which person is which, so one of the conventional distinctions between the second house and the eighth has no meaning here. The eighth house has other meanings that have little to do with finances, but you should consult both the second and the eighth for information on all financial matters in a relationship.

The Composite Third House

The composite third house has essentially the same meanings as the third house in a conventional birthchart: communication, mind, routine day-to-day environment, and relatives. In the composite chart the communications aspect is especially important. If the people in a relationship cannot communicate, they are in real trouble. Very often in a close personal relationship, each partner expects the other to understand him or her on some deep, intuitive level that does not involve words. When the couple discovers that this deep understanding does not exist, they are most upset and hurt. An afflicted third house usually indicates lack of communication in some way. This should be watched for.

This matter is related to another problem. The third house is the house of the "lower mind," that is, the mind in its routine day-to-day operation, usually on a low level of consciousness, involving habitual patterns of thought, unquestioned opinions, and unexamined notions. The composite third house tells a great deal about how these patterns will operate within the relationship. Will they constantly be a source of conflict, or will they be a source of compatibility, binding the relationship together? Very often they are a source of conflict. The only way to deal with these patterns is to have a neutral third party help bring them out into the light, because people are often not even aware of their own habitual attitudes.

A relationship with a strong third house usually comes about because of mental affinity. The two people are fond of talking with each other and exchanging ideas. Their only real problem arises in a close personal relationship, for mental exchange may become a substitute for a much-needed deep emotional exchange. Otherwise, a third-house relationship is perfectly fine.

The Composite Fourth House

The fourth house represents more than the home, especially in the composite chart. Many relationships have nothing that could be called a home, and yet the fourth house remains important.

First of all, it is one of the angular houses, which gives it added significance. But more fundamentally, the fourth house indicates the basic roots of a relationship—both literally, in geographic terms, and figuratively, in terms of mental and emotional background. The fourth house signifies the innermost depths of a relationship, which may be so far within as to be invisible at the surface.

The fourth house should be checked to see if there is an underlying compatibility between the two people. Do they have compatible backgrounds in the senses just described, and are their basic emotional and psychological characteristics compatible?

On top of this, the fourth house does mean collective "home" if such a notion is appropriate. The home is where a couple's deepest emotional and psychological attitudes have their strongest impact. The home is in many ways the physical embodiment of one's innermost being, and is therefore influenced by anything that affects the inner life. Afflictions to the fourth house have a negative effect upon the home, if there is one, and upon the deepest levels of compatibility.

A composite chart with a strong fourth house usually indicates that the two people share their innermost lives and that they probably share their actual place of residence.

The Composite Fifth House

The fifth house in the composite chart has many of the same meanings that it has in a conventional chart—love affairs, children (where this is appropriate), creativity, self-expression, and so forth. The interpretation of self-expression, however, is especially critical in a composite chart.

The composite fifth house represents, first of all, to what extent the relationship provides a setting for the individuals to be themselves in the most genuine and honest way possible. Many relationships survive only because each partner puts up a false front to the other. Each one tries to be what he or she thinks the other wants, rather than what he or she really is. When the truth becomes known and disillusionment sets in, such a relationship must collapse. The fifth house signifies the ability of the individuals to be real in each other's presence, which is not always easy. And being real should not be an effort. An ideal relationship allows each person to be real and to feel that it is easy to do so. When the fifth house operates smoothly, it is easy to enjoy oneself with the other without feeling that something unnatural is expected. A badly aspected fifth house, on the other hand, indicates the opposite.

A strong fifth house signifies a relationship that is very concerned with the issue of self-expression. In a fifth-house relationship a couple is not together to form a team or partnership, but because they enjoy being themselves in each other's company and because they enjoy each other. For this reason, this is the house of love affairs and of friendships (which are also ruled by the eleventh house). But the very nature of this house means that it is not for people who are trying to operate as a single unit. In a fifth-house relationship the two people are together but still individuals. For this reason it may not be the best house for a marriage, although it is not harmful to one. The staying power needed for a marriage or other long-term partnership may not be provided by a purely fifth-house relationship.

The Composite Sixth House

The composite sixth house can signify real obstacles to a satisfactory personal relationship. Somewhat like the sixth house of a conventional horoscope, it refers to the duties and responsibilities that the relationship must fulfill. Of course, all relationships have obligations, and in most cases they are not likely to be harmful. Duties become a problem only when they are the major element of a relationship, with no room for necessary self-expression as ruled by the fifth house. When the sixth house is too strong, the two people see the relationship as a duty to be met, not something to be enjoyed. In a business relationship this is not a great problem; there are tasks to be done and obligations to be met. But in a personal relationship, which is supposed to be a voluntary and natural expression of each partner's self, such a dutiful attitude can ultimately weaken a relationship. Only if the circumstances call for work to be done does a strong sixth house become an advantage. To make good use of these energies requires that the two people approach even a personal relationship from a strong sense of personal duty.

Health, the other traditional meaning of the sixth house, seems to have little relevance to a composite chart, except as it may indicate a business or professional relationship relating to health.

The Composite Seventh House

The composite seventh house, like the first, is a sign of a relationship in which the two people are truly trying to function as a unit. The seventh is the house of intimate one-to-one encounters. If a chart is on the whole favorable, a strong seventh house is a good indication that any kind of partnership, including marriage, can survive. A strong and well-aspected seventh house is not absolutely necessary for a marriage or business partnership, but it helps. In a strong seventh-house relationship, the two people are likely to think of themselves as one, as "we" and "us." It is not simply a matter of enjoying each other's company, as in a fifth-house relationship. They should enjoy each other, but more important is the fact that they complement each other and make a strong whole.

A clearly seventh-house relationship that is not well-aspected will still be an intimate encounter, but the people may be enemies or at least competitors. This is because the seventh is also the house of one's open enemies.

Obviously a strong seventh house cannot guarantee a marriage between two people who love each other, but because they will think of themselves as a unit, it is quite likely that they will get married or at least live together.

A strong seventh-house chart is also favorable to any one-to-one relationship in which one person consults the other, such as a patient and doctor, patient and psychotherapist, client and astrologer, client and lawyer, or client and any other type of professional. Needless to say, the seventh must be well aspected in these cases.

The Composite Eighth House

In traditional astrology, one meaning of the eighth house has been joint finances and property, or the "partner's" finances and property. In a composite chart it is difficult to distinguish between the meanings of the second and the eighth house, because one cannot clearly distinguish between the two partners. One difference is that the eighth house can refer to finances and property of people outside the relationship. Otherwise it is difficult to separate the two houses, insofar as they both refer to value and things that are valued. The same issues can arise with both houses. Therefore the reader is urged to review the second house for further information.

However, the eighth house also has a quite different meaning all its own. Traditionally it is the house of death, but this meaning is not limited to actual physical death. It really means the passing away of any old order and the building up of a new one. Therefore we refer to the eighth house as the house of major transformations.

A strong eighth house may signify some great involvement with property, but it is more likely to mean a relationship of great significance that will bring about major changes in the lives of the two people, especially at the psychological level. A strong eighth-house relationship will very likely make a considerable impact on both partners.

Whenever you encounter a strong eighth-house chart, be sure to keep in mind the double nature of this house. Its effects can be manifested at either level or both at once.

The Composite Ninth House

The composite ninth house signifies the overall view of the world taken by the persons involved in a relationship. The phrase "consciousness-expanding" is often used in the delineations, because a ninth-house relationship usually broadens the views of the two people. They are exposed to new ideas and forced to think in terms of a broader spectrum of possibilities than before.

Since the ninth is the house of ideas and consciousness, a strong ninth house enables people to communicate at a very high level. They can really understand each other and share their views with one another. Exchanging ideas plays a very important role in their relationship, and they will make more than the usual effort to understand each other. Of course, difficult aspects to this house, especially involving Saturn, can turn this around so that failure of communication becomes a major factor that weakens the relationship. Similarly, some planetary combinations, particularly Mars and Pluto, can create intense competition on the intellectual level and great resistance to each other's views. The one certainty is that a strong ninth house will make it very important that the two people have a strong intellectual relationship. If they do not, that fact will be the major source of difficulty between them.

The Composite Tenth House

The tenth house in the composite chart has much the same significance that it has in the conventional natal chart. However, "career" seems to have little relevance for a relationship, unless it is a business or professional relationship. But even in an individual horoscope the tenth house has a much deeper meaning. It tells about a person's development as an individual, a unique human being, and how he or she establishes that uniqueness in the world. Because of this, the tenth house refers to status and reputation. It also tells about the directions of a person's evolution and the principal occurrences of that process. All these matters apply in a composite chart, especially the uniqueness and evolutionary purpose of a relationship, both for the persons involved and for the outside world.

A strong tenth-house relationship will be more than normally concerned with directions. The two people will often ask, "What purpose does this serve in my life?" And often the encounter with each other will help them find out exactly what they are doing in this world.

A tenth-house relationship is not likely to be a professional one. Profession is only one aspect of life direction, and one that has been rather overemphasized. What one does for a living may have little or nothing to do with the central purpose of one's life, especially in a composite chart. Consciousness of objectives is the main theme. The issues of the tenth house are more than ideals and hopes, which are ruled by the eleventh. They are plans that will probably be realized, because they are the real intention of the relationship.

The Composite Eleventh House

A strong eleventh house is very appropriate in a composite chart, for it is the house of friendship. It does not limit a relationship to friendship, but it helps two people to be friendly in whatever they are doing together. This is especially important in a sexual relationship; lovers who have a strong eleventh house will also be friends. Businessmen with a strong eleventh house will be friends as well as professional associates. A strong eleventh is an excellent house for a marriage composite.

Because it is also the house of hopes and wishes, a good, well-aspected eleventh house gives a relationship a strong sense of shared ideals. Both persons are looking for the same things in life.

Difficult aspects, especially those of Saturn, may bring about conflicts of ideals in a relationship. Or friendship may be denied, limiting a relationship to a purely professional one or a purely sexual one, without friendship.

In any case, a couple with a strong eleventh house must be able to share with each other a great deal of their lives. Otherwise it is not likely to be a very successful relationship.

The Composite Twelfth House

The composite twelfth house has many of the same meanings as it has in an ordinary birthchart. However, as stated in the old texts, some of these are so cloudy that it is worthwhile to state them here in a new way.

Basically, the twelfth house represents repressed thoughts. It signifies once-conscious ideas that have been eliminated from the waking mind because the mind has chosen not to deal with them. The twelfth also clearly indicates the environmental factors that has caused the thoughts to be repressed. These are the aspects of the twelfth house that have the most significance for the composite chart. The traditional meanings concerning hospitals, prisons, and other places of confinement do not really apply here.

The problem with repressed ideas is that they give rise to unconsciously motivated actions that are often harmful to an individual or to the relationship. Because the actions are automatic, they are often inappropriate to a given situation and serve to undo rather than aid the relationship.

In a strongly twelfth-house relationship, the persons involved do many things to and with each other that do not make sense in terms of what is really happening between them. As a result, they wind up dealing with behavior patterns automatically when they should be making a thorough, conscious evaluation of them. Even when a couple makes a great effort to deal with problems consciously and openly, there is often more going on that is raw, intimate, and heavily psychological than most people can deal with in a personal relationship.

If people can handle what comes up in a twelfth-house relationship, fine, and some people even enjoy such a relationship. Marriage is not normally recommended for a couple with a very strong twelfth house. But there are those who benefit greatly from intense, day-to-day psychological encounters. And there are individuals whose unconscious acitons—one is tempted to call them "programs"—dovetail with their partner's so perfectly that they are indispensable to each other, no matter how miserable they seem. For this reason, twelfth-house relationships must be evaluated very carefully. They cannot be rejected out of hand, even though they are among the most difficult of all relationships.

The Composite Ascendant

Because of the mechanics of casting a composite chart, the cusp, or beginning of the first house, does not coincide with the midpoint of the two natal Ascendants. Nevertheless, the midpoint of the two natal Ascendants does have an importance of its own, aside from being a house cusp. It is a sensitive point in the horoscope, which can be aspected just like the planets. It is called the composite Ascendant to distinguish it from the first-house cusp, which is called the composite first-house cusp.

The composite Ascendant has two sources of importance. First, it has the effect of increasing the importance of any planet that is conjunct or opposed to it in the composite chart. Second, it describes through its aspects ways in which the energies of the relationship affect you and your partner. Its significance is very similar to that of the first house in general. The main difference is that it is a point that can be aspected by planets in other houses.

The composite Ascendant may not always fall in the first house of the composite chart. In fact, it can fall anywhere from the eleventh house to the second, depending on how different the latitude of the composite chart is from the latitude of the two (or three or more) birthplaces. The house position of the composite Ascendant may tell something about the kind of effects the relationship will have upon the outer world but it is not as significant as the house position of the composite Sun and Moon. In the delineations that follow, the composite Ascendant will be treated as an axis, a line running completely across the horoscope. This is done because the composite Ascendant actually includes in its symbolism the composite Descendant, the degree that is setting in the west exactly opposite the Ascendant. Together, these two points signify the total exchange of energies between the two of you and the world around you.

Chapter Five

Sun

The Meaning of the Sun in the Composite Chart

The house position of the Sun (along with that of the Moon) tells a great deal about the basic thrust of the relationship, what it exists for, and the major issues it will revolve around. The aspects to the Sun refer to the most important energy patterns in the horoscope, the kinds of behavior that will be most important between you.

A badly placed Sun with difficult aspects can be an important factor in making a relationship difficult or even unbearable. It indicates that the basic energies of the relationship are not being handled well and that something is fundamentally wrong between you. On the other hand, a well-placed and well-aspected Sun will help a relationship survive even in difficult times.

In any chart the Sun provides the energy for whatever entity the chart represents. In a composite chart it shows what kinds of energies each of you contributes. If the proper expression of this energy is blocked, the relationship will seem inhibiting and repressive to each person's free self-expression. It will be an effort to maintain the relationship, and you will not feel at ease with each other. If the Sun is well placed in the chart, the relationship will be experienced as free and spontaneous self-expression, requiring little effort. Of course, other factors can create difficulties, even when the Sun is well placed, but a good Sun in a composite is very desirable.

Composite Sun in the First House

Composite Sun in the first house often signifies a relationship that is unusually important in terms of your own lives. The first house signifies an entity's personality and the way a person or a relationship impresses others.

The two of you complement each other in such a way that as a pair you may make a stronger impression on those around you than you would as individuals. Even if neither of you is an especially strong or dominant personality, you will be strong as a couple. Together you may be able to accomplish more in life than you could have separately. And you will be especially strong in an adversary situation in which the two of you are pitted against someone else.

The first house is a very strong and favorable position for the composite Sun. It is usually an indication that you will be able to accomplish whatever you have come together to accomplish. But as in most relationships, some difficulties can arise if the energies of this placement are not properly handled.

First of all, the two of you may tend to worry too much about how you appear to others. This can lead you to neglect the real problems that are not visible to others, for you consider such problems to be less important. They may be more important than you think.

Second, if as individuals you are intrinsically forceful people, the energy of this position may make you come on too strong with others, which could provoke active opposition to anything you want to do as a couple. If this is the case, be careful to control your energies toward others.

For an intimate relationship such as a love affair or marriage, this is an intrinsically excellent position. It is characteristic of the first-house Sun that the two of you will become very much a unit, which can bind you together closely. Assuming that in the aspects of this horoscope there are some good indications of love between you, this is likely to be a meaningful relationship.

Composite Sun in the Second House

The Sun in the second house of the composite chart is the best possible position for any business or professional relationship whose primary aim is to make money or to gather material possessions. For a personal relationship this position is neither good nor bad. However, it does mean that the relationship focuses rather heavily on material advantage, possibly at the expense of psychological, emotional, and other intangible factors.

The second house is the house of values, or rather, of things that are valued, either tangible or intangible. The Sun in this house gives you a strong drive to seek whatever it is that you collectively value. Usually these are material things, although in some cases they may be philosophical or spiritual values. The point is that you will go after whatever you want, and you are likely to succeed simply because you put so much energy into the effort.

In a personal relationship such as marriage, in which you own things together, these things will be very important to the security of the relationship. Even if you would not normally acquire property together, you may do so with this placement. Friends with this position in the composite chart may go into business together or become involved in a common living situation in which possessions such as furniture and appliances are owned jointly. However, although a second-house Sun may suggest that you will live together, this is usually more characteristic of a fourth-house Sun.

One danger of this placement is that there may be a conflict of values between you. If this is so, it will be a serious problem, because your relationship is based so much on values. It will not be easy for the two of you to compromise on such issues, so it would be best to decide whether your values are compatible before you embark on any kind of joint venture. Unfortunately, the second-house Sun does not necessarily indicate compatible values; it only indicates that values as such are an important issue in the relationship.

Composite Sun in the Third House

The Sun in the third house of the composite chart favors relationships in which communication and exchange of ideas and opinions are important. In business and professional relationships, this position favors associations in commerce and in the communications field.

For a personal relationship this position has great strengths as well as great weaknesses. The strengths are as follows. You will have a strong ability to communicate, for you share many of the same ideas and opinions, and you will be able to speak openly with each other. There will be few barriers to mutual understanding, except perhaps at the emotional level. You will enjoy having good conversations with each other.

The greatest weakness of this position is that even a personal relationship will function primarily on an intellectual or mental level. It is not likely to be a very profound emotional tie. Clearly, then, the Sun in the third house is a much better position for friendship than for a love affair. You will relate to each other by talking rather than by feelings, as a love relationship requires. When an emotional situation arises, there is the danger that you will intellectualize it or try to figure it out instead of just living through it and learning from the experience. The knowledge gained by this kind of experience cannot be replaced by logical analysis. But this is a lesson that the two of you may have some difficulty in learning, because the third-house Sun inclines you to logical analysis.

There is nothing wrong with an intellectual relationship, but there are times when it is inappropriate. Fortunately, your strong commitment to communication will aid you in approaching the problems you may have to face together. Just be sure that you don't stop at the purely mental level. You should enjoy an unusually good mental rapport and be more able to talk to each other than many couples can.

Composite Sun in the Fourth House

Composite Sun in the fourth house favors a strong emotional involvement. In a personal relationship, you and your partner are likely to seek out everything that you have in common—past experiences, shared tastes, standards of right and wrong, and particularly, shared ideas about home and domestic life.

The fourth is the house of your most personal and intimate life, your home, your past and origins in general, as well as your inner feelings and emotions. The Sun in this house of your composite chart will make you focus particularly upon these factors in your life together. Thus, this position favors a relationship in which you settle down together and share each other's personal lives as intimately as possible.

This is one of the best positions for marriage. It will not necessarily bring about marriage, but should it happen, your domestic life will be very important to you both. You will work very hard to create a stable home life and a personal world to which you can retire from the pressures of everyday existence.

Because this is an angular house, the position makes for a very strong relationship. This position indicates a concern for owning a home or real estate together, which may manifest itself as a desire to own land. If you live together you will not be satisfied with a small city apartment but will want plenty of room and, if possible, land.

On the psychological level, you are likely to experience profound emotions together and to become deeply involved in each other's innermost mental and emotional depths. This is not likely to be a superficial relationship. But try not to become so wrapped up in each other's psyches that you lose all perspective and the ability to see things clearly. The fourth is a subjective house, and the composite Sun there reinforces all subjective tendencies in the relationship.

Composite Sun in the Fifth House

The Sun in the fifth house of the composite chart is one of the best positions for a sexual relationship, because the fifth is the house of love affairs, among other things. It is also the house of creativity, children, self-expression, amusement, and good times in general, as well as of speculation and gambling. The Sun in the fifth house gives a strong emphasis to any of these elements.

In a personal relationship, a composite fifth-house Sun implies that your relationship will give you good opportunities for self-expression, for being yourself and enjoying it. You will like each other and enjoy being together. This is not truly a position of partnership, but rather of being yourself with others. For this reason, although this position is good for love affairs, it is not so good for marriage or any partnership that requires a greater feeling of oneness between you. The Sun in this house is not harmful to marriage and partnership, but by itself it does not produce staying power for the long haul. But if other positions make up for this lack, it can be quite good for marriage, especially since it gives a strong concern for children.

This is a good position for friendship because it indicates a light-hearted relationship in which you genuinely enjoy each other's company. Also, you will learn to be yourselves with others and discover more about how you affect others.

In a relationship with this placement, you must give each other room to be what you are. Fortunately a fifth-house Sun relationship usually has this capacity. If you do not give each other sufficient room, you both may feel that the other is placing clamps on your self-expression. Neither of you can remake the other, so do not try. In any case you must learn to let each other be and still stay together.

Composite Sun in the Sixth House

The sixth house is one of the more difficult positions for a composite Sun, because it is inherently a house of inequality. In most relationships there must be some balance between taking and giving. Even if each person does not contribute exactly the same thing, each one must contribute in equal measure, if the association is to work. But in a relationship with a sixth house Sun, one partner gives and the other takes. It is the house of your service to others and of others' service to you.

The great danger of this position is that one of you is likely to feel taken advantage of by the other. In fact, it is quite likely that each one is somehow using the other and is in turn being used, which both of you will ultimately resent. You will find yourself asking the question, "What am I getting out of this relationship?" When a question like that comes up, there are serious problems.

A sixth-house relationship is one in which normal ego drives seem to be particularly disruptive. Perhaps the best way to deal with the problem may be by going into such a relationship in a spirit of service and help for your partner, with as little thought for yourself as possible. But recognize that to really do this is extremely difficult, and you will probably be deluding yourself if you try.Maybe you're just looking for warm pats on the back for your "selfless" endeavor, but even that much recognition may not be forthcoming. Remember that each of you may be doing the same thing in this relationship.

Another way of dealing with this position would be to have a common task or goal that you can work toward together. Even in this instance, accomplishing your objective should be the only reward you seek. Other rewards may come, but you must not consciously seek them, or you will endanger the relationship.

Composite Sun in the Seventh House

The Sun in the seventh house of the composite chart is usually an excellent position for any kind of relationship in which two people are trying to work as a unit in an equal partnership. You will work together on a basis of total sharing, with each of you making your own contribution to the strength of the whole.

In most cases, this is the best position of all for either marriage or a business partnership. It denotes a complementarity that makes the whole stronger than either of the parts. Unlike a relationship with the composite Sun in the first house, the strength of your relationship is real as well as apparent to others.

One warning, however. The seventh is the house not only of partnerships and marriage, but also of open enmities and intimate conflict. In fact, the best overall description of it is the house of intimate one-to-one encounters of any kind. With this placement, if your relationship is not going well, you may compete with each other in a way that is disruptive and produces antagonism between you. Even in a healthy relationship you can expect this to some extent, but usually such competitiveness should bind the two of you together rather than drive you apart.

Composite Sun in the Eighth House

Composite Sun in the eighth house may give the two of you a feeling of "fatedness," that this relationship is going to play an important role in your lives, even if it is not a long-term relationship. The eighth is the house of major transformations, involving the destruction of an old way of being and the birth of a new one. In conventional natal horoscopes it is the house of death. But this should not be taken to mean that a relationship with an eighth-house Sun will end quickly. Instead, it will probably cause something in each of you to die and something new to be born. Obviously both of you will experience this relationship deeply.

You will be exposed to the most basic and profound aspects of your own and your partner's inner nature. In addition you will likely confront each other in such a way as to force changes in the areas of your lives that are not working out well. Both of you will experience psychological changes through this relationship.

In a sexual relationship, physical sex assumes an unusual importance, although not entirely for its own sake. Sex is likely to be seen by both of you as an experience that transcends ordinary reality—not as an escape but as something that gives greater depth to everyday life. Consequently, your attitude toward sex is not likely to be casual.

The eighth house is also the house of joint resources and property. Somewhat like the second-house composite Sun, this position can give the two of you a strong drive to acquire material possessions, or it can mean that possessions are a very important element in the security of the relationship. Here again it is necessary not to overdo this emphasis, because it can distort your perspective. Emotional needs are actually more important than possessions. However, because the eighth house is more basically emotional and profoundly psychological than the second house, this is not so likely to be a source of difficulty.

Composite Sun in the Ninth House

Composite Sun in the ninth house indicates a relationship that involves the growth of consciousness. Particularly in a personal relationship, the experiences that you undergo will give you greater understanding and insight into what is going on in your world. Together you will have a great interest in philosophy, metaphysics, religion, and all other routes to expanded consciousness and understanding. The relationship itself is likely to be quite idealistic. With the Sun in this position, a relationship between the sexes may tend to become platonic. Even if sex is involved, a platonic feeling will still be present.

The two of you will be very interested in communication and the sharing of ideas. Community of thinking is one of the dominant drives created by this position. You may travel quite a bit or at least be interested in foreign or distant places. "Travel is broadening," as they say, and you both view it as a positive force in expanding your consciousness.

For a personal relationship the only possible defect of this placement is that the relationship is likely to be more intellectual than emotional.

In a business or professional relationship this position is excellent for associations involving foreign countries, for businesses concerning travel—especially over long distances—for importing and exporting, and for intellectual enterprises such as "think tanks." This position is useful in any type of relationship because it indicates that together you have foresight and the ability to plan ahead for the long haul.

Composite Sun in the Tenth House

A relationship with composite Sun in the tenth house is likely to be a significant one. The tenth house, one of the most important houses of the horoscope, rules overall life direction or purpose. This is manifested in such areas as reputation, career, sense of self with respect to the outside world, and the general direction that something must take in order to evolve.

First of all, this position indicates that the two of you have an identity of purpose in your lives together, or at least that you are able to help each other attain the goals you have set for yourselves. Obviously this position is particularly useful for a business or professional relationship, but it is also very important in a personal relationship. If this relationship goes anywhere at all, it will have a strong effect on your life purpose. It may help both of you to define yourselves and answer the question of who you are, or it may take you further on a path that you have already chosen. At the very least, you will feel a strong community of purpose and direction, that your egos somehow complement each other.

Since the tenth is also the house of status, some couples may become excessively concerned with how they look to others—in other words, their social image or their importance in the community—while ignoring serious emotional problems that may be destroying the relationship. With this position there is a general danger that you may be much too concerned with the outer world in general and not enough with your own subjective concerns, which are valid in their own way. This is the exact opposite of the problems that can arise with the fourth-house Sun. Here the danger is that the two of you may deal with difficulties by trying to adjust matters in the external world, when their origin is within yourselves.

Even so, this placement is a good indication of an important relationship, one in which you will find a strong identity of life purpose and direction, which will enable you to work well together.

Composite Sun in the Eleventh House

Composite Sun in the eleventh house is an excellent position for almost any type of relationship because the eleventh is the house of friends. The composite Sun here indicates that no matter what the purpose of the relationship, the two of you will be able to get along with each other.

It is an especially good placement for marriage, because in the long run, friendship is one of the most important elements in cementing a marital relationship. This position does not by itself indicate sexual attraction; that must be provided by other components of the horoscope.

The Sun in this position is a good indication that you will share common hopes and ideals for the future, and you will work together to attain them, which is a desirable trait in any relationship. In fact, shared hopes and ideals may be the main element that binds the two of you together.

The eleventh is also the house of one's social self-expression and your ability to fit into groups. A well-placed eleventh-house Sun indicates that the two of you can function as a small group in your own right and that together you will find it easy to relate in larger groups. When you are together, you enjoy the company of others and are glad to have people around you. This is in contrast to those couples who like to be together without others.

With this placement, even a business or professional relationship is likely to develop a strong personal dimension as well, which in most cases should aid rather than inhibit the other functions of the relationship.

Composite Sun in the Twelfth House

Composite Sun in the twelfth house is a significant position, but it presents challenges that many people find difficult to deal with.

It indicates that through this relationship both of you will encounter aspects of your inner selves that you would normally keep hidden from yourselves as well as from others. It is also possible that the relationship itself may be hidden from others in such a way that either they are not aware that it exists or they do not understand what it is about.

The most difficult result of this Sun placement is that it may make the relationship self-defeating for both of you, particularly if you are not completely honest with each other. Unless you disclose all secrets, they will cause one or both of you to behave in a way that will undermine not only the relationship but your own self-esteem as well.

In any personal relationship this placement demands that you thoroughly search your innermost selves to understand how previously hidden psychological traits are operating within the relationship. This encounter will make each of you grow as individuals, and the growth it can bring about is more important than your survival as a couple. If you are at all dishonest or if you shrink from the psychological truth in order to keep the relationship going, it will only serve to further undermine the partnership. And a breakup brought on in this way will thoroughly destroy any possible potential for growth.

With this Sun placement, do not enter into any legally binding relationship such as marriage until you have thoroughly worked out all the hidden psychological patterns that may weaken it. This placement represents a potential for psychological repression, so separations and breakups can be particularly disastrous as the hidden pressures surface.

No one position or element in a chart is sufficient to destroy a relationship, but this position of the Sun in a composite chart is a call to be especially careful.

Composite Sun Conjunct Composite Moon

With Sun conjunct Moon in the composite chart, the two of you will have a single-mindedness of purpose that is usually lacking in other relationships. This aspect is especially good in the chart of a love relationship, because the Sun is the masculine principle and the Moon is the feminine. Conjunction is the symbolic marriage of the two, indicating that you are truly complementary partners. Because of the complementarity of masculine and feminine, a man and woman with this aspect in the composite chart are likely to have a strong sexual attraction. In friendship, this aspect is also helpful, for just as in a love relationship, complementarity can be a strong binding force.

Just as the Sun-Moon conjunction is the beginning of a new cycle, so the conjunction in the composite chart indicates that your relationship has the potential for bringing something new into the world. This attribute is important, especially in a business or a professional association. The complementarity factor indicates that you are somehow more complete as a partnership than as individuals. Therefore the two of you will be more formidable in the contests you enter together in life.

Composite Sun Sextile Composite Moon

The sextile of composite Sun and Moon is a very good indication that the two of you are basically compatible, regardless of the kind of relationship you have. The more personal and intimate the relationship, the more favorable are the effects of this aspect. The Sun indicates the active or masculine energies of this relationship, while the Moon indicates the feminine or passive energies. These descriptions should not be taken as comments on the nature of the sexes but as manifestations of a metaphysical polarity that is active in any relationship.

The sextile is an aspect of balance, indicating that neither of you will always take the dominant, assertive role. Instead, you will exchange the active and passive roles, and as a result your relationship will be more truly a partnership between equals.

In most cases, communication between you should be good. You will feel an overall intellectual and emotional compatibility as well as a conviction that your views complement your partner's views.

In a sexual relationship, the "maleness" of the Sun and the "femaleness" of the Moon do express themselves. Sexual attraction will be coupled with a genuine feeling of friendship, a quality not always found in such a relationship.

Composite Sun Square Composite Moon

Composite Sun square composite Moon indicates a fundamental tension within the relationship. The Sun and Moon symbolize the archetypal masculine and feminine functions, the most important complementary pair in the universe. In a larger sense the Sun and Moon signify all complementarity. The fundamental meaning of this aspect is that the two of you are not totally complementary. This can be quite a problem in a sexual relationship, which depends upon complementarity.

There is a sense of tension on the psychological level, which prevents you from being really at ease with each other. However, this can also work in a positive way by making the relationship challenging and creative, so that it doesn't fall into stale patterns and behavioral ruts.

Sometimes, for reasons that are not entirely clear, the Sun-Moon square can create a rather strong mutual fascination. It is as if each of you sees in the other something you want very much, even though you cannot handle it very well. In fact, the energy may be so strong that you are unable to relax into the casualness that is desirable in a long-term relationship. A Sun-Moon square is quite likely to be found in the composite chart of an intense love affair.

In any case, there will be considerable differences of opinion between you, which should be hashed out whenever they occur. In this relationship, repressed feelings are likely to cause potentially disastrous outbreaks of emotion when the pressures become too great.

Composite Sun Trine Composite Moon

The trine of Sun and Moon in the composite chart is an excellent indication of compatibility. It makes true love and friendship possible, partly because the two of you are able to accept each other and allow the other person to be whatever he or she is.

The Sun and Moon represent on the planetary level the basic polarity of the universe, expressed as male and female, active and passive, energy and matter, or any other such pair of opposites. The principle represented by the Sun and Moon together is wholeness. The trine of these two means that as a couple you are capable of that same wholeness. In this relationship, you each are completed by the other, or perhaps it would be more accurate to say that each of you is allowed to experience your own wholeness. Such a relationship is characterized by a lack of tension and conflict. You are not inclined to play games of "one-upmanship" with each other nearly as much as other couples.

Any type of relationship is favorably affected by this aspect, but a sexual one is especially favored, because sexuality is one of the most basic expressions of the Sun-Moon polarity. This aspect does not necessarily guarantee that you will have a sexual relationship; the whole chart must be analyzed to see whether that is likely. But it does help to make a sexual relationship easier and more rewarding.

Composite Sun Opposition Composite Moon

Sun opposition Moon in the composite chart is a double-edged aspect, capable of bringing about much good or much difficulty, particularly in a love relationship. With this aspect, there may be tremendous polarity, which results in either-or situations that can cause great tension, even a feeling of competitiveness between you. On the other hand, this aspect can bring together two radically different elements of your lives and make a higher and more dynamic entity of the two of you.

In a love relationship, you can expect this aspect to generate a lot of energy. You will be tremendously attracted to each other, in spite of the differences between you that this configuration represents. But although you will be drawn to each other very strongly, you will not feel entirely at ease, because there is a tremendous energy imbalance between you. For example, one of you may be extremely energetic and dynamic, while the other is more inclined to act slowly and deliberately. The differences are likely to be a source of irritation, even though they are, paradoxically, the source of attraction between you. That is the chief difficulty in this composite aspect.

Much the same interaction will be found in the chart of friends. In a business or professional relationship, you will have to ask yourselves how much tension and irritation you are willing to put up with in order to obtain the very great benefits the relationship can provide. In all situations this is a very energetic but unstable combination.

Composite Sun Conjunct Composite Mercury

The conjunction of composite Sun and Mercury signifies that there will be a great deal of mental activity in this relationship. This aspect is good for verbal communication between you, but it does not especially favor nonverbal, emotional forms of communication. Do not make the mistake of thinking that your ability to talk means that all channels of communication between you are open. They may or may not be. Feelings and emotions are not readily reduced to the forms of communication ruled by Mercury. You both should be wary of the tendency to intellectualize your emotions rather than deal with them at the gut level.

But your verbal communication should be excellent. You have an unusual similarity of thinking, or at least a better than average ability to understand each other's thinking.

Mercury is a planet of travel, not always in the literal sense of the word, but in the metaphorical sense; that is, you like to be continually exposed to new ideas and experiences together. To others this may appear to be restlessness, but it is really only curiosity aroused by being together.

One of the most positive attributes of this aspect is the ability to be detached from what you are discussing. Because of this detachment you may even be able to talk about your relationship and arrive at understandings that will help you both to get more out of it. But in the process, do not neglect the emotional sides of the issues.

Composite Sun Conjunct Composite Venus

The conjunction of Sun and Venus in the composite chart is one of the strongest indications of a love relationship between two people, even in a friendship. It does not primarily indicate a sexual relationship; instead it signifies love, pure and simple. In a friendship your feelings will have a depth and intensity that most people associate only with a sexual relationship. The attraction indicated by this aspect is so powerful that it can bring together people who are incompatible by ordinary criteria. They may succeed in making each other quite miserable, but they will still love each other.

A Sun-Venus conjunction usually means that you will almost certainly have one of the deepest and most loving relationships of your life, but there are some possible dangers. Love is closely related to hate, and if the relationship is laden with conflicts, even a strong feeling of love between you may turn to hatred. The reason for this is that the two of you are so involved with each other at such a fundamental level that you cannot get away. While this is a possibility, it is not likely to occur in a relationship with this aspect. In most cases this will be a very fine personal relationship.

Composite Sun Conjunct Composite Mars

Composite Sun conjunct composite Mars is a very energetic combination. A relationship with this aspect in the composite chart is not likely to be entirely peaceful and quiet, but it can be very creative. This relationship will arouse strong energies within you, energies that can be used for getting a great deal of work done or for making changes within yourselves.

You will have many discussions about your relationship or other subjects that will border on or actually be fights. However, this is not as negative as it sounds, for these "battles" can help to clear the air and prevent serious strains from developing. If you have this aspect in your composite chart, it is important that you express these energies. Do not suppress your legitimate angers and complaints because of a misplaced desire for peace and quiet. This relationship can grow through creative conflict. If you do suppress your anger or express it indirectly, the relationship could become very uncomfortable or turn into an endless stream of arguments.

Since Sun conjunct Mars is an indication of physical vitality, you should take part in vigorous physical activity together whenever possible.

This is a tricky aspect to handle in a business or professional relationship. It can be an indicator that you will work well together and accomplish much with dynamic vigor. But if the energy between you is very strong, it can indicate disputes, conflicts, and disagreements, as well as destructive ego competition.

Composite Sun Sextile Composite Mars

Sun sextile Mars in the composite chart will bring about great energy within your relationship. Being together will make you feel more vigorous and active. Together, you will be able to accomplish more than you can separately, especially if you are not normally very high-energy people. You will find that your egos complement each other very well and that you will be able to work cooperatively on most things.

Physical activities will be important when you are together, even if you are not physically oriented as individuals. Other people will regard you as a team in any physical activities you take part in together. You should avoid sitting around and doing nothing, although that is not likely to be a problem.

In doing any kind of task together, your ability to work cooperatively will be especially useful, as will be the balanced relationship between your egos. You will save your competitiveness for people outside the relationship rather than exhibit it toward each other.

You are very likely to discover that together you have an excellent sense of timing and that you are good at recognizing and taking advantage of opportunities. Use this trait to help you work together as a team.

Composite Sun Square Composite Mars

Composite Sun square composite Mars is a difficult aspect for almost any relationship. Such great energies are generated that it is difficult to channel them constructively. Usually these energies surface as intense ego competition, disputes, disagreements, and other forms of hositlity.

The trick is to channel this energy outward instead of allowing it to operate within the relationship. If you are physically very active together or if you work very hard for a common goal, you may be able to bring this aspect under positive control. If you let the energy stay within your relationship, however, you will have many problems.

The energy signified by this aspect will make you quite active together, but certain problems may arise when this energy is released. In a positive sense, this aspect can produce a healthy sense of competitiveness between you, which should bring about good results. But if you are not careful about how you use this energy, your relationship may not hold together at all. This aspect favors situations in which intense competition between you is useful rather than disruptive. In such a case, all the energy is used, not wasted in useless conflict and disagreement.

Composite Sun Trine Composite Mars

Sun trine Mars in the composite chart indicates that as a result of this relationship you both will have great energy for accomplishing work or tasks of any sort. This is not to say that your relationship will necessarily be work-oriented, but only that the energy is available should you need it. You will enjoy all forms of physical and athletic activity together, even if singly you are not especially active.

If you do work together on any kind of task, your egos will not conflict and you will complement each other very well. Through this relationship you will be able to improve your understanding of yourselves and even reinforce your inner selves.

It would be good to find some outlet for the collective energies symbolized by this trine. The energy will express itself in a healthy manner if you let it. However, even the most benevolent energy can turn sour if it does not have an adequate outlet. Either some kind of work or some physical activity together would provide an excellent release for this energy.

This aspect signifies a lack of ego-conflict between you and an ability to work together creatively, accomplishing much. You will be competitive with others but not with each other. This aspect favors any activity involving athletics or physical fitness and any tasks that require hard work.

Composite Sun Opposition Composite Mars

Composite Sun opposition composite Mars could be extremely useful in a relationship if its energies were not so difficult to harness, for this is the most competitive, argumentative, and pugnacious of all Sun-Mars combinations. All opposition aspects indicate some kind of polarization between two entities, but this is especially so with the combination of the Sun and Mars. The Sun represents the will in general, while Mars represents that side of the will known as the ego-drive.

This aspect in your composite chart is a probable source of arguments, fights, and all kinds of ego competition. It indicates particularly that the two of you have very different energy levels, which can cause all kinds of conflict. One of you will want to do something in one way at one rate of speed, and the other will want to do it another way at a different pace.

The negative and disruptive effects of this aspect can be mitigated if you both are very secure in yourselves. In that case, instead of regarding this competitive energy as a threat, you will take it as a challenge and spur each other on to greater heights of accomplishment. You will still be competing, but the results will be creative instead of destructive.

Needless to say, this energy would be most difficult to harness creatively in a love relationship. In a business relationship or a friendship it would be easier to deal with. One exception should be noted, however. If one of you has to counsel the other in any way, this aspect would be extremely counterproductive. In such a situation you should be trying to put your own ego in the background. Such a relationship is not furthered by flare-ups of ego conflict, which are often indicated by this aspect.

Composite Sun Conjunct Composite Jupiter

Sun conjunct Jupiter is one of the most useful configurations in a composite horoscope. It is an indication that you will grow through your relationship. In fact, there will be growth, expansion, and luck in many areas of your lives together.

First, you will have a general sense of well-being, of comforting each other when you are together, even of nurturing and protecting. A Sun-Jupiter conjunction is a sign of contentment.

Second, there is likely to be material prosperity. In fact, one of the few negative attributes of this aspect is that within the relationship you may become overly concerned with acquiring wealth and possessions. But this will not happen in most cases. Even if you are not wealthy, you will feel that together you have enough. At the very least this is a highly optimistic configuration.

Third, this aspect will have the effect of broadening your horizons, of expanding your consciousness of yourselves and each other, and of increasing your understanding. It might possibly cause you to travel or have connections with foreign countries.

This aspect is a strong indication that whatever the basis of your relationship, it will be a good one, with fortunate consequences for you.

Composite Sun Sextile Composite Jupiter

Sun sextile Jupiter in the composite chart is an excellent aspect for friendship. You will feel very much at ease when you are together, and you will gain a great deal of satisfaction from the relationship.

You will be fond of discussing things and exchanging ideas with each other. But even your everyday conversations will concern important subjects, because the broadening influence of Jupiter tends to minimize small talk. All your thinking and conversation together will relate ultimately to larger spheres, such as your philosophy of life and your view of the world.

In addition to broadening your mental outlook, this relationship will also broaden your range of opportunities in the real world. This configuration is associated with what people usually call luck. But it isn't really luck so much as a positive attitude, which attracts good fortune simply because you are open to it and can recognize opportunities when they arise.

Jupiter's influence will permeate the relationship with a strong air of optimism and positive thinking, which will probably lead to much success for you as a team. There is also the likelihood of considerable travel with this aspect.

Composite Sun Square Composite Jupiter

Composite Sun square composite Jupiter will produce a great deal of energy in your relationship. If you do not establish adequate outlets for this energy, it could manifest itself as restlessness and instability. The reason for this is that the Sun-Jupiter square creates within you a sense that there are things that must be done. You will make great demands on yourselves and on each other in your efforts to achieve growth and development. Not satisfied with the status quo, you will constantly be trying to improve and perfect your relationship with each other, as well as trying to make it look good to others.

Fortunately, the effects of this combination are such that you should be able to achieve your goals. But do not try to give others the impression that your relationship is better than it really is or that the two of you are better off than is actually the case. This seldom convinces people and instead makes them believe that you both have a superiority complex.

However, you must learn to be patient; you will probably try to do too much too fast. As a couple, in your dealings with others you may overextend yourselves and go too far in various kinds of projects. Avoid the tendency to act on such a grand scale. You have the necessary ability to do what you want together, so simply try to be a bit more patient.

Composite Sun Trine Composite Jupiter

Sun trine Jupiter in the composite chart gives your relationship a good start, and it will be a favorable and positive experience for both of you. You will have whatever you feel you really need in your life together. Even if you have nothing in a material sense, you will believe that your life together is all that is necessary.

You will find that together you are able to express yourselves more adequately to the world than you can as individuals. Your understanding of each other will constantly broaden, giving you the wisdom and openness to deal creatively with any difficulties that arise in your relationship. Communication between you will be open and free, and your conversation will deal largely with matters that both of you believe in and consider important. But even when you discuss important subjects, either together or with others, there is no sense of weightiness or solemnity. You have a sense of cheerful optimism and a feeling that together you can handle anything the world may throw at you. And the chances are good that you can.

It is likely that you will travel together and perhaps go abroad or have connections with foreign places and people. Even if you don't actually travel, you will certainly go places together in your mind, exploring new ideas, new concepts, and new dimensions of living.

Composite Sun Opposition Composite Jupiter

Sun opposition Jupiter in the composite chart has very strong potentials for your relationship, but to get the most out of them will require some effort. The problem with this aspect is that it causes you to make great demands upon each other in terms of personal growth and evolution. You will have very high ideals about what your relationship should be and will not readily settle for less. This can result in either a pulling apart or a coming together.

Oppositions in general indicate a struggle between two forces that are in some kind of competition. The danger of this opposition is that in demanding so much of each other, neither is able to give easily to the relationship. On the other hand you may come to understand that the best way for you to grow and realize your ideals together is to help each other rather than simply make demands. In that case this aspect will provide more than enough help. This positive side of the aspect, if properly used, should make you grow as people far more rapidly together than you would separately.

Composite Sun Conjunct Composite Saturn

Sun conjunct Saturn is a very powerful aspect in a composite chart. It indicates that you have come together to have an important learning experience. Nothing else matters very much, really. Your relationship may or may not be long-lasting or ultimately satisfying in terms of what you now expect of it. The dynamics of the relationship will change your expectations.

The experience of this relationship may expose you to truths about yourselves that you would rather not face, which may cause you to be discouraged. But instead of reacting negatively, try to learn about yourselves, even about your shortcomings and weaknesses. The point is not to judge yourselves or each other, but to see clearly and with detachment and then try to make changes where necessary.

In many respects you may find this relationship confining and limiting. You must ask yourselves whether the relationship is giving you a necessary discipline that you would not otherwise have. Or is it cutting off legitimate self-expression that is really an intrinsic part of you? You may be inclined to feel that the latter is the case, but be very careful. It may well be that you do need this discipline and that you are not facing your responsibilities. If you need this experience, the relationship may last a lifetime. But if it is really too confining, it will probably not last very long. A Sun-Saturn conjunction can operate either way.

Composite Sun Sextile Composite Saturn

The sextile of composite Sun and Saturn gives a sober and rather restrained tone to your relationship but at the same time makes it stable. Other relationships may be more flamboyant and uninhibited, but with a Sun-Saturn sextile, yours will probably outlast them, assuming there is a basic attraction between your personalities.

This relationship should give your life a sense of stability and positive structure, as well as knowledge of where you stand with each other. If either of you is inclined to be impulsive or to act rashly, this aspect indicates that you will have a positive restraining effect upon each other. It will teach you a lot about yourselves and will have a great effect on the way you think about things. But in this strength there is a possible danger. With this aspect you can get so set in a rigid thought pattern that as a couple you do not grow at all. Don't allow the structuring tendencies of Saturn to become rigid. If you can maintain some degree of flexibility, this relationship should work out quite positively, even though it will be comparatively quiet and restrained.

Composite Sun Square Composite Saturn

Composite Sun square composite Saturn is likely to present some problems. First of all, it is an indication that your lives are presently at cross purposes to each other. It may be that you get in each other's way and then are not flexible enough to let the other do what he or she wants. One of you is very likely to become a repressive influence upon the other, constantly criticizing and condemning. There is a real question as to whether or not you can accept each other as you are.

It would be good if creative changes could occur spontaneously in each of you that would make your relationship more stable and pleasant, but you should not make this a condition of the relationship. You must be able to accept each other here and now, although this aspect makes it difficult to do that.

Try to avoid criticizing each other excessively, and do allow more freedom of self-expression. If you really cannot accept each other's annoying characteristics, it is probably best to get out of the relationship. The interpersonal warfare that this aspect can bring about will make you less complete as a couple than you are separately. And the only valid reason for a relationship is to make your lives more complete together than they are individually. Too much criticism and tearing each other down may make that impossible.

Composite Sun Trine Composite Saturn

Composite Sun trine composite Saturn operates as a positive restraining influence on your relationship, giving it structure and form. Eventually you will know exactly what to expect from each other and what you must give. At the same time, this aspect provides that through your relationship you will both learn a great deal about yourselves and each other.

Although your relationship will not be very flamboyant, it will have a quiet and sober dignity that others will admire, for this is a sign of stability. As you grow to understand each other better, your experience of this relationship will affect your thinking and give your outlook on life a stable foundation.

As a couple, you will prefer peace and quiet and established living patterns. You may be reluctant to experiment and encounter new aspects of yourselves. But be careful not to let caution become timidity, or fondness for familiar patterns become rigidity.

You will be rather reserved in the way you express your feelings for each other. People may even think there is a kind of coldness between you. But you probably do not need frequent superficial reassurances, preferring the deep and sincere expression of feeling that is seldom put into words.

This relationship should outlast many others that may seem more energetic and vigorous. Because the energies signified by this aspect are released slowly, you will be able to stay together for a long time, no matter what kind of relationship you have.

Composite Sun Opposition Composite Saturn

Sun opposition Saturn in the composite chart presents real problems. Among them are: lack of mutual understanding, temperaments so different as to cause difficulties, a tendency to work against rather than with each other, a tendency for one of you to inhibit and limit the other unnecessarily, and excessive criticism of each other. With energies of this sort, it is most difficult to make a relationship work properly.

The greatest danger is in criticizing and limiting each other. The one who is temperamentally stronger is quite capable of depriving the other of any strength he or she might have. Because of this, the relationship can gradually make both of you less strong than you would be otherwise.

It is possible for a relationship with this configuration to survive, but several conditions must be met. First, criticism must be limited to really important problems and not be allowed to turn into constant carping and harassment. Second, the relationship should be open enough so that you can get away from each other in your daily lives and lessen the tension between you. Third, the two of you must broaden your viewpoints and become more tolerant of what you reject in each other. And fourth, aside from the problems you may cause each other, you must have feelings of genuine love or friendship for each other.

If you cannot meet these four conditions to a considerable degree, it is unlikely that your relationship will survive or be of any real benefit to you in the long run.

Composite Sun Conjunct Composite Uranus

With Sun conjunct Uranus in the composite chart, this relationship will challenge the very core of your beings. All your ideas about yourselves and how you fit into other people's lives, as well as life in general, will be tested very severely. If you are strong and secure in yourselves, you both will learn a tremendous amount through this relationship. But if you are not strong, you will probably find it somewhat frightening.

Do not expect this relationship to follow any particular established patterns, for you will define for yourselves new behavior patterns that fit only the two of you. If you are looking for a conventional, predictable relationship, you will probably be disappointed. In a marriage, for example, you would both have to be very open. Your only goal must be each other's happiness, not adherence to community standards. Any effort to force each other into an ordinary marital pattern will create such a feeling of frustration that you both will want to wander elsewhere. This is also true for nonmarital love relationships. If you are friends, be prepared to surprise each other frequently with new facets of yourselves.

If you find this relationship frightening or upsetting, you should examine your expectations and try to determine whether you are a victim of rigid thinking. However, even with the best will in the world and the most open consciousness, a relationship such as this may not last. Indeed, permanence is one of the concepts frequently challenged by Uranus. Make as few demands as possible on the relationship, assume an open attitude, and allow yourselves to be changed and opened up by the experience.

Composite Sun Sextile Composite Uranus

The sextile of composite Sun and Uranus indicates that this relationship will seek out a path of its own, defining new standards of behavior and changing your thinking. While most relationships are very much restricted to the two individuals involved, this one will be open to contact with others, almost as if you must share what you have with as many people as possible. If it is a sexual relationship, therefore, it will be quite open and free. A friendship with this configuration will constantly challenge and stimulate the world-views of you both and of those around you. Even if neither of you is particularly unconventional, you will be amazed at the new aspects of life and experience that this relationship will open up.

There will be a continuing exchange of ideas and new concepts between you, always lively and stimulating. And the more you allow this exchange, the better the relationship will be. Otherwise you both will find that you are easily bored and restless in each other's company. Don't allow laziness or fear of experimentation to let this partnership fall into conventional patterns. To do so would be to weaken something that should be a highly stimulating and creative experience for both of you.

Composite Sun Square Composite Uranus

Sun square Uranus in the composite chart means that this relationship will be the source of many surprises for you, some of which will be quite difficult to deal with.

Most important is the problem of instability. You are likely to find that this relationship makes one or both of you extremely restless, impatient, and likely to behave in ways that fly in the face of tradition. Clearly this is not a relationship in which either of you can be possessive; you must give each other maximum freedom. And if this results in one of you drifting away to someone else, then that is the way it must be. This aspect is not especially good for any relationship, such as marriage, that involves traditional expectations. Marriage is possible, but it would require much more flexibility than most people have.

A persistent difficulty that you may have to face is the nervous, electric quality in your interaction with each other. This quality will make it difficult to relax and take it easy when you are together. On the other hand, at least you will never be bored with each other.

This relationship must be allowed to take its own course, unhampered by restrictive expectations. Even so, it will probably be a very unstable and unpredictable experience.

Composite Sun Trine Composite Uranus

Sun trine Uranus in your composite chart means that you will be strengthened by seeking out new paths of self-expression together. Do not allow your relationship to fall into conventional patterns; instead, explore new ideas, new horizons. If you can, you should travel to new places to find experiences together that would not be possible outside your relationship.

If this is a love partnership, you should keep yourselves open to encounters with others. Narrow conceptions of fidelity or possessiveness should not prevent you from having valid relationships outside of this one. However, this should not be interpreted as a license to be dishonest with each other.

On the contrary, this encounter calls for even higher standards of honesty. You must be honest not only with each other but with yourselves at all times. In this way, as you come to each new experience, you will be able to deal with it openly, not from a fearful or narrow position. Be assured that this relationship will expose you to new areas of life with each other and within yourselves.

Composite Sun Opposition Composite Uranus

The opposition of composite Sun and Uranus suggests that this will be an upsetting relationship in many ways. Not that it cannot be rewarding and worthwhile, but it is not likely to be very conventional or predictable. Whether this relationship will be too upsetting for the two of you depends largely on how flexible you are and how open you are to new kinds of experience. The more traditional your ideas about the roles you play with each other, the more disturbing the relationship will be.

The central problem here is that one or the other of you will constantly challenge the other's most cherished ideas. The experience will be one of constant, unremitting revolution. It would almost be better to have this aspect in a composite chart with one's psychiatrist, rather than with a lover or friend. The ceaseless challenges will make it difficult to attain any kind of stability between you. One moment you will feel you have the situation well in hand, only to have the whole pattern changed by new events.

Another possible effect of this aspect is that the relationship will present a challenge to the standards of the community in which you live. Others may see it as a very unusual and eccentric relationship, one that even poses a threat. In a sense, this problem could help your relationship, because outside pressures might drive the two of you closer together. On the other hand, the situation may become too hot to handle. If other people oppose your relationship too strenuously, the pressure may be too great to withstand.

Composite Sun Conjunct Composite Neptune

With Sun conjunct Neptune in the composite chart, there is either a lot of idealism or much self-delusion in this relationship. The challenge you face is to determine which of these is true in your case and to come to terms with this reality.

Note that if idealism is carried too far, it comes very close to self-delusion. It is one thing to have a strong sense of how things ought to be. But it is something else if you believe that your ideals are being met when they are not.

At any rate you will probably feel that the two of you have a highly spiritual union, which may in fact be so. This aspect can indicate a soul-union in which the two selves are so perfectly matched that verbal communication is unnecessary. But it can also mean that you only believe this is true, even when it is not. The action of Neptune is very nonphysical, so that a love union under its influence is likely to be platonic rather than physical.

The second possibility, that of self-delusion, simply means that the two of you are not confronting each other but instead are projecting visions of what you want on your partner. One manifestation of Neptune in a relationship is that one of you may be trying to "save" the other from himself or herself. This is especially true if one of you has a severe psychological or physical problem that the other tries to cure. Often there is .a strong martyr quality in such a relationship.

All these tactics represent insincere or self-delusive efforts to avoid the real people in the relationship—you and your partner. If there really is a strong spiritual or philosophical element in your relationship, that is very fine and beautiful. But if not, don't try to deceive yourselves that there is.

Composite Sun Sextile Composite Neptune

With composite Sun sextile composite Neptune, your relationship tends to be very idealized. In some ways it is best suited to friendship, because it tends to make a love relationship platonic. But if both of you are on a spiritual path, this aspect will reinforce your efforts to be together.

No matter what kind of relationship it is—friendship, love affair, marriage, or something else—you will have very high ideals about what you should be to each other. Since you will be caught up in this ideal, you may be reluctant to deal with the ordinary, mundane aspects of life. Others may see your relationship as impossible or at least impractical, but that won't disturb you particularly. You will go right on, seemingly with your heads in the clouds. Obviously, this can be carried too far if you are not careful. You have to deal with the real world one way or another. Also you must learn to communicate with each other about all areas of your relationship, not just the ideal parts.

In the long run, this is not a particularly difficult aspect to deal with. The idealism it signifies can make a relationship quite beautiful. It is not so much a matter of suppressing idealism as of learning to deal with reality.

Composite Sun Square Composite Neptune

Be extremely careful with a relationship that has the square of Sun and Neptune in the composite chart. This aspect implies that the relationship tends to be unrealistic and impractical. In particular there is a danger that one of you will deceive the other, which could result in disappointment and disillusionment when this is revealed. No matter how beautiful the relationship seems at the beginning, there is a real possibility that it will end with a major let-down.

Often, one person is victimized by the other's constant deceptions. But the so-called victim may be partly to blame because of a subconscious desire for martyrdom. No single aspect can make a relationship completely impossible; however, this one demands that you both be extremely understanding about the real reasons for the bond between you.

This aspect can mean that both of you are very unclear about what you are doing with your lives, not only together but as individuals. If you do not know where your own life is going, it is very unlikely that the experience of this relationship will help you very much.

A relationship with this aspect could possibly have a solid basis and a strong sense of spiritual union. That is the goal toward which you should strive, but first make sure it is a realistic possibility.

Composite Sun Trine Composite Neptune

The trine of composite Sun and Neptune indicates that there is a good deal of idealism in this relationship. You will feel that it is an extraordinary union between two souls, perhaps even a spiritual union. Many of the thoughts you want to communicate to each other will not have to be spoken, for you will know beforehand what the other person is thinking. Often one of you will start to say something, only to find the other saying it too. In other words, there is a strong likelihood of a psychic bond between you.

The spiritualizing power of Neptune tends to negate the physical realm. For this reason, a relationship with a strong Neptune, such as this one, is likely to be platonic rather than physical. Nevertheless, the great feeling of beauty in such a relationship usually compensates for the fact that it does not operate on a physical plane as well as on a spiritual level.

Your lack of concern with the physical and material realms constitutes the major problem here. In a friendship it is perfectly all right to commune at such a high level, ignoring practicality. But in a love relationship, especially marriage, practical concerns have to be dealt with, and it may be difficult to bring yourselves down to that level.

But because Neptune rules self-sacrifice, one of the strongest bonds between you will be your willingness to give selflessly to each other at any time.

Composite Sun Opposition Composite Neptune

The opposition of Sun and Neptune in a composite chart presents a number of problems. First of all, it means that one or both of you is refusing to evaluate the relationship realistically. One manifestation of this problem would be that you each project your own ideal images onto the other person; or it could appear as outright lies and deceitfulness.

Second, of all combinations of the Sun and Neptune, this one is the most susceptible to savior-victim behavior. As a noted astrologer expressed it, the relationship is that of "a savior looking for a victim or a victim looking for a savior." Neptune denies the drives of the ego and therefore may cause you to look for a friend or lover who will be saved by your wholehearted sacrifice. Needless to say, the person who is being saved must pay by being constantly reminded of the martyr's sacrifices.

Or it may be that one of you wants to be the one who is saved and looks to the other as a savior. If he or she does not take the savior role, there will be terrible disappointment.

The main problems presented by this aspect are learning to relate realistically, which will be difficult, and learning to relate to each other as equals. Sacrificing yourself will never improve anything or anyone, and it may well sour the whole relationship. Relate to each other as you really are. Do not impose unrealistic goals on each other, for they inevitably lead to deceit and disappointment. This brings us to the strongest warning: be honest with each other and with yourselves, for dishonesty, either inadvertent or intended, is the greatest danger of this aspect.

Composite Sun Conjunct Composite Pluto

The conjunction of composite Sun and Pluto signifies that this relationship will have very deep and long-lasting effects on you, for Pluto rules deep, profound, and inevitable transformations.

This aspect will work in one of two ways. The first possibility is that your relationship will have a very powerful effect on other people. You may find that together you can control and manipulate others in ways that would never be possible individually. The effects of Pluto are always powerful. Use that power carefully, because if it is misused, others will respond violently and join together to put you down.

The second possibility, which may happen quite independently of the first, is that the relationship will have a powerful internal effect and cause you both to go through important changes and transformations. Pluto rules depth psychology and psychotherapy in general, for the aim of these techniques is to bring about a thorough regeneration of the self. This relationship may have that kind of effect on both of you.

One warning, particularly for love relationships and marriages! At times you both will feel that everything is collapsing and that the whole relationship is over. With a strong Pluto, this may simply mean the beginning of a major change; when it is complete you may enter a new phase that will be better than ever for both of you. Try to be patient when such crises occur. You can't afford to act impulsively.

Composite Sun Sextile Composite Pluto

The sextile of Sun and Pluto in the composite chart indicates that there is a powerful force for regeneration and growth in this relationship. Concretely, this aspect makes it possible for the two of you to revive your relationship after periods of difficulty, either between the two of you or between you as a couple and the outside world. It gives you staying power.

At the same time this aspect ensures that the experience of this relationship will have a strong effect on your views of the world and your ways of thinking about it. For the most part, these effects should be positive, involving greater understanding of yourselves as individuals and as partners in a relationship. You will continually be made aware of new aspects of yourselves, as they are brought to the surface and examined by both of you. In most respects this is a serious relationship, meaning that you will be involved with each other at a very deep and profound level.

It may be that others will be somewhat afraid of the level of intensity between you, but don't pay any particular attention to their fears. They will come to see that there is nothing to be afraid of. The changes brought about in you through this relationship are good, necessary, and natural products of your own evolution.

Be prepared for the fact that your normal patterns of doing things will be altered by this relationship. This aspect signifies that new insights about yourselves will be revealed to you, but do not be afraid to deal with them. The results can only be good for both of you.

Composite Sun Square Composite Pluto

The square of composite Sun and Pluto indicates that this relationship will have profound effects, but they will not be especially easy. The combination of the Sun and Pluto signifies power, and in its simplest and most blatant form it usually means power struggles between you. The problem is that one of you has a strong desire to transform the other into something that he or she is not. Even if a change is called for, the style in which it is done is likely to provoke the other partner to active opposition.

Pluto always operates on a relationship at a very deep level. There is absolutely nothing superficial about its operation. If this aspect is one of many that indicate conflict, then this will certainly be a difficult relationship. If other aspects are more harmonious, the effects of this one will be less destructive. But the relationship will still be experienced as a very intense and deep transformation through and by each other. Even if you are not trying to change your partner, you will. And the changes will be felt from the innermost depths to the outermost reaches of your lives.

One problem that can arise with this aspect is a serious conflict of life directions. It is not simply that you have different courses to pursue in your lives, but that your life directions actually conflict. This is likely to be the source of considerable ego conflict between you.

The only way to deal with the energy of this aspect is to avoid all ego games. Confine yourselves to real sources of conflict and don't indulge in mutual harassment over small matters that you do not really care about but are using to score points at the other's expense. There will be enough real issues to deal with that you will not need to invent any.

Composite Sun Trine Composite Pluto

The trine of composite Sun and Pluto is a sign of an emotionally intense relationship that will transform you both for the better if you learn to move with its flow.

Your overall life attitudes and philosophy will be very much affected by the emotional and psychological changes brought about by this relationship. The effect on both of you will be as profound as could be achieved through any kind of therapy or psychological analysis. Pluto rules psychological transformations, and you can be sure of profound changes wherever Pluto is involved.

Not only will this relationship change you inwardly, it will also have a visible effect on your personalities and the way you express yourselves to others.

This is not an extremely difficult aspect to deal with, but if you are seeking a casual, light-hearted relationship, it would not be good. Because of Pluto, it will be a significant partnership and not light in tone, although potentially quite creative.

In a sexual relationship, the effect of Pluto is to increase the emotional intensity as well as the emphasis on sex. The interest in sex will not be just for physical reasons, but also for the profound emotional effects that go with it. You both feel that sexual contact is an experience that affects you at all levels of your being and enables you to transcend ordinary reality. This attitude makes sex much more important to the two of you than it would be to others.

Composite Sun Opposition Composite Pluto

In a relationship with composite Sun opposition Pluto, the most difficult problem will be power struggles. At times such a relationship will seem more like a competition than a love affair, marriage, or friendship. And there is a real danger that if this relationship breaks up it will degenerate into open warfare.

One or both of you must learn to curb your desire to dominate the other. Even if you justify your need to dominate as being for a good cause, still it must be curbed. When the power of Pluto is misused, the response tends to be violent, and no matter what you think, with this aspect the power is likely to be misused.

It is also possible that together you may stir up opposition from other people. The energy that this aspect brings out often makes others afraid of what is going on between you. This possibility, however, is not so great as the chances of conflict within the relationship.

There is a danger that through struggles for domination one of you may emerge so much the loser that you will not easily be able to recover a sense of pride and self-confidence. You must be quite careful about any relationship that has this aspect in the chart. Although it may not be impossible by any means, the dangers described above must be watched for.

Composite Sun Conjunct Composite Ascendant

The conjunction of composite Sun and Ascendant signifies a relationship that is likely to have a considerable impact on its surroundings. Other people will be very much aware that something is happening between the two of you. This is because Ascendant rules the kind of energy that the two of you transmit to your surroundings, as well as saying much about the relationship itself, while the Sun rules the basic energy drives of the relationship. The consequence of this placement is that the fundamental energy of your relationship is directed at your surroundings in some way.

It may be that you are simply a striking pair of people who impress others easily without making any special effort to do so. But it may also be that the two of you are trying to make an impact on those around you for reasons of your own. In a business relationship, for example, you might want to have it known that you are a partnership to be reckoned with, that you are an important team. This might also be the case in a personal relationship, although for different reasons.

In any case, it is certain that you both will insist that others allow you to be what you want to be as a couple. You are not likely to bow to social pressures. In fact, you are more likely to apply pressure to others than you are to knuckle under yourselves.

The most important point about this relationship is that it will have considerable integrity. You will be true to yourselves, and that will certainly help to win you the admiration of others.

Composite Sun Sextile Composite Ascendant

Composite Sun sextile Ascendant indicates that the two of you enjoy social exchange with others. You are not a couple that likes to retire by yourselves and avoid others. In fact, you are more likely than most to seek out friends who become a very important part of your relationship with each other.

Not only do you like to be with friends, but also it is very important to both of you to have opportunities to talk with people and exchange ideas and communication. In a similar way, the two of you place great importance on communication between yourselves.

You will probably be good friends. If this is a sexual relationship, you may be lovers, but you will be friends as well. This is very important in a relationship between the sexes and not always achieved.

You are likely to experience a certain restlessness in this relationship, but not a difficult kind. It is simply that the two of you like to seek out new experiences and new opportunities for doing things together. This leads you to range far and wide, either literally through travel or figuratively through pursuing a curiosity together. As a consequence, the two of you are likely to have more varied experiences than many couples have. The successful search for variety is a keynote of this relationship.

Composite Sun Square Composite Ascendant

When composite Sun is square composite Ascendant, the two of you are not so concerned with how the energies of your relationship affect others in your environment. You are much more concerned with your own identity within the relationship and how it might further your own development. You will be very concerned about the nature of your own personal lives, or of your professional lives, if this is a professional relationship. Or it may be that you will be concerned to find some overall purpose in your lives through the experience of this relationship.

In most cases this is not a particularly difficult square. There is no reason why the two of you should not concentrate on your own development rather than worrying about how your relationship affects others. If carried too far, however, this attitude can cause some troubles by disrupting relationships with other people. Others may regard the two of you as being overly concerned with yourselves, possibly too withdrawn or, at the other extreme, too concerned with dominating others.

Fortunately, because the two of you are not very concerned about the impression you make as a couple, it should be easier to deal with the pressures that you may inadvertently arouse in others. You should try not to stir up so much trouble with others that you find it difficult to get along with them. But this is not likely to happen unless you both go to extremes to outrage others, which is not a normal consequence of this aspect.

Composite Sun Trine Composite Ascendant

The trine of composite Sun and Ascendant is a very easy combination in the composite chart. It indicates that you find it easy to express yourselves to each other and to others. The two of you radiate good energies, and other people like being in your company because you enjoy being with them. This is not likely to be a withdrawn relationship that takes place largely in secret.

At the same time, the trine means that the two of you find it easy to be yourselves with each other. This is not a relationship in which you have to pretend to be something other than what you are in order to get along with each other. As a consequence, this is a good aspect to have in the chart of a love relationship or close friendship.

The trine also means that this relationship will have a strong effect on your consciousness. You will have new experiences together that you might not have had otherwise, and you may even travel a lot more than you did before you came together. Since your philosophies of life are compatible, you will not find it necessary to argue about the different ways in which you see things.

In general, this aspect will help a relationship to survive, because it allows the two of you to be at ease with yourselves and others.

Composite Sun Opposition Composite Ascendant

The opposition of composite Sun and Ascendant is similar to a seventh-house composite Sun. It means that the two of you place great stress upon being together as a team and facing the world as a couple. Instead of thinking of this aspect as an opposition of Sun and Ascendant, think of it as a conjunction of Sun and Descendant. In most cases, this is an excellent placement for an intimate relationship such as marriage or one in which the two of you must operate as a unit, as in a business partnership. It is also favorable to any relationship that involves giving and receiving advice, such as a lawyer-client, psychologist-patient, or astrologer-client relationship.

Others will look at the two of you as a team or partnership, even to the point that they would find it strange for you to be apart.

Sometimes the energies of this particular combination can go outside the relationship and produce conflict between yourselves and others. Sun opposition Ascendant can be a sign of open conflict as well as intimate togetherness, although the conflict is not so likely to be between yourselves. It is necessary to examine other aspects of your relationship; if the overall potential for conflict is high, this aspect is likely to produce conflict rather than togetherness.

Chapter Six

Moon

The Meaning of the Moon in the Composite Chart

The Moon, the natural complement to the Sun, represents the medium through which the Sun's energy expresses itself. Whenever there is a manifestation of the Sun's energies, the Moon's influence is also operative.

The Moon is the "planet" that most relates to emotions and feelings. Of course, it is not really a planet but a satellite of the Earth. Nevertheless, it operates as a planet in the horoscope.

In a composite chart, the Moon indicates how well the relationship acts as a medium of emotional expression for the two of you. Can you be honest and open with each other about your feelings? Can one of you reveal his or her feelings without being rejected by the other? It is often difficult for others to deal with the lunar aspects of one's being, because the level of intensity of feeling is so basic that they do not fit into the formalized way that people usually relate to each other. Yet in a close relationship it is very important to be able to deal with each other on this level. For this reason alone the position of the Moon is very important for describing compatability.

The Moon also represents basic structures within one's personality: habits, unconsciously motivated behavior, and their sources—one's past, origins, family, and home life. If the Moon is well placed in the composite chart, the two of you will feel that you have something in common. Even if your origins are quite different, you will feel that because of your experiences you can understand each other better than most couples. A badly placed Moon, however, can create a sense of alienation, of being different from each other, that will make it difficult for you to get along.

The house position of the Moon in the composite chart shows the area in which you feel, or ought to feel, that you have the most in common. If the Moon is badly placed in the chart, its house position will show the area of greatest emotional stress.

The aspects to the Moon show the quality of the emotions that are experienced in the relationship.

In contrast to the Sun, which shows what the relationship does, the Moon indicates the subjective feelings of harmony and empathy that you have for each other, even in difficult times.

Composite Moon in the First House

Composite Moon in the first house makes clear that in this relationship your feelings and emotions are very prominently involved. It is not a cool or distant relationship in which the two of you treat each other as distant objects. You will be in there with all your feelings working.

Obviously, this placement is favorable to any relationship in which you want to relate on a close, intimate level. However, it can create some problems that must be dealt with if you want to derive the greatest benefits from this configuration.

As the planet of emotions, the Moon emphasizes the subjective side of any matter. A prominently placed Moon can, at its best, indicate a very sensitive relationship in which the two of you know intuitively what is going on inside each other. You have a deep emotional understanding of how you get along. But the Moon can also create such a strong emotionalism that you are unable to stand back and look at yourselves clearly in terms of your relationship. In other words, your subjectivity overwhelms your ability to see each other objectively. Be careful to avoid such extreme emotional involvement.

The Moon also rules the past and the contribution each of you makes from your individual experience, so these factors will be very important to you. A first-house Moon is usually a strong indication of an important personal relationship. It should give the two of you a strong sense of emotional compatibility. You will feel that you belong together and that you have much in common, which will indeed be true.

Composite Moon in the Second House

Composite Moon in the second house indicates that this relationship will bring out the needs you both have for emotional and material security. In fact, you may have come together because of those needs.

You will have a strong sense of shared values, which will help to reinforce you as a couple against the undependable and changeable outside world. Because of this shared feeling, your relationship will grow strong even when there are considerable difficulties between you. You will be reluctant to give up the emotional security granted by the Moon in this position, even when things get tense. But the need for security could keep you together even when that is not the best solution for either of you.

One minor problem that this placement can bring about is that your need for emotional security can lead to a compulsive gathering of physical objects. You may try to satisfy your need for emotional security through owning things together. In this case your relationship will come to be symbolized by great quantities of material possessions. Beyond a certain point, possessions can become a millstone around your neck that limits your freedom of movement. Particularly if this is a marital relationship, you might be trapped into staying together because of what you own rather than because the relationship is working well. Like everything else, possessions must be kept in their place.

Nevertheless, the security that this relationship can offer should be one of its strongest points and should help keep you together when the going gets tough.

Composite Moon in the Third House

Moon in the third house implies that this relationship is based largely on feelings. The third is the house of the mind in its day-to-day functioning, and in a relationship it indicates the normal attitudes and opinions that you share. When you are together, you think about yourselves more subjectively and are more influenced by your emotions. You communicate with each other primarily through feelings rather than through intellect, so communication between you is likely to be mostly nonverbal.

Because you have a strong sense of shared opinions and viewpoints, you may not really need to communicate so much on an intellectual, verbal level. But at the same time, because communication within the relationship is so subjective and emotional, it may be difficult to discuss things rationally and objectively when you have to.

You may talk quite a bit about your collective feelings, which obviously is good in a personal relationship if you keep your sense of perspective and don't overdo it. Do not let this tendency degenerate into making mountains out of molehills.

In a marriage or love relationship you are likely to be involved to an unusual extent with relatives, who may in some way contribute to the emotional stability of the partnership.

Composite Moon in the Fourth House

The fourth house is in some ways the most natural position for composite Moon, for there is a strong analogy between this house and Cancer, the Moon's sign.

With this placement it is extremely important that the two of you share a common background or experience, for it is likely to be a strong force binding you together. You may feel that you are alone together in a crazy world, protected only by your shared attitudes and origins. However, it is not so important that your backgrounds be truly similar as that they have given you similar basic attitudes to the world.

Even more than in a relationship with a second-house Moon, you are together to give each other emotional security. And here again your security is very likely to take the form of sharing real estate or a house. This is an excellent position for marriage partners or roommates because of the strong sense of sharing it can induce.

However, it is necessary to warn you that your desire for emotional security and the related tendency to seek material security should not become the sole factors binding you together. Also your need for a secure relationship must not lead you to repress the legitimate gripes you may have with each other. Let your partner know how you feel; your relationship is probably strong enough to stand the strain.

A fourth-house Moon is most favorable in a relationship in which you set up housekeeping together. For this reason it is a good position in the chart of a marriage.

Composite Moon in the Fifth House

Composite Moon in the fifth house suggests that your relationship exists because it makes you both feel good, especially emotionally. Traditionally, the fifth is the house of amusement, love, and children. One could also call this the position of recreational relationships, in which self-expression is a principal aim. Obviously this is a good house position for any kind of personal relationship, especially a love affair. You will enjoy each other's company immensely, and together you will seek out parties, the theater, nightclubs, and all kinds of good times. These experiences will be important in your feeling of what you share with each other.

The major deficiency of this position is that you may find it difficult to settle down to anything serious. This can be especially difficult in a marriage or long-term love relationship, for you can't always have fun and games; at some point you have to work at the serious business of building a relationship together.

If this is a marriage, children are likely to assume an important role in your life together. With this position of the Moon, you will probably want to have children, and you will have them.

For pleasantness in a relationship, this is one of the better Moon placements. It ensures that you will be able to express yourselves emotionally with each other easily and fully.

Composite Moon in the Sixth House

The sixth house is a rather somber and serious placement for composite Moon. It suggests that you have a sense of having come together for a specific and necessary task or purpose that may not be completely pleasant. One of you may feel subordinated to the other in some way. Therefore, this is a difficult placement for any relationship that requires you to give and take equally, as most relationships do. One person may feel like a doormat for the other; he or she is likely to get tired of that position and revolt against the other.

The only way to make this position work is for the two of you to exchange services equally, thus preventing it from becoming a one-way affair. This may be more difficult than it sounds if one of you is determined to be a martyr, especially since a martyr usually demands some kind of repayment that is very difficult for the other to make.

A related danger is that if one of you is giving more to the relationship emotionally than the other, you could become quite resentful about it.

Whatever the costs, you both must strive to be more nearly equal in giving and receiving. Otherwise, this relationship will become quite unpleasant.

Composite Moon in the Seventh House

Composite Moon in the seventh house is a good indication that in this relationship shared feelings will be very important. The seventh is the house of intimate one-to-one encounters, both positive ones such as partnerships and marriage, and negative ones such as open enmities. However you encounter each other, it will be with feeling.

In general, the seventh-house Moon favors any intimate relationship, especially marriage or other love relationship in which sharing emotions is important. You will have a strong feeling that you belong together as a unit, and your emotional attitudes toward the outside world will be similar. The symbolism of this position is that you feel as if you were one person.

Somewhat like the first-house composite Moon, which is the polar counterpart of the seventh-house Moon, there is the danger that in times of emotional stress you will not be able to keep your relationship in perspective. You are likely to become too involved in your personal feelings and not be able to see what is really going on between you. Try to stay somewhat detached from difficult situations so that you can deal with them objectively and not get completely carried away. If you can do that, this should be a very good emotional relationship for both of you.

Composite Moon in the Eighth House

Composite Moon in the eighth house indicates that your relationship is very introspective. You will spend much time examining what you are as a couple and trying to arrive at a complete psychological understanding of it. Obviously, this is a good attribute in any relationship, if it is not carried too far. Just make sure that you do not become lost in the emotional intricacies of your relationship.

This is a position of transformation, which means that your relationship will undergo extensive changes, partly because of what you will learn about yourselves, partly because of the pressure of your emotions. Sometimes you both will feel that the relationship serves much the same purpose as seeing a psychiatrist or counselor; that is, it gives you new understandings about yourselves.

In addition, this placement of the Moon in the composite chart makes you very concerned with values. If you do not start out with a common set of values, it will be very important that you develop one. Your shared values may be purely on a psychological level, or they might exist more on the material plane as a great concern for possessions and property.

The greatest strength of this Moon placement is the contribution it can make to your self-understanding. Its greatest difficulty is the tendency to emphasize the heavy, moody aspects of your relationship and to dwell excessively on serious matters. Try not to fall into a "slough of despond" or become too introspective. Explore the new and constantly changing features of your life together, and welcome such changes instead of fearing them.

Composite Moon in the Ninth House

With composite Moon in the ninth house, there is a strong feeling between you that you share basic attitudes about the world and philosophies of life. Consequently you like to discuss your ideas and opinions with each other. You feel that being together greatly expands your awareness. Even if your backgrounds are quite different, communication between you will not be difficult. You will see differences of that sort simply as an enjoyable challenge to your understanding of each other. It is possible that you may travel long distances together, or that you met in a place foreign to both of you, or that you are from different countries.

At its best, this is a good position for learning and growth within a relationship. You will continually teach each other, and even if the relationship does not last, you both will feel that you have benefited from it.

While this position is good for any type of relationship, it is strongest in situations that emphasize communication and exchange of ideas. It is especially good for people working together on some project, writing together, or negotiating in any way.

In a personal relationship, this placement by itself works more to produce friendship than love, but even in a love relationship there will be a strong intellectual affinity between you.

Composite Moon in the Tenth House

Composite Moon in the tenth house indicates that you will share a concern for getting ahead in life. You both want to get somewhere, and you feel that together you can do it better than you could separately. Fortunately, the Moon in this house is traditionally associated with making a favorable impact on the public, so your public image is likely to be good. Because of that fact, the potentials of this position can be exploited better by a professional relationship than by a personal one, although it is quite good in either case.

However, in a personal relationship, one factor must be kept in mind. The tenth house is an external house; that is, it deals with matters that are normally part of the external world. Having an important element of the chart in the tenth house indicates that you tend to see things too much in terms of externals. The Moon, representing the feelings and emotions, is particularly damaged by this tendency, because the feeling aspect of a relationship should be an internal concern. It should be between the two of you rather than outside.

There is a danger that you will look to factors in the outside world—your life situation, your jobs, property, or whatever—to explain problems that arise between you. You may look out when you should look in. Or you may concentrate on externals and superficial matters to the exclusion of internal matters. This is not an inevitable result of this placement, but it is a danger that must be recognized and dealt with.

In general, the tenth house is a good position for the composite Moon because it is an angular house, which gives the Moon strength and importance. It also gives the relationship a dynamic, active quality that can prevent stagnation.

Composite Moon in the Eleventh House

Composite Moon in the eleventh house indicates an underlying emotional sympathy between you that is good for both love and friendship. You have a strong feeling of shared goals and objectives in life, which will contribute to your ability to get along with each other. You will spontaneously think of yourselves as a unit rather than as two separate individuals, which obviously is a plus for any relationship.

Since the eleventh house is the house of friends, this position is a good indication that the two of you will have friends outside of the relationship. You will be fond of company and enjoy sharing good times with others. Not only will you have friends in the literal sense, but many factors in your lives together will support your relationship in a friendly way without any special effort on your part.

In general this is one of the better positions for a personal relationship and should enable you to share both love and friendship.

Composite Moon in the Twelfth House

Composite Moon in the twelfth house is a demanding position in that it requires the two of you to do a great deal of work that most couples are unwilling to do. Any relationship is helped by such work, but with this position it is absolutely necessary that you do it.

If left alone, the two of you would be very likely to keep your feelings hidden not only from each other but also from yourselves. When you do this, the feelings become the source of actions and behavior that neither of you understand but that are very detrimental to your relationship. At the same time, you will tend to shy away from other people or at least to keep your feelings hidden from others, perhaps because you fear that if they get too close they will discover your secrets.

With this house position of the Moon, the greatest danger is emotional dishonesty at the very least and sometimes open and outright dishonesty. Very often this happens because you don't really know what is going on inside your relationship. There may be repressed fears that you do not know how to face or that you can't face directly.

The need here is for both of you to plunge into the relationship, find out the truth of what is going on, and face it squarely and honestly. Do not shrink from what you find, because the consequences of not being honest with yourself and each other are far worse than anything you may be hiding.

If you don't seek out the truth, your relationship will make you lesser people than you really are and will give you the feeling that you have been defeated in life by forces you don't understand. And when the repressed feelings finally do emerge, they will explode destructively and perhaps violently. If, however, these feelings gradually emerge from an honest search for understanding, the wisdom you gain will make you much wiser than people who haven't had to face such a challenge.

Composite Moon Conjunct Composite Mercury

The conjunction of composite Moon and Mercury can contribute many strong and useful features to a relationship. Very simply, it means that the two of you can talk about your feelings instead of keeping them bottled up inside. Therefore you will be able to sit down and hash out a problem in a reasonable way whenever things get rough. However, this aspect does not guarantee that you will be able to deal with everything in a totally rational way. That ability depends largely on the kinds of habits you have developed together. Moon conjunct Mercury may have two different kinds of effects, depending on whether the lunar tendency or the mercurial tendency dominates.

If the lunar tendency triumphs, you will be able to discuss your emotional situations, but you will be very emotionally involved and subjective. On the other hand, you will really live and feel your emotions, so that something real is communicated between you, even if it is not too clear.

If the mercurial tendency dominates, you will be more detached and rational but also less involved. You will intellectualize your feelings instead of living them and working them out. Consequently your communication, even if easier, will be less meaningful.

Obviously the best tactic with this aspect is to create some kind of balance between these two extremes. If you can achieve a balance, you will have the best of both worlds. This position does provide that potential, which makes it a good aspect in a composite chart.

In any case, avoid going to the other extreme—spending all your time examining your emotions together. That can have a very distorting effect on your perspective.

Composite Moon Sextile Composite Mercury

The sextile of composite Moon and Mercury means that you can discuss your feelings openly and easily with each other. However, with this aspect there is less risk of being extremely subjective about yourselves and excessively introspective.

This aspect indicates that you will be able to communicate both intellectually and emotionally. It creates an emotional and intellectual compatibility that enables you to combine your feelings and your ideas so that you communicate with your whole being. Through this ability you will come to know and understand each other and become friends with much in common. This relationship will give you both an opportunity to grow intellectually as individuals.

When emotional difficulties arise between you, your ability to talk to each other will allow you to work out your problems better than most couples. Using and defining words in different ways is one of the worst barriers there can be between people, but for you it will not be a problem.

Regardless of your objectives, if you take advantage of this characteristic, you should be able to build your relationship into something fine and meaningful for both of you.

Composite Moon Square Composite Mercury

The square of composite Moon and Mercury raises certain problems for your relationship. It indicates that the emotional bonds between you are somehow working at cross purposes to your intellect. Normally this means that for each of you the intellectual and relatively detached part of your understanding is overwhelmed by the emotional and subjective part. The result is that when you try to talk about a problem it becomes an emotional contest instead of a discussion. You must try to become more objective about yourselves and each other when you talk things over.

On the other hand, it must be said that you don't keep things secret. You do express your emotions openly, which is an advantage even in a difficult relationship, for you know what is going on between you. And your emotional communication is not limited to arguments and disagreements; you communicate your good feelings for each other also. But again the problem is that the communication may not be too clear on a rational level. You will have to develop understandings in nonintellectual terms in order to solve your problems. If you do this and also try to attain a higher level of detachment in your relationship, you should be able to overcome the problems that this aspect can bring about. It is not one of the most difficult squares, for it can signify great depth of emotional understanding between you.

Composite Moon Trine Composite Mercury

The trine of Mercury and Moon in a composite chart indicates that there is great potential for intellectual and emotional growth through this relationship. It means that you can communicate in a positive way about your feelings and opinions and that your basic philosophies of life are compatible, which reinforces your emotional compatibility.

When a situation arises that requires the two of you to sit down and discuss your problems, you can do so easily and with the proper blend of objectivity and involvement. You understand that it can be dangerous to overintellectualize emotional matters, and you are able to communicate through your feelings as well as about them.

As a couple, you are open to new ideas and experiences and consequently enjoy exploring different areas of your lives together. At the same time you are not afraid to express your ideas freely and completely. There will be few barriers between you, at least as far as communication is concerned.

With any effort at all, you should be able to exploit the potentials offered by this aspect and to grow tremendously through this relationship.

Composite Moon Opposition Composite Mercury

With composite Moon opposition Mercury, the challenge for your relationship is to learn to balance rational communication with communication of feelings. If the relationship is allowed to follow its natural tendencies, you will probably find it difficult to bring the two kinds of communication together. It will not be easy to discuss matters in which you are emotionally involved with any degree of detachment and objectivity. When you do talk rationally, it will tend to be about matters that aren't really important to either of you, so nothing is actually being communicated.

On the plus side, however, you probably won't hold back on discussing matters that you feel must be talked about. But the problem will be in how these matters come out into the open. Usually such a discussion will be a very emotional experience with a good deal of sound and fury and not much true communication. You must learn to make the discussion useful for understanding as well as for letting off steam. In fact, you will have an overall problem in objectively understanding the fundamental truth of this relationship. It is not that your understanding is false, but that it is formulated in such personal terms that no one else, including your partner, can share it.

Nevertheless, it is possible to bring about a balance, so that real feelings can be communicated clearly and objectively. But you both will have to learn to look at things in a new and different way by standing outside of your involvement and seeing your partner's position.

Composite Moon Conjunct Composite Venus

The conjunction of composite Moon and Venus is a most positive aspect for any personal relationship, especially for a love affair or marriage. It indicates a strong feeling of love between you that you will express openly. The relationship may even have something of a dreamy quality, as if it were too beautiful to be true. But the nature of this aspect is such that this relationship should be as good as it looks. Other aspects can give a relationship a feeling of beauty that is actually an illusion, but this aspect should make the feeling quite satisfactorily real.

This quality of beauty may be envied by other people. It may seem to them that there are no rough edges in your relationship, although that will not be entirely true, of course. But the basic inner strength of this relationship should be great enough to overcome all but the worst problems.

If this is a marriage, you may have a strong desire for children, because this aspect reinforces your parental instincts. It also indicates that you probably will have children, although that is not a basic concern of this aspect.

Beauty and art are also promoted by this aspect. People who work together in the arts often have this aspect in their composite charts.

In general, this is one of the most positive and useful aspects that a composite chart can have for a successful personal relationship.

Composite Moon Sextile Composite Venus

The sextile of Moon and Venus in a composite chart indicates warm and positive emotions between you. It is a good aspect for friendship and love in any kind of personal relationship. Furthermore, it indicates that you communicate your affections to each other easily and that you are emotionally compatible in general.

The effects of this aspect are very quiet and easy. It will not produce a sudden mad, passionate attraction between the two of you, but rather a relaxed feeling of affection. This kind of energy is better for a long-term relationship than for a short-term, possibly stormy affair.

In a love relationship with this aspect, you will find that you are friends and lovers simultaneously. Friends with this aspect will have an affection for each other that is deeper than is usual in a friendship.

In a marriage the sextile of Moon and Venus indicates that you want children and probably will have them. The Moon and Venus configured in an easy angle such as the sextile signify fertility and motherhood. It is the sign of the earth mother. Love is strongly linked to parenthood with this aspect.

On the whole, this is one of the most beneficial aspects in a composite chart, although its effects are rather quiet.

Composite Moon Square Composite Venus

Unlike most squares, the square of composite Moon and Venus cannot really be called a difficult aspect. It presents some problems, to be sure, but on the whole it is a rather benevolent aspect in a composite chart. Its major effect is to give an air of compulsion when this relationship is beginning; that is, you both have an urgent feeling that you should get together. This aspect creates a strong and lasting attraction between you, and like all Moon-Venus aspects, it acts as a buffer against bad times within a relationship.

The only real difficulty here is that even if you are not really suited to each other, you may be drawn together almost as if by a fatal force. This force of attraction is undiscriminating but strong enough to bind you together in what might otherwise be a very unstable, short-term affair. By itself this aspect will not tell you whether a relationship will be a good one; it only designates the presence of this powerful attraction. Therefore you must evaluate your relationship carefully. But if you are getting along well with each other, the feelings of love between you will be greater than average, and your relationship should endure.

Composite Moon Trine Composite Venus

The trine of composite Moon and Venus is an excellent indication of a relationship based on love and affection. By itself, this aspect suggests that you are very compatible emotionally and that your relationship will have a positive effect on both of you. Not only will it be pleasant but it will also help each of you in your personal growth.

This is an excellent aspect for any relationship based on feeling, and for a love affair it is superb. But that does not necessarily imply a short-term affair, for it can also mean a long-lasting relationship. This aspect simply creates a strong and intense feeling of love between the two of you. Needless to say, it is also an excellent aspect in the composite chart of married people, indicating that the marriage will start out and continue as a love relationship.

In a marriage, this aspect may create a strong desire for children, because the love generated here includes a strong need to protect and nurture. Children satisfy a need created by a strong Venus-Moon combination, which represents biological fertility.

On a very different level, this aspect can indicate that the relationship will be materially prosperous, particularly if it involves investments and speculation.

This aspect is most desirable in the composite chart of any kind of relationship, but particularly in a love partnership.

Composite Moon Opposition Composite Venus

By and large, the opposition of composite Moon and Venus is a good aspect in the chart of any relationship, especially a love relationship. But it has some peculiar properties that should be noted.

First of all, it indicates a certain instability. Although your relationship may be a long-term one, it will have considerable ups and downs of feeling. However, these should not destroy it.

Second, this aspect can bring the two of you together even though you are really quite different and would not usually get together. Your differences actually make you complements of each other, but that will not be apparent at first. Once you come together, you will discover your complementarity, which will bind you together. The instability mentioned above comes from learning to relate your differences to each other.

This aspect creates a strong magnetism, which is why it can bring together two people who appear so different. This magnetism will help to hold the two of you together even when the going gets rough, but at the same time it has created some of the roughness, because of your differences.

On the whole, this aspect in a composite chart should prove to be a considerable asset.

Composite Moon Conjunct Composite Mars

The conjunction of composite Moon and Mars has a double-edged effect. On the one hand, it indicates that you arouse very strong feelings in each other, but by itself it does not indicate whether they are good or bad feelings.

In a love relationship, for example, this aspect indicates that you will have a very strong emotional involvement. The relationship will probably stir up both positive and negative emotions in both of you. You will have vigorous disagreements and even fights, but your reconciliations will be equally intense.

By itself this aspect does not tell whether this is a good relationship in other ways. If your relationship is basically good, you will simply experience a heightened emotional involvement, although with a greater tendency to quarrel. But if your relationship is not otherwise very sound, it will be destroyed by the fighting that this aspect produces. In any case the two of you will have some heated moments, which simply have to be taken in stride along with all that is good in the relationship.

One of the strong points of this aspect is that in a sexual relationship it creates a good deal of sexual energy. This can make sexuality a strong bond between you. Although you will probably have many fights, even these are a reflection of the underlying sexual energy.

Composite Moon Sextile Composite Mars

The sextile of composite Moon and Mars indicates that your relationship is based on feelings. There is a great deal of emotional energy here that makes it difficult for you to ignore what the other person does or says. Fortunately, however, the energy is not especially negative. In fact, in a sexual relationship this aspect is a positive indication for success, because Mars rules certain portions of the energy complex that makes up sexual energy. The Moon, of course, rules the feelings. The result is that this aspect arouses the energies needed for a positive sexual relationship.

Except for sexual contact, this combination of Mars and the Moon is not especially physical in its expression. But physical activity provides a good outlet for the energies it generates. Consequently you should not sit around together but should try to be active in all possible ways. If there is work to be done, the energy of this aspect can help. This is not a particularly good aspect for mental work, however, because the subjective nature of the Moon makes it difficult to understand ideas with logic and detachment. Also, the energy of Mars is too vigorous for the quiet reflection needed for most kinds of mental work.

This is a good aspect for a relationship based on feeling, but not so good for one that requires much mental activity or communication of clear, ordered, and objectively presented facts.

Composite Moon Square Composite Mars

The square of composite Moon and Mars is a somewhat difficult aspect for a relationship. The Moon rules the basic feelings and emotions present in the relationship, while Mars indicates its vital energies. More precisely, Mars is the energy one uses to assert one's individuality. The result of the square is likely to be emotional conflicts between you and a sense that your individuality is constantly being challenged by your partner. Fights, disputes, and general disagreement are the probable result, unless you make a great effort to overcome this problem.

Whenever the two of you have a disagreement or communication problem, your immediate response is to get hot under the collar. But this tendency must be curbed, because once that happens, all your ability to objectively analyze and solve the problem goes out the window. You lose any chance of understanding the other person's position; a fight ensues; and the relationship is driven further apart. Only by maintaining some degree of calm, difficult as that may be, can you arrive at a creative resolution of the problem. Anger and extreme subjectivity go hand in hand in your relationship.

If you really want to solve your problems, avoid getting angry with each other. Obviously there are times when an honest expression of anger is useful and constructive, and you should not always repress it. But try not to overdo your honest expressions of anger; chances are, with this aspect, you both fly off the handle too readily. Keep cool and save your anger for times when it is really justified. Otherwise the relationship will not survive or be productive.

Composite Moon Trine Composite Mars

The trine of composite Moon and Mars is a sign that the two of you have a great emotional involvement in this relationship. You each evoke such strong feelings in your partner that you can't ignore each other. For the most part, these feelings will be positive, but it is important that your relationship have ample outlet for emotional self-expression. This would not be a very good aspect for a professional relationship that required mutual feelings of detachment. The combination of the Moon and Mars, even in a trine, implies that the feelings evoked are strong enough to make the relationship extremely subjective and personal.

This aspect acts most positively in a love relationship, where it can make an otherwise quiet and subdued affair into something much more emotionally rich and involving. Also, in a sexual relationship, the energy of the Moon combined with Mars helps to stimulate physical sexuality.

One point must be kept in mind, however, and that is that neither of you must repress the other. There must be complete freedom of emotional expression between you. If held in too long, the energy of this trine would probably come out in an explosive way.

Composite Moon Opposition Composite Mars

The opposition of Moon and Mars can be a very explosive aspect in a composite chart. It is an indication of anger and hostility breaking out, which can transform any kind of relationship into open warfare. The question is, do you want to be friends and/or lovers? Or do you want to be competitors and/or enemies? If the energies of this aspect are given free rein, you are more likely to be the latter.

One certainty is that you will never have to worry about repressing your feelings when you ought to express them. The problem is to make the expression creative, so that it can help the two of you grow, instead of just being a destructive outburst.

When difficulties arise, try to keep calm for a little while and make some kind of rational sense out of what is happening. Only in this way can you keep a tight rein on the energies of this aspect. You will have one thing going for you, at least; when people with this combination do blow up, it's all over with quickly, because all the negative energy is expended. But because the energies arise so often, quite a bit of damage occurs anyway. You should ask yourselves whether the two of you are really compatible enough to make a go of this relationship. The answer may be either yes or no, but you should ask the question.

Some people have a great deal of difficulty expressing anger or hostility in any form, even if the relationship tends to trigger it. If you are one of these people, you must learn to express your feelings.

If you do succeed in repressing the energies of this configuration, which is quite difficult, the results will be most destructive. Expressing your real feelings honestly is essential with this aspect. Simply try to keep it under control.

Composite Moon Conjunct Composite Jupiter

The conjunction of Moon and Jupiter in a composite chart is a very favorable indication for any kind of personal relationship. Its symbolism can be described in general as good feelings; that is, the two of you feel good together. You feel warm toward each other, and you can express your feelings easily and with enthusiasm. If one of you is sad or depressed, the other person will cheer you up.

At the same time, you respect each other's emotions. You feel quite protective of your partner and try to keep him or her from being emotionally hurt by others. It may even get to the point of mothering each other; however, this will be experienced as supportive rather than oppressive. In fact, the effects of this aspect are quite far removed from the kind of mothering that may be better described as smothering, for you have a great deal of respect for each other's freedom and individual rights.

When disputes do arise, you will try to deal with them in a very high-minded manner, not allowing yourselves to be petty or small. You will discuss the issues openly and try to resolve them in a way that is fair to both of you.

A Moon-Jupiter conjunction in a composite horoscope is often an indication that the two of you will be quite prosperous in a material way if you have the kind of relationship in which you own possessions in common.

Composite Moon Sextile Composite Jupiter

The sextile of composite Moon and Jupiter indicates that your relationship has excellent potential for happiness and good feelings. There will be considerable emotional exchange between you, most of it positive.

In a sexual relationship, this aspect signifies emotional interaction rather than love. In any other type of relationship it indicates feelings of contentment and happiness with each other.

You feel that you are supportive of each other and that you share similar hopes for the future. And you find it easy to believe that your goals will be fulfilled, because the Moon-Jupiter sextile is one that generates optimism. In turn, your attitude of optimism makes it easier to attain your objectives. Others may regard you as lucky, but your luck actually results from positive thinking.

The expansive effect of Jupiter upon the Moon means that both of you will grow emotionally and personally in this relationship. In a business or professional partnership this aspect indicates successful dealings with the public and possible financial success. Either a personal or a professional relationship with this aspect will probably have a good image in other people's eyes.

Composite Moon Square Composite Jupiter

This square of composite Moon and Jupiter is one of the few squares that is not especially difficult to deal with. Like all combinations of Jupiter and the Moon, it indicates basically good feelings between you. Your relationship will have a quality of exuberance that will make others glad to be with you. Also, you will be tolerant of each other's faults. In fact, the only real difficulty this aspect might raise is that you may be too uncritical of each other. The result might be that your personal growth would be lessened, but it is unlikely that such an attitude would break up the relationship.

You will enjoy each other's company and may be quite fond of going out together socially and having a good time. This is an expression of the emotional exuberance of this square, which is an active aspect that requires some form of activity to make it work out well. Therefore, take every opportunity to do things together, so you can enjoy the energies of this aspect to the fullest.

There is one other effect of this aspect that should be noted. If as individuals you tend to overdo in some way, that tendency is likely to be reinforced by the relationship. As a couple you probably won't deny yourselves anything you want.

Composite Moon Trine Composite Jupiter

The trine of composite Moon and Jupiter will have a good effect upon your relationship in several areas. First of all, it denotes that the two of you have a generally good feeling for each other. You feel happy together and enjoy each other's company. When you are depressed or low, being together will make you both feel better.

Second, this aspect will help to create a warm sympathy and deep emotional understanding between you, which will help you through any problems you may have to face.

Third, this relationship is likely to have a spiritually and morally uplifting effect upon you; it will make the world look better and will actually help you both understand what the world is all about, in a spirit not of resignation but of positive optimism.

In a marriage, this aspect instills a desire for children and makes it more likely that you will have them.

Because of the feelings of optimism and happiness that you have with each other, you will always feel that you benefit from being together.

Composite Moon Opposition Composite Jupiter

The opposition of composite Moon and Jupiter is relatively easy to handle. It may bring the two of you together even though you are quite different, but it also provides the energy for you to adjust to each other. Any Moon-Jupiter aspect indicates that you will be able to tolerate the differences that exist between you.

An opposition is an active aspect, which means that the two of you will have to be active together. Neither of you will be very fond of sitting around waiting for something to happen. You will want to go out and look for things to do. Probably you will be fond of going out together and socializing. Jupiter is gregarious and likes company.

Other people are likely to see you as a very outgoing and happy couple. You are also very generous to others, although you may be a bit overextravagant.

Sometimes with this aspect there is a compulsion to be "happy-go-lucky" all the time. You like to do exciting things and are fond of rather boisterous activities. You may be reluctant to settle down and deal with serious concerns that you should be facing together. As a consequence, you may let important matters slide. This is perhaps the most serious negative tendency of this aspect and the one you should watch out for most. By and large, however, this is not an especially difficult opposition.

Composite Moon Conjunct Composite Saturn

The conjunction of composite Moon and Saturn produces two different kinds of effects, both of which are somewhat difficult to deal with in a personal relationship.

On the one hand, it can create an emotional barrier between you, so that you have trouble communicating with each other on a feeling level. Without the aid of that largely nonverbal and subjective dialogue that cements a personal relationship, the two of you will have to spell out the emotional messages that should be understood intuitively. Consequently you will spend a great deal of time trying to express in words what should be obvious without them.

You will do a lot of analyzing, both of the relationship and of each other. The danger is that you will make things seem worse than they are. Beware of this tendency, because it can make a perfectly viable relationship seem impossible. At best, analyzing your relationship can help you understand what you have together, but it cannot completely replace intuitive communication.

On the other hand, this aspect may cause the two of you to subordinate emotional considerations to supposed necessities, duties, or responsibilities, denying yourselves the joy and pleasure of open and relaxed self-expression. Try to relax together and not be so serious about things.

At its worst, this configuration can bring about such a sense of emotional alienation between you that the relationship will never get off the ground. Even though purely verbal or intellectual analysis cannot totally substitute for the subtler kinds of communication that this aspect prevents, such analysis is the best course to take in trying to get along with each other.

Composite Moon Sextile Composite Saturn

The sextile of composite Moon and Saturn suggests that you both are very serious about your relationship, which you have probably entered for practical as well as emotional reasons. As a result, you handle the relationship very carefully and probably develop it rather slowly. Because of your care and caution, the partnership you build will probably outlast many others.

You are very sober in the way you deal with each other, which may justifiably give others the impression that you are too serious and do not look at life with enough humor. It isn't necessary to be so careful; you can afford to take a lighter view of things. In fact, you can take liberties that others cannot take because you have prepared yourselves so thoroughly and carefully.

This aspect gives a relationship an emotional stability that is truly to be envied. It is not likely to be an especially flamboyant or demonstrative affair, and other people may think you are somewhat cool to each other. That does not mean there is no real affection between you, but that as a couple you have a different way of showing it. Go on doing things your own way, and pay no attention to what others think.

Composite Moon Square Composite Saturn

The square of Moon and Saturn in a composite chart is an indication that there is a lack of emotional affinity between the two of you. You may be able to work together as business associates on various projects and even be quite friendly. But you are not likely to have the in-depth understanding needed for a deep personal friendship or love relationship. This aspect is least detrimental in a relationship that requires no great emotional communication.

In a close personal association, this aspect is likely to produce a sense of emotional alienation, as if you cannot quite get into each other. The close warmth and togetherness that is basic to such a relationship is just not there.

An emotional relationship may survive for a long time in spite of this aspect, but it will not be completely satisfying, and you may feel lonely with each other. When you are together you will seem rather serious and somber, causing other people to wonder exactly what you do for each other. Introspection and deep examination of your relationship can compensate to some extent, but intellectual understanding is not an adequate substitute for what should be an unspoken emotional understanding. In addition, the depressive effects of the Moon-Saturn square may cause you to overemphasize the difficulties you actually face.

If you both feel that you need the relationship for personal growth, by all means pursue it. But you should modify your expectations for deep satisfaction on the emotional level. If you are just beginning such a relationship, it may be that for the time being you need a rather detached kind of commitment.

Composite Moon Trine Composite Saturn

The trine of composite Moon and Saturn produces a highly stable and consistent relationship. In a love relationship, this aspect makes your love for each other steady and sober. If this is a friendship, it will be an enduring one. What you won't have with this aspect is the wildly romantic, unstable kind of love that many people seek out. This is an indicator of a serious relationship, one that is only for those who are tired of playing around and want something real and enduring. This aspect neither creates nor denies affection and love. It simply makes whatever feelings there are steady and solid.

You are likely to share the attitude that although you both have emotional needs, they must always be governed by a realistic, pragmatic approach to life. You accept what you have and do not make excessive demands upon the other. As a couple, you take seriously what the relationship offers.

The two of you are also probably quite reflective about the nature of your relationship and quite self-critical. It is as if you are constantly asking, "What are we together, really?" While it is beneficial to reflect on the real nature of a relationship, do not overdo the criticism. You have solid virtues working for you with this aspect. Do not negate them with pessimism.

Composite Moon Opposition Composite Saturn

The opposition of composite Moon and Saturn can be quite difficult for a personal relationship, especially in terms of your emotional interaction. The Moon and Saturn are opposite principles, and the opposition aspect emphasizes their oppositeness.

The chief danger is that you will not interact emotionally at all, or you will have no mutual understanding of each other's emotional nature. If you have managed to establish an intimate relationship in spite of this obstacle, you will feel lonely with each other at the times when you most need understanding and warmth. You seem to be emotionally alienated. At best, you act distant, and at worst you are hypercritical and intolerant of each other's faults. The more you need intimacy and warmth, the more unsatisfying it is likely to be. It may even get to the point that you handle each other as objects in a cold and detached manner.

With this aspect in the composite chart, it is best not to expect too much of an emotional relationship. A business or professional association that does not require much emotional exchange is not severely affected, however; the opposition of the Moon and Saturn indicates detachment rather than hostility. But an intimate personal relationship with this aspect will prove to be severely limited or totally unsatisfactory.

Composite Moon Conjunct Composite Uranus

The conjunction of composite Moon and Uranus is bound to create a certain amount of excitement; what it will not provide is stability. You seem drawn to each other for the excitement and stimulation that this relationship offers, which you both depend upon. If the relationship ceases to be stimulating, it may very well come to an end. And this is perhaps as it should be, for Uranus challenges your preconceptions and drives you out of your established ruts. This relationship may exist for the same purpose.

On the other hand, it is possible that this conjunction signifies something unusual or atypical about the relationship itself. In a love relationship it could mean that the two of you would not ordinarily be expected to get together. Perhaps your backgrounds are radically different—racially, ethnically, or socially—or there is a great difference in your ages, or possibly you are both of the same sex. Whatever the case, Uranus makes it unusual. This quality may also be characteristic of a friendship.

The unusualness of the relationship may actually overcome the instability brought about by Uranus. That is, if the relationship itself is unusual, it may be more stable than a more ordinary partnership.

In a marriage or love relationship, this aspect demands that you give each other more than the usual amount of freedom. Any attempt by either of you to be very possessive is likely to jeopardize the partnership.

This is likely to be an unusual relationship. Accept it as such and allow it to teach you something new about life.

Composite Moon Sextile Composite Uranus

The sextile of composite Moon and Uranus indicates that there is an open and free quality to this relationship, or at least there should be. It should change your thinking and give you new insight into the creative possibilities of a relationship. Either as friends or as lovers, you should allow these new ideas to enter your consciousness and open up new worlds.

Under no circumstances must you force this relationship, whatever it is based on, into established patterns governed by regular rules. This partnership may be a totally new hybrid. A sexual relationship, for example, is likely to be very open and may even include other people. Or this aspect may produce a friendship that is also sometimes a love affair. Two people with this aspect in their composite chart may be very intensely involved with each other, then separate for a while, then come back together, always conscious that the other is there in spirit if not in body.

This aspect may bring together two people who have rather different opinions and ways of thinking. Should this be the case, however, you will be able to get along together if you are open enough to allow each other to creatively challenge and possibly alter your thinking.

Composite Moon Square Composite Uranus

With the square of composite Moon and Uranus, this relationship is not likely to be a stable, enduring, long-term one, at least as far as love is concerned. This is an aspect of emotional change and instability. A love affair with this aspect may flare up suddenly and then cool off with equal suddenness. Or one of you may continually challenge the other's ideas and feelings, so that there seems to be no peace or stability.

Nevertheless, considerable good may come from such a relationship, as long as you try only to find what it can offer rather than how long it can last. It will challenge your basic patterns of thinking on an emotional level. You will open up and explore new ways of relating to each other. If you give it a chance, this relationship will expand your consciousness.

A friendship with this aspect may be quite enduring because it doesn't demand such constant intimacy as a love affair. Because friendship is not by nature possessive, it does not challenge the rebellious, free nature of Uranus so much. But even a friendship with this aspect will change your preconceptions and established ways of relating.

If you are at a stage of your life and consciousness when you are seeking to build a stable and reliable relationship with someone, this is not a very favorable aspect. But if you are open to any experience that a relationship can offer, this will be a creative learning experience, although a bit crazy at times.

Composite Moon Trine Composite Uranus

The trine of Moon and Uranus in the composite chart signifies that both of you must be free in your emotional expression in order to bring out the best in this relationship. This aspect demands that you allow new experiences and ways of feeling about each other to affect your consciousness. Even the relationship itself may take on very unusual forms. You should have the courage to deal with each other in different and exceptional ways. Otherwise you will have wasted an opportunity for growth.

By the same token, this relationship is likely to have a strong consciousness-altering effect upon both of you, changing your attitudes about your own and your partner's emotions. Your world-views and philosophy of life may very well be changed.

Certain attributes of a conventional relationship, such as stability and predictability, may not exist here. Yet despite the unpredictability, there will be much of value. And the more freedom you allow each other within the structure of this relationship, the more you will get out of it, to the point that whatever instability exists will not be of any importance to either of you. In this relationship, freedom of self-expression is absolutely essential

146

for both of you and should be your first priority.

Composite Moon Opposition Composite Uranus

With the opposition of composite Moon and Uranus, this relationship will be a constant challenge to both of you. It will be rather difficult and probably very unstable. Neither of you will know quite what to expect from the other, and you will not be able to count on having traditional role expectations fulfilled. As individuals, each of you will have to seek a unique and different place to find yourself in regard to each other. Even then, however, you are not likely to settle down to a constant and reliable way of relating to each other. As a consequence, a relationship with this aspect in the composite may not be long-lived.

Indeed, if longevity is one of your principal criteria, as in a marriage, it might be best not to enter into the relationship at all. At least you should establish a real and reliable arrangement with each other long before entering a legal marriage. Even then, the legal contract of marriage, which alters any relationship, may turn it into something quite different from what you expected. You both may be disappointed or feel unduly restricted.

This aspect is least destructive, in fact it is actually positive, in a relationship that has no expectations placed upon it; both of you are simply encountering each moment as a unique experience to be savored for itself and not as a promise of some hoped-for future. With Moon-Uranus configurations, no moment can be counted on for anything, particularly as a building block for the future.

You will constantly challenge each other, which will cause you to question your most cherished preconceptions about the nature of life and of relationships in particular. This fact alone would produce some instability, as you reel from the shock of new discoveries that alter your awareness.

This is certainly not an aspect for a reliable, safe relationship, but it can be productive of great learning experiences, if you are open to receive them.

Composite Moon Conjunct Composite Neptune

With the conjunction of Moon and Neptune in your composite chart, you both should be very careful to understand the true nature of your relationship. It is not necessarily a bad relationship; in fact, it might be extremely beautiful and high-minded. But there is a problem because of the idealistic nature of Neptune when combined with the Moon.

This aspect signifies the highest evolution of emotional and spiritual idealism. You will not be satisfied by the ordinary and mundane ways in which people usually relate to each other. What you both want is something much more than that, a complete union of two souls in a cosmic oneness. The difficulty is that you may think you have achieved this state when you haven't. Both of you may be in a complete psychological fog about the relationship and may not understand it at all. Consequently you must be very careful to find out what the truth is. Don't allow yourselves to wander about in a beautiful haze that has nothing to do with reality.

On the other hand, you must try not to fall into the trap of making excessive and unrealistic demands on the spiritual quality of your relationship. You both are only human and must accept your frail humanity as you try to relate to each other.

If you succeed in striking the balance between these two extremes, you may be able to build an extremely high and spiritual kind of relationship.

One final note. In a relationship between the sexes, the nonphysical and idealistic influence of Neptune often results in a platonic union that is never consummated on the physical level. Usually one or both of the partners feels inwardly that a physical union would corrupt the high purity of the relationship. It is difficult to make a sexual relationship live up to the Moon-Neptune idealism, but it is worthwhile to try to spiritualize your sexuality without denying its physicalness. Only then can you achieve the total union on all levels that is Neptune's ultimate object.

Composite Moon Sextile Composite Neptune

The sextile of composite Moon and Neptune gives a relationship a strongly idealistic, antimaterialistic, and nonphysical flavor. It is probably more suitable for a friendship or platonic love affair than for a physical relationship between the sexes. The spirituality of the relationship will be emphasized very strongly. Both of you may be inclined to use the other to get away from normal, everyday reality and to get in touch with a higher, more ideal realm of existence.

Communication between you will be largely intuitive and nonverbal, with looks and subtle gestures often taking the place of words. Yet you will feel that you communicate very well, even better perhaps than those who are limited to words. If this is in fact true, you have a very high type of relationship, indeed. However, look carefully to make sure that this is really the case with your relationship and that you are not merely deluding yourselves. Make sure that you really understand each other and are not living in some fantasy you have constructed about yourselves.

The potentials of this aspect are good if the advice given above is heeded, and you should have a relationship that is in many ways ideal and spiritual.

Composite Moon Square Composite Neptune

Be very careful if you have the square of Moon and Neptune in your composite horoscope. This aspect creates a great danger that one or both of you will deceive yourselves or each other, either about the nature of the relationship or about outside matters that affect it. It can produce a situation in which one of you has come to "help" the other with a very difficult psychological problem, such as alcohol or drugs. But with a Moon-Neptune square, the so-called helper is often motivated by the desire to escape from some personal problem by relating to someone whose problems appear to be worse. This situation creates a savior-victim relationship that can be quite unhealthy, because the real issues are never faced.

The relationship may also take on a very unreal idealistic tone, with the two of you creating beautiful illusions about yourselves and each other. But eventually you are likely to find that you have not faced all the facts about each other, and you may become completely disillusioned and embittered. Disappointment of one's ideals is perhaps the greatest danger presented by this aspect. Its negative effects can be prevented only by the most hard-nosed, pragmatic, and practical evaluation of the relationship. And unfortunately, that is the very thing that the Moon-Neptune energy tends to block.

Composite Moon Trine Composite Neptune

In any kind of relationship with the trine of composite Moon and Neptune, idealism will be a dominant theme. You will feel that the spiritual union between you is higher and more soulful than in any ordinary relationship. Such a union is a real possibility, which the two of you should strive for, but it will not come automatically. What will come with this aspect is the expectation of spirituality, not necessarily the fact. All Moon-Neptune combinations carry the seeds of self-delusion, which should be watched for very carefully. But the trine provides an energy that can help bring about the ideal as well as its vision. You both must be very realistic about yourselves as well as compassionate for each other's weaknesses.

The love you experience together will be a very ideal and spiritual love, and it may be platonic rather than sexual. There will be a strong feeling that you have a true soul union. Much that would ordinarily be expressed in words about your feelings will be communicated in a subliminal and intuitive way that others will not even be aware of. If you have really established the ideal bond that you desire, you will be able to communicate more through intuition than other people can with words.

This relationship will also affect your philosophy of life by making you more idealistic and concerned with spiritual matters than you were before. Faith will become a stronger element in your views of the universe.

The demands this aspect can make upon a relationship are great, but so are the potentials. A truly ideal and spiritual relationship of a most uncommon sort is a real possibility. But remember—so also is a relationship in which you wander about in an idealistic romantic fog. The choice is yours.

Composite Moon Opposition Composite Neptune

The opposition of composite Moon and Neptune can present many difficulties in a relationship, all stemming from one central problem. Namely, you have very little clear understanding about the true nature of your relationship. The lack of understanding can take many forms, but two of the more usual ones will be discussed.

First, of all Neptune-Moon combinations, this one is most affected by a desire to escape your own problems through a "savior-victim" relationship. That is, both of you are looking for ways to escape your own problems, but one does so by "saving" the other from himself or herself, while that person plays the complementary role of wanting to be saved. Since neither of you will face your real problems directly, nothing is solved. You should try to relate as equals, giving and receiving alike, with neither of you martyring yourself to the other.

A second result of this aspect may be that the two of you have radically different views about the relationship. While one of you idealizes, the other may take advantage and act quite treacherously behind the first one's back. The result may be that what you believe is friendship or a love relationship is really not that at all. The surreptitious actions of one against the other may lead to great disappointment and disillusionment.

The main problem is one of illusions. When this aspect occurs in a composite, only the most hard-headed and pragmatic evaluation can determine the true nature of the relationship. Detachment and objectivity are needed at every turn. Perhaps the best answer is to rely more than usual on a third party to help you come to a true understanding. But be careful whom you pick, and don't let your idealism and romantic imagination get you into a situation you cannot deal with.

Even if neither of the two manifestations described above is at work in your relationship, beware of other self-delusions that can weaken the valid basis of your relationship.

Composite Moon Conjunct Composite Pluto

The conjunction of composite Moon and Pluto is a very intense aspect. It means that your feelings will be extremely intense, and the relationship is not likely to be a casual one.

Not only will the emotional content of the relationship be intense, but both of you will discover in yourselves emotional depths you may not have been aware of. You will experience feelings you have never had before, but do not worry; they will not necessarily be bad feelings. The principal effect of this aspect is simply to intensify whatever feelings exist already.

There are some effects, however, that you should watch out for. This aspect can create an unnecessary degree of possessiveness in one or both of you. If you do not allow each other enough freedom of self-expression, the relationship may become too stifling.

It is possible that your feelings about this relationship will run so high that you will not be able to evaluate it or each other rationally. On the other hand, if there is a strong feeling of love between you, this aspect will make it a most intense and enduring kind of love.

Just be careful that you do not go to work on each other's feelings too much. You will need a little peace and quiet with each other, without the constant analysis that this aspect tends to provoke. Do not become too heavy in the way you relate to each other; try to lighten the atmosphere and enjoy each other quietly. If you always operate at an intense level, you are likely to burn out each other as well as the relationship.

Composite Moon Sextile Composite Pluto

The sextile of composite Moon and Pluto indicates a great deal of intense introspection and self-examination within a relationship. You will reflect and consider various aspects of your relationship, and this will allow you to arrive at a deep and lucid understanding of what you are to each other and to yourselves. You have a greater potential than most couples for doing this successfully. At the same time, your self-examination will probably lead both of you to make great changes in the way you deal emotionally with life. Your everyday ideas about the nature of the world will also be strongly affected by this relationship.

A Moon-Pluto aspect of this kind is very psychotherapeutic; that is, the results of your encounter can be very much like the experience of psychotherapy: an increased understanding and awareness of your innermost selves.

The result of all this is that both of you are likely to regard this relationship as one of the more important and significant in your lives, because it has made you grow in awareness.

Composite Moon Square Composite Pluto

The square of composite Moon and Pluto can lead to a very intense encounter. Whether or not it will work out positively depends very much upon how you handle it.

This is an aspect of uprooting, in that it brings matters up from the depths of your unconscious minds to the surface so that they have to be dealt with. But the effects of this aspect are so intense that the relationship may burn itself out before anything positive can be accomplished. One point that must be noted is that you both have a great penchant for working upon each other's psyche. But don't overdo it or try to be your partner's psychotherapist. Such tactics are often a disguise for a not-so-subtle power game between two people who profess to be only trying to help each other. As a result, one of you is very likely to feel emotionally dominated and overwhelmed by the other.

The emotional intensity of this aspect can also work in another way. It can create such a strong involvement between you that you cannot let go of each other for a moment, resulting in a smothering relationship in which neither of you can grow.

Beware of emotionally manipulating each other. Try to be a bit more detached in your attitude and leave each other alone a little, no matter how strong the temptation is to interfere and make changes. Love each other for what you are now rather than for what you think you can make the other person into. If you cannot do this, perhaps it would be best to dissolve the relationship.

Composite Moon Trine Composite Pluto

The trine of composite Moon and Pluto in the composite chart indicates that your relationship has an unusual emotional intensity, which makes it difficult for you to react to each other in a detached manner. In itself this is not at all bad and can, in fact, produce a very meaningful and significant relationship. But it will sometimes be hard to avoid being too emotionally involved with each other. You may find it difficult to stand back and make an objective evaluation of the situation, which is necessary at times in any relationship.

Nevertheless, if you want intimacy, this combination provides an intensity that will bind the two of you together for a long time. This relationship may cause you both to go through very profound emotional changes, in which you will discover aspects of yourselves that you may not have known existed. What comes out, if properly exploited, will enable you to express yourselves more fully in many different areas of your lives. If either of you has a tendency to be too intellectual or to live too much in the mind, this relationship can greatly increase your capacity for emotional experience.

The only other difficulty that this aspect may bring about is a tendency to be possessive and jealous of each other. Outside of this problem and the need to be more objective about each other, this is a good aspect to have in a composite chart, especially if your relationship is an intimate, personal one.

Composite Moon Opposition Composite Pluto

The opposition of composite Moon and Pluto is an aspect of extreme emotional intensity, calling forth great involvement and strong feelings. You certainly won't worry about not having a strong effect on each other; the problem will be to avoid having too strong an effect.

If improperly handled, this combination can give rise to extreme jealousy, struggles for dominance, and excessive possessiveness. As a result, one of you may completely strangle the other's individuality, or at least attempt to do so. If this occurs, the one being dominated will find it very hard to deal with, because the tactics used to dominate will be subversive rather than direct. For example, one of you may appeal to the other's sense of guilt in order to coerce the other. The aggression will often be passive rather than active; that is, the manipulator may pretend to be hurt by the other in order to get his or her way.

Such a situation must be avoided at all costs. The power of this aspect can lead to emotional violence, which could destroy the relationship and leave much bad feeling in its wake. If you are tempted to use these tactics, don't. Be as straightforward and direct as possible. The results will probably be better than you imagine, and at least they will be less destructive. Every time you win by being manipulative, you actually lose, because the other person is building up a long-lasting reservoir of resentment that may explode when you least expect it.

If you are the victim of such methods by your friend or partner, be direct and call your friend's bluff. Declare that you know what is being done and that you won't stand for it. If emotional manipulation is being used to prevent you from doing something you have a right to do, say so and go right ahead with your plans. Don't allow yourself to be the victim of any kind of emotional blackmail.

Composite Moon Conjunct Composite Ascendant

The conjunction of composite Moon and Ascendant signifies a relationship in which your emotions and feelings play a very prominent role. Therefore, this aspect is more favorable to a personal relationship than to a professional one, because the subjectivity that is characteristic of the Moon is not very helpful in a relationship that requires clear thinking and detachment.

On the other hand, in a personal relationship, the Moon close to the composite Ascendant signifies that the two of you can achieve an emotional rapport and depth of shared feeling that will be the envy of many other couples. You will share your moods, emotions, and feelings with each other at all times, so that it will be easy for you to know each other on an inner level as well as an outer one.

Of course, this attribute can also be a problem. It may prevent you from seeing each other clearly at those times when a certain degree of objectivity and detachment are called for. During periods of stress in the relationship, you may get so wrapped up in your emotions that neither of you is capable of sorting out who is responsible for what. You each may blame your partner for situations that are really your own doing, which can lead to disruptive arguments between you. It is very important with this aspect of the Moon and composite Ascendant that there be many indications of harmony in the relationship. This could be a difficult aspect, but if other indications are good, it can also be an excellent aspect.

Composite Moon Sextile Composite Ascendant

The sextile of composite Moon and Ascendant means that it is easy for the two of you to share your feelings and communicate them to each other. You are able to strike a balance between your need to have emotional rapport and feelings in common, on one hand, and the ability to be clear and objective about the relationship, on the other. The sextile means that you can probably verbalize your feelings for each other, and even when you cannot, you get the message across.

Although you may not verbalize this feeling, you both have a deep sense that your objectives are similar. You have similar attitudes about many things, which gives you a strong sense of community with each other. Many problems that other couples would have to spend a long time straightening out with each other seem to have obvious solutions to the two of you and are understood intuitively.

You may have similar habits also, and these will be hard to break if you want to break them. The reason is that the Moon, which operates on an unconscious level most of the time, signifies a kind of "programming" that has been built into you since early childhood. This should not be too much of a problem, because the sextile of the Ascendant and the Moon helps to make you compatible in your habits. However, if conflicts arise because of bad habits or unconscious attitudes, you will have some difficulty making the necessary changes.

Any friends that you have as a couple will be persons to whom you both can relate on an emotional level. You will not be happy with people who provide only intellectual stimulation. You will want communication at all levels.

Composite Moon Square Composite Ascendant

The square of composite Moon and Ascendant places great emphasis on emotional fulfillment within a relationship. This is a relationship that will get nowhere without strong emotional interaction between you. Because of this, it is necessary that you both feel that your backgrounds are similar, even if they are not actually the same. The important point is that your backgrounds give you compatible attitudes about the world.

This relationship will very likely cause each of you to be very attached to elements in your past, so it is important that these be elements that bring you together rather than drive you apart. Unfortunately, you cannot tell from this aspect alone which of the two it will be. Your overall compatibility is the only way to judge this. An any rate, watch out for unconscious attitudes from your past that affect the way you get along together now. Live in the here and now with each other, and do not let the past get in your way.

If your relationship is not running smoothly, people around you will find out very quickly. Your emotions as a couple are very quickly transmitted to others, even without any particular idea of conciliating them. You both are more concerned with the relationship between you at all levels than with how it looks to others. Nevertheless, you will probably get along well with people outside of your relationship.

Composite Moon Trine Composite Ascendant

The trine of composite Moon and Ascendant is a good aspect in any personal relationship. It indicates that it is easy for the two of you to fully express yourselves to each other on an emotional level. You are able to show your feelings with complete confidence that the other will understand or at least accept them. And this is important, for the trine makes emotional expression very important in a relationship. You are not likely to be detached and cool toward each other.

In a love relationship this aspect indicates a very positive emotional rapport between the two of you. You understand each other's feelings, and expressing them makes you both feel good. At a very deep emotional level, you are able to feel as one, which makes the bond between you even deeper.

You deal with people outside the relationship on an emotional level also. Others see the two of you as a couple with strong emotions, which you express easily.

Through emotional self-expression and through experiencing each other at such a deep emotional level, you both will grow in understanding and tolerance. Even though you are not generally very critical of each other, you will become even more tolerant of each other's quirks, even those that might have irritated you in another situation.

Composite Moon Opposition Composite Ascendant

It is better to think of this aspect, composite Moon opposite Ascendant, as the composite Moon on the Descendant. In other words, its effects are not truly those of an opposition.

Like all Moon-Ascendant aspects, this one indicates a very strongly emotional relationship. However, when the Moon is directly on the composite horizon, as in the case of the conjunction and opposition, the emotional factor is emphasized. This is a sign of two people who can feel as one, who may at times totally transcend the feeling of separateness that usually exists between two people. As a consequence, this is a very valuable position for any personal relationship. It is not quite so good for a professional relationship that requires you to be somewhat detached and objective about each other. The extreme subjectivity of the Moon's effects is not always good in such a situation.

You must watch for subjectivity in a personal relationship also. There is a fine line between feeling a strong emotional affinity, on one hand, and relating so emotionally that the intellect is completely sacrificed, on the other. In the latter case you may become so extremely subjective that you cannot evaluate matters concerning your relationship. This is most troublesome when other factors bring about difficulties, for then it is necessary to see clearly in order to do what must be done. The Moon-Ascendant opposition may make it impossible to see clearly. If this problem can be transcended, however, this aspect is excellent for all kinds of personal relationships.

Chapter Seven

Mercury

The Meaning of Mercury in the Composite Chart

Mercury is the planet of mind and communication. In a relationship it signifies the quality and manner of communication between the two of you. It also tells something about the way you affect each other's thinking and how you think as a couple, collectively.

A well-placed Mercury in the chart indicates that you have some degree of intellectual understanding and can communicate with each other. While it is desirable, especially in an emotional relationship, that two people have an intuitive, unspoken understanding, it is also highly desirable that you be able to talk easily with each other. Even in the most compatible relationship, it is impossible for each partner to figure out what is on the other's mind without some kind of verbal exchange.

Unfortunately, very often, especially in a love relationship, people think that if they truly love each other, they should be able to feel what the other is thinking without having to say anything. What happens if you do this, however, is that you act according to what you guess about each other, and eventually you are dealing with your partner as if he or she were a creation of your own mind. If there is no communication between you, all you have left is the image created in your mind in the absence of real understanding. This is what a badly placed Mercury often signifies.

Basically, Mercury signifies your ability to speak each other's language, to express your thoughts in ways that the other can understand. This requires that your minds be attuned to each other in some way, so that you can share ideas, concepts, and words. A well-placed Mercury is a great benefit to any relationship.

Composite Mercury in the First House

Mercury in the first house of the composite chart indicates that in this relationship communication and community of ideas should play an important part. Not that the relationship will be just an intellectual one, but communication and intellect will be important factors. Therefore this is an excellent placement for all relationships involving business or commerce in any form. However, it does no harm in a personal relationship, which often suffers from a lack of real communication. That should not be a problem for you. The first-house Mercury is usually a sign that your minds are compatible, and you are capable of thinking almost as one person.

Of course, this placement is also excellent for any relationship that involves writing or working on a cooperative intellectual venture. It will be important to keep alive the intellectual interests you share. Together you will be interested in the world around you and constantly wanting to explore and examine new aspects of its variety.

Composite Mercury in the Second House

Composite Mercury in the second house has two different meanings. Either the two of you value things of the mind, or you put a lot of mental effort into what you possess or otherwise value.

If the first of these is true in your case, it means that as a couple you value books, musical instruments, radios, television, audio equipment, or other materials with which you can entertain or stimulate your minds. Or on a more abstract level, the two of you may value ideas and intellectual principles.

If the second possibility is more correct, you both will spend a good deal of time managing the property that you own in common, and you will put a lot of effort into it. In an individual's birth chart, a second-house Mercury signifies cleverness and intelligence in the handling of money. That should also be the case in a composite chart.

Since it is likely that the two of you do value things of the mind or have rather strong opinions about what you do value, it is very important that you come to some kind of agreement about these matters early in the relationship. Otherwise, disputes over such matters are likely to crop up later on.

Composite Mercury in the Third House

Composite Mercury in the third house can be extremely valuable in a relationship, because it assures easy and complete communication between you. Many otherwise sound associations are weakened because two people cannot say the simple things that keep a relationship going smoothly. This should not be a problem for the two of you. In fact, you have a strong need to communicate with each other, and it is likely that you first came together because of some intellectual affinity.

Not only do the two of you have a strong need to exchange ideas and opinions, but you also like to be with others and exchange ideas with them. You have a great liking for all kinds of mental and intellectual interaction with your environment. You do not like to stay off by yourselves but prefer to get out and talk and have a good time.

The only thing you should be wary of is letting the cheerful and often superficial banter of Mercury replace the deeper, more significant communication that any successful relationship requires. Mercury works so easily on a light level that you may be reluctant to delve any deeper. If you can avoid intellectual and emotional superficiality, you should have an excellent mental and intellectual rapport with each other.

Composite Mercury in the Fourth House

Mercury in the fourth house of a composite chart indicates that the two of you are able to communicate about your deepest feelings and the most deeply buried attributes of your relationship, matters that normally would be unconscious. This is because the fourth house rules the deepest, most internal aspects of things. You can share your thoughts about how your relationship is working and what is at the heart of it. You should have an unusual intellectual awareness of each other's feelings.

The fourth house also rules one's home—in this case the home you set up together, if that is appropriate to your relationship. Since Mercury rules thought and communication, this placement means that you are likely to make your home as intellectually stimulating as possible. You will surround yourselves with fine books or whatever else interests you, such as materials for hobbies or crafts. You are also fond of having people get together in your home for good stimulating conversation.

As is usual when Mercury is in a position that concerns feelings, the only real danger here is that you may overintellectualize the deep inner aspects of yourselves. Your inner feelings may come to exist purely as ideas rather than as part of your daily experience. Try not to analyze yourselves or your relationship too much.

If this warning is heeded, a fourth-house Mercury can be very helpful, precisely because it does help to improve communication about your feelings and inner selves, which in most relationships are difficult to discuss.

Composite Mercury in the Fifth House

Mercury in the fifth house of the composite chart indicates that as a couple you are attracted to intellectual modes of recreation and self-expression. You enjoy talking to each other, not just to communicate what must be said, but also because you really enjoy talking. You both enjoy conversation with others and activities such as going to the theater and concerts or just being together and reading good books.

The fifth house is also the house of children and their education. If you have children, you will pay close attention to their education, making sure that they have all the right opportunities and are surrounded by the proper influences. Just be sure that you do not educate them intellectually to the point of neglecting their emotional growth. They must learn to be complete individuals.

The fifth-house Mercury indicates that your attraction for each other is based at least partly on your intellectual affinity. This position doesn't indicate whether your thinking is similar at all levels, but at least you should enjoy intellectual compatibility. Since one requirement of a successful personal relationship is that you communicate easily, you have an excellent start.

Composite Mercury in the Sixth House

Composite Mercury in the sixth house indicates that the two of you expend a great deal of mental energy on the problems or tasks that you have to accomplish together. You will analyze, consider, and explore all the various ways to deal with the matters that are important to you both, which may be either material concerns or emotional ones.

If this is a business relationship centered around accomplishing some particular task or series of tasks, you will go about them systematically, rationally, and carefully.

If your relationship is an emotional, personal one, such as friendship or a love affair, you will do what you have to in a systematic and careful manner. Here, however, the issue will be making your relationship work better so that the two of you will get more out of it. Be careful that this habit of dealing with problems in a reasonable way doesn't turn into an overconcern with your problems. It could get to the point where your whole viewpoint is overwhelmed with analyzing your relationship.

Planets in the sixth house tend to emphasize duties and responsibilities at the expense of the pleasure and fulfillment that should come out of any personal relationship. Obviously a balance must be struck, particularly with Mercury, because Mercury's location in a chart very strongly affects the overall attitudes of the relationship.

Composite Mercury in the Seventh House

Mercury in the seventh house of the composite chart indicates that your relationship will work well as a partnership in mental and intellectual concerns. For example, if you came together to write a book (which this placement of Mercury does not indicate especially), you would be able to work together as a team very well. Similarly you would work well together in any kind of business or commercial activity, particularly those involving electronics, communication, data processing, or transportation.

In a personal relationship this placement indicates the ability to think as a team and to provide a united front, at least intellectually, to the rest of the world. The two of you are generally able to share your ideas and opinions about everything.

Because the seventh is an angular house, the planet that occupies it is more important than it would be otherwise. When Mercury is strengthened, as it is in the seventh house, communication between you is easier and is a more prominent part of the relationship.

Composite Mercury in the Eighth House

The position of Mercury in the eighth house of the composite chart will enable you to examine in depth the psychological forces that are at work in your relationship. These forces will be brought out and examined in the full light of consciousness. For this reason, the two of you should be more capable than most people at working out problems that may arise between you. Just be sure that you keep some sense of perspective about the whole process and do not allow yourselves to get carried away by it.

This placement of Mercury also means that the relationship will probably have an important effect upon the intellectual development of both of you. Your way of thinking about the world will be changed, although it is not possible to tell from this placement alone whether the change will be for good or ill. In general, however, the potential for understanding yourselves and each other is very great.

Composite Mercury in the Ninth House

Composite Mercury in the ninth house grants a relationship a great deal of mental aliveness and interest in all new ideas that expand your collective awareness.

Together you may be interested in travel, literature, philosophy, or religion—interests that you did not have to the same extent before you came together. You will want to explore and range widely, either in the real world or in the world of the mind. At the very least you both will find that your way of looking at the world has changed because of this relationship.

Others will recognize that the two of you have the intellectual capacity to rise above the daily concerns of life that so often bog people down and overwhelm a relationship with a mass of trivia. Together you will be concerned about larger issues that affect the world in general, and you will understand how these issues affect individuals, especially yourselves. Consequently you will have unusual foresight as a couple and will seldom be trapped by unforeseen circumstances.

In general, this relationship should enable your mind to grow and expand.

Composite Mercury in the Tenth House

The key idea of Mercury in the tenth house of the composite chart is consciousness of life direction or purpose. This position implies that you both have a very strong feeling of purpose within your relationship. At the very least, you will discuss and think about your aims a lot. Mercury in the tenth house does not tell a great deal about what that purpose may be, but it does indicate that the issue will be important.

If your relationship exists for a business or professional purpose, this position suggests that you will work together successfully in such fields as communications, transportation, education, or writing.

In a personal relationship, nothing so specific is implied, except that communication at all levels will be important in fulfilling the purpose for which you have come together. There will be a strong intellectual bond between you. You will enjoy sitting and talking and sharing your ideas with each other. And the more you do this, the more you will grow as a couple.

This placement signifies that through reason, logic, communication, and thought—the functions of Mercury—you will achieve your maximum growth as a couple.

Composite Mercury in the Eleventh House

Mercury in the eleventh house of your composite chart gives the two of you a very hopeful attitude. You like to think about the future and make plans together. This position is likely to make you optimistic about your future as a couple.

Friends will play an important role in your life together, especially friends with whom you can exchange ideas and have witty and stimulating conversations. You will like people who are intelligent and also very lively, who can constantly present you with new ideas, rather than people who seem to be stagnant or stodgy. Younger people appeal to you especially.

At the same time, Mercury in the eleventh house is a sign that the two of you have similar intellectual goals and ideals. This increases your capacity for communication because you do not have to spend a lot of time defining basic issues for each other. Because your minds are compatible, you are able to understand each other much more quickly than you would otherwise.

Composite Mercury in the Twelfth House

Composite Mercury in the twelfth house indicates that the two of you will do much thinking and talking about the inner psychological aspects of your relationship. There will be considerable mental probing of yourselves and each other. At the same time, you are not likely to share this process with people outside the relationship. Others may view you as rather secretive or even clandestine in the way you communicate with each other. You will try to work out whatever problems you have within the relationship without appealing to outsiders. This is a good position for psychological self-understanding within a relationship.

However, ceaseless probing into each other's minds can degenerate into playing games with each other's emotions. Be careful how you use the understandings you gain. If you use them to manipulate each other, you are likely to unleash forces that can undo the relationship. In particular, you may stop communicating and start keeping everything secret from each other. This is extremely dangerous in a relationship, because with a twelfth-house Mercury it is very likely to generate suspicion.

Composite Mercury Conjunct Composite Venus

Mercury conjunct Venus is an excellent aspect in a composite chart, for it indicates that you both are able to express affection easily. If you love each other, you will have no difficulty expressing it, and there will probably be some kind of affection between you.

This aspect also is an indication that the two of you share a love of beauty and a strong sense of aesthetic appreciation, such as a common interest in art, which you will probably discuss at length.

Another fortunate attribute of this conjunction is that it gives you sensitivity to each other's feelings and the ability to say what must be said nicely. This position helps to prevent the kind of disagreements that are caused solely by verbal clumsiness. That is to say, you may have conflicts about ideas and opinions, but you will not have petty fights about how an opinion was expressed.

This aspect should help smooth out the roughness that occasionally comes up in any relationship, but it may also make you keep quiet for the sake of preserving harmony when you feel angry. Go ahead and say what you feel, for you will be able to express what must be said in the right way. Don't hold back.

Composite Mercury Sextile Composite Venus

Mercury sextile Venus in the chart of your relationship makes communication between you much easier and more pleasant than it might otherwise have been. You both regard your relationship as something beautiful, and you want to keep it that way. Consequently you try to avoid unnecessary disagreements and petty arguments. Just be sure that in your desire to avoid unpleasantness you do not back off from the real confrontations that are necessary in any relationship. Sometimes the affability of Venus causes people to shrink from saying anything unpleasant, not so much from cowardliness as from a simple desire to avoid anything distasteful. But this should be a minor problem and not a source of great difficulty.

On the plus side, this aspect confers an easy ability to express your feelings for each other. If this is a personal relationship you will probably be quite affectionate with each other. This aspect also favors relationships that are motivated by literary or artistic interest. You both will have a strong love of beauty and good times, and this attitude will be reflected in the ways you express yourselves to the world together.

Composite Mercury Conjunct Composite Mars

With Mercury conjunct Mars in your composite chart you can be sure that you will express your feelings to each other with vigor and that you will react strongly to each other's words. The effect of this aspect can range from petty irritations with each other to constant fighting. It is this second effect that you must learn to control.

It is possible that the two of you may actually enjoy fighting, at least on the verbal level. Certainly you will let off quite a bit of steam this way, which may help preserve the relationship. It is unlikely that you will repress your resentments and brood upon them, but if you feel tempted to do so, try not to. Let your emotions out, or they will destroy your relationship. Repressing anger is always destructive, of course, but with the energy of this aspect it is especially dangerous.

On the plus side, this aspect indicates that you will stimulate each other intellectually and uproot each other from your mental ruts. In the long run this can be quite beneficial, although the disagreements it causes in the early phases may appear at first to weaken the relationship.

Composite Mercury Sextile Composite Mars

With Mercury sextile Mars in your composite chart, you will be able to hold your own verbally and intellectually better as a couple than you could separately. Your minds seem to complement each other and make a stronger and more aggressive whole. You will also stimulate each other intellectually and become more active mentally than you have been.

You are likely to express your feelings to each other quite forcefully, but not necessarily destructively. In fact, this forcefulness will cause you both to say things that ought to be expressed between two people but often are not. Unexpressed feelings can cause a relationship to break up, because they turn into negative psychological energies that can undermine the bond between you. Expressing your ideas and feelings openly will be one of the strong points of this relationship. Neither of you is likely to feel put down by the other, and you will be able to strike a balance between you.

In a business or professional relationship this aspect signifies competitiveness and the ability to stand up for yourselves in any commercial activity, particularly the communications media.

This aspect also denotes people working together in shared effort. It is excellent for any enterprise that involves a good deal of mental work.

Composite Mercury Square Composite Mars

Mercury square Mars can be quite difficult in a composite chart unless you both are willing to make a concerted effort to overcome its effects. By itself, this aspect can indicate a great deal of verbal arguments and fighting between you. You may even reach the point of fighting purely for the sake of fighting, rather than for some real issue. In every relationship, hidden feelings have to be expressed, but don't overdo it. Otherwise the two of you could become so battered and bruised mentally—or even physically—by arguing that it will be hard for you to justify continuing the relationship.

The effect of this aspect is not real incompatibility between you, but it does make you too sensitive to each other's irritating qualities, so that you overreact to actions that are not really so bad. The danger of this aspect is that it can allow trivialities to destroy a basically sound relationship.

What must be done is to strike a balance. You must be able to get your problems out into the open, but make sure that you are arguing over something significant, not merely finding an excuse for recreational arguing. Save the energy for a real dispute and then let it all out.

In general, this aspect in a chart indicates that if the relationship does not have a solid basis, there will be considerable difficulties. But if there is a real bond between you, you must learn to control your energies a bit, especially in what you say to each other.

Composite Mercury Trine Composite Mars

Mercury trine Mars in a composite chart indicates a mentally active and vigorous relationship in which neither of you will allow the other's mind to become lazy. You will stimulate each other's ability and desire to learn and have new experiences.

If you are doing some kind of mental or intellectual work together, this aspect will prove extremely useful. At the same time, if one of you has a problem that must be aired, this aspect will enable you to express your feelings openly and get it over with. There should not be any of the sullen, bitter, unexpressed resentment that so often poisons a relationship. It may even be that you will enjoy arguing as a way of keeping each other sharp and not being taken for granted (although that is quite unlikely to happen).

Fortunately you will be able to keep your arguing under control.

The openness between you and the stimulation you give each other, which you both know you need, should be a strong factor in keeping this relationship healthy for some time.

Composite Mercury Opposition Composite Mars

The energies of Mercury opposition Mars in a composite chart are somewhat difficult to deal with. This aspect is an indication of verbal disagreements and disputes that can be quite damaging to the relationship if not handled correctly. There will be times when arguments arise between you not because of a real issue but simply because something in each of you triggers the other's argumentative instincts. In such a situation, both of you must learn to count to ten before flying off the handle.

If your relationship has other good qualities, it will be worth working this problem out. Try not to take yourselves so seriously when you get angry. Recognize that most of what sets you off is trivial. If necessary, when you feel this anger coming on, leave the room for a moment or two.

One good point about this type of Mercury-Mars energy is that its effects do not last long, unless there is really something serious at stake. In that case it is best to get it out into the open and deal with the problem. Above all, do not deal with your anger by suppressing it. Either employ some kind of cooling-off technique, as described, or have it out. Suppressing this energy can be quite destructive, for when the energy finally emerges, as it eventually must, it may very well destroy the whole relationship, regardless of how good it is otherwise.

The two sets of tactics you should concentrate on in dealing with this aspect are first, getting a better perspective on your irritability, and second, getting the anger out into the open when the issue is important.

Composite Mercury Conjunct Composite Jupiter

The conjunction of composite Mercury and Jupiter is an indication that the two of you are very compatible intellectually and mentally. That does not necessarily mean emotional compatibility, however, which is brought about by other combinations. Nevertheless, this aspect will help to ensure that your relationship will survive and that both of you will benefit from it. More than other couples, you two will have the capacity to put your relationship into proper perspective and see what is really important.

Also, you will find that your relationship enormously stimulates the development of your consciousness; that is, you will become more and more aware of the world about you and your place in it. If the two of you do any extensive planning for the future, this aspect will help you greatly. In this regard, you will work better together than you would separately.

Being together may very well stimulate an interest in philosophy, religion, or metaphysics; or it may bring about opportunities for travel. At the very least you should both feel that your being together has been a positive learning experience, even if other factors in your relationship eventually cause it to break up.

Composite Merucry Sextile Composite Jupiter

Mercury sextile Jupiter in the composite chart helps to create a positive feeling of friendship between you because of your overall mental and intellectual compatibility. You will notice striking parallels in the way you both think about things. Even when you differ, your ideas complement each other in such a way that together they make up a whole that is greater than its parts.

Being together will stimulate your feelings of idealism about the world. Because of the positive viewpoint that this aspect signifies, you may actually find it easier to make your plans come true, even if your plans are seemingly idealistic and impractical.

You both will find that this relationship expands your awareness of the world about you and makes you see things more clearly than you did before. You may help each other see patterns in life that were not clear before. At the same time, this relationship will broaden your views about the way people ought to be. You will be inclined to be tolerant of each other, because something about this relationship makes you realize that there is room for all kinds of differences in this world. In many ways you will be each other's teacher.

Composite Mercury Square Composite Jupiter

The square of composite Mercury and Jupiter is one of the easier squares to deal with. About the only serious problem it indicates is a possible tendency to be overly idealistic. It may lead you to expect more from your relationship than it can deliver. However, this aspect also creates an optimistic and positive frame of mind, which makes it more likely that matters will turn out as you want them to, even if that is quite demanding.

Jupiter often acts to make something happen simply because you assume that it is going to happen. This is the power of positive thinking.

Another effect of this combination is that when there are problems between you, it may be hard to figure out what is wrong. This happens because Jupiter makes you look to big issues for the cause of the problem, even when it has arisen from some routine, apparently insignificant event. If things are going wrong, do not always assume that it is because of some great cosmic difficulty between you. The real cause may be something that strikes both of you as quite trivial, which it may in fact be. But pay attention to it—think how much more easily you will solve the problem if it really is trivial.

Outside of these two small areas of difficulty, this aspect should make the two of you very optimistic about your relationship, and that attitude should be most helpful in smoothing out any difficult times that arise.

Composite Mercury Trine Composite Jupiter

Mercury trine Jupiter in the composite chart is an excellent indication of a good intellectual and mental relationship. You should find that your outlooks on life are very similar or at least complementary. Even while you are getting to know each other, you will not have to spend a lot of time defining basic issues for each other. At least on an intellectual level, you will get to know each other very quickly.

At the same time, this relationship will have a great consciousness-expanding effect upon you, and you will be able to see the world in ways that you have never seen it before. This may be true in a literal sense, in that you may travel together more than before, because of opportunities arising from knowing each other. At the very least this relationship should awaken in both of you a curiosity and interest in the world that you did not have before.

This aspect is also particularly good for any kind of professional or business relationship. Mercury and Jupiter in combination rule success in commerce. As a team you will have the ability to see the overall picture and interpret what is going on in a way that is very useful in business.

Composite Mercury Opposition Composite Jupiter

The opposition of composite Mercury and Jupiter is one of the less difficult oppositions. Like all the aspects between Mercury and Jupiter, it broadens your consciousness, making both of you more tolerant and broadminded, especially about faults in each other that might otherwise be sources of disagreement. At the very least it minimizes pettiness when you do disagree. You confine yourselves to the more serious issues that arise between you.

One effect of this aspect that you should watch for, however, is that you may get into ventures that are simply too big or grandiose to be realized. This is especially fatal in a business or professional relationship. Mercury and Jupiter together are the combination of big ideas—ideas that are not always truly practical but seem tempting at first. In a personal relationship this is not so serious, although in a marriage it may affect financial management.

Another area of possible difficulty is that you may expect too much of the relationship. Although you are tolerant of each other, you expect to accomplish things that cannot be accomplished in any relationship. Try to keep your expectations down to earth.

But outside of these two possible sources of difficulty, this is not a bad aspect in a composite chart. You both should learn a great deal from this relationship without having to go through very hard times.

Composite Mercury Conjunct Composite Saturn

Mercury conjunct Saturn in the composite chart has great potential and also great dangers. Both possibilities are equally likely, and the two of you will have to choose your own course.

To deal with the dangers first, Saturn is the principle of limitation and discipline. At its worst, it can have a narrowing and inhibiting effect upon anything it is connected with—in this case, thought and consciousness as symbolized by Mercury. With this aspect, the attitudes and opinions that you hold jointly about the outside world and about yourselves can become fixed and rigid. As a result, you could fall into ritualized games and patterns of behavior that gradually have less and less connection with reality. While you are standing still, reality is changing.

This rigidity does not have to occur, if you can be very conscious of your patterns of thinking and communicating. At all times you must communicate with each other, and you must be explicit and clear. This aspect is not good for successful intuitive communication, so say what you mean. If as a couple you can do these things, you should be able to reap the benefits of this aspect.

The positive side of this aspect is that your communication with each other should have a great deal of form and discipline. You are able to plan for the future more effectively than most, because you consider every possibility. Together you plan very carefully, thoroughly, and methodically. Although other people may think of the two of you as a bit too careful, pay no heed. You must go about your affairs in the way that is best for you.

Composite Mercury Sextile Composite Saturn

Mercury sextile Saturn in a composite chart can have a most beneficial effect on the way you think and analyze matters as a couple. It makes you cautious in planning for the future and in approaching various areas of everyday life, and this can help ensure your success. When the two of you go about a task, you will succeed, not through blind luck but through careful and methodical planning. You leave nothing to chance, so you get very few unpleasant surprises. But be careful that being cautious does not also eliminate the possibility of pleasant surprises. Remain open to new experiences while you retain your carefulness.

At first, most relationships have to overcome some barriers to mutual understanding and arrive at a common ground of opinion. After that phase you will find that your thoughts and feelings about each other will remain constant and grow further along the lines you have established. That can be either bad or good, of course, depending on what kinds of feelings you have established in the beginning. With this configuration, if you get off to a bad start it will be difficult to change your point of view. But if the start is good, the relationship will continue that way.

Composite Mercury Square Composite Saturn

Mercury square Saturn in the composite chart can present real problems in a relationship, for it symbolizes basic difficulties in communication. Most commonly the problem is not that the two of you cannot communicate but simply that you do not try. But you can get around the worst effects of this aspect if you make the effort to communicate. Do not assume that the other person knows what is on your mind. Try to say whatever you are thinking, and say it clearly.

You must be careful, however, for if this aspect does not cut off communication, it may make you dwell on negative subjects. You may say nothing to each other except to complain, and then communicate in the most irritating way possible. Or, on the other hand, you may carp about minor issues and say nothing about real ones.

As a couple, you must communicate regularly about all things, not just complaints and criticisms. Otherwise you each will feel that there is no reason to keep the relationship going, that it is not worth the effort. But if you keep in touch with each other, it will not be this way.

Composite Mercury Trine Composite Saturn

Mercury trine Saturn in your composite chart gives the two of you a serious and sober but realistic view of the world. You are not prone to fantasies about each other, but build a mutual respect based on the solid reality of what you are to each other. A relationship with this aspect is likely to be based on pragmatic considerations rather than ideals, fond hopes, or romantic illusions. Something about the solidness and certainty of this association will appeal to you, especially if you have had other relationships that did not work out. This aspect can be very good in a business or professional relationship, for your kind of practical concern can make it very profitable.

In a personal relationship, this concern for practical reality helps to keep things straight, but do not let it limit your ability to enjoy each other and experience the lighter pleasures of life. Do not become overwhelmed by pragmatic concerns to the exclusion of creative self-expression within the relationship. You may feel that self-expression serves no useful purpose, but if it isn't there, the relationship will seem dead.

The effects of this aspect can often help a relationship survive difficult times; since you are not inherently idealistic, you are less likely to be disappointed when there are problems between you. Instead of dreaming about how things ought to be, you will work together to build something real.

Composite Mercury Opposition Composite Saturn

Mercury opposition Saturn in a composite chart means that the two of you will have to work very hard on communication in order to build a common point of view. This will not occur naturally without some work on your part.

If you make no effort to control what is happening, this combination will create disagreements, for your viewpoints are fundamentally different and not easily reconciled. To deal with this problem you will both have to make an effort to recognize the other's point of view and to understand what it is based on, rather than just rejecting it out of hand. It may not ever be possible for you to agree completely, but at least you can respect each other's opinions.

To do this, it is necessary to communicate, but this aspect may prevent you from even making the initial overtures toward communication. On a mental level you could be like two ships passing in the night that don't even notice each other. Or if you do attract each other's attention, it may only be to exchange verbal barrages.

So communicate, and do so with the positive intent of at least understanding the other's position. If you cannot do that, you will certainly have problems with each other, no matter what you try to do.

Composite Mercury Conjunct Composite Uranus

The conjunction of composite Mercury and Uranus makes for a relationship that is stimulating, at least on the intellectual level. You will both constantly challenge each other and point out new ways of looking at the world. One thing you can be sure of is that you will not fall into a rut.

There is only one danger this aspect can present; you both may become so addicted to the excitement you give each other that you cannot settle down to the routine, everyday concerns of your relationship. Fortunately this aspect works most strongly on the intellectual level, so it need not affect the emotional basis of a personal relationship.

This aspect is most helpful in a professional relationship based on mental and intellectual creativity, such as two people working together to produce something new and inventive. Mercury and Uranus together relate to technical and mathematical disciplines and to inventions in general.

For a personal relationship this aspect may be a bit nerve-wracking because of the constant stimulation. It may be hard to find an easy and comfortable level of being together, which most couples need. However, some people really like the unending excitement this aspect brings, and perhaps the two of you will enjoy it.

Composite Mercury Sextile Composite Uranus

Mercury sextile Uranus in the composite chart indicates that this relationship will have a stimulating effect on both of you. You will find that you challenge each other's accustomed ways of thinking in a way that is interesting and rewarding rather than annoying or difficult. Your conversation and exchanges have a vital, alive quality that is not found in many relationships. When you are together you enjoy going out and finding new experiences, particularly intellectual and mental ones.

This aspect works to best advantage in any kind of business or professional relationship that requires intellectual creativity and innovativeness. No matter to what extent you have these qualities as individuals, you will find that being together brings them out.

In a personal relationship, this aspect can help prevent you from falling into ruts and thereby help your relationship to stay alive and vital. It also is a good indication of basic intellectual compatibility, which is good in any personal association.

Composite Mercury Square Composite Uranus

Mercury square Uranus in a composite chart indicates restlessness and unquiet in the mental life you share. This may take one of two forms.

It may be that as a couple you find conventional ideas and opinions very unsatisfactory, and you are in a constant state of rebellion against them. People might see the two of you as intellectual eccentrics who never take any idea at face value but are always probing and analyzing to find the deeper meaning and hidden implications of what others say. This manifestation of the aspect is the easier one to handle, because the energy is directed outward and doesn't become a force that divides you.

The other manifestation is more difficult to handle for it does tend to divide a relationship. This aspect may make you very restless and rebellious against each other's ways of thinking. Whenever one of you says something, the other automatically disagrees with it. And you do so with the dogmatic vigor that is characteristic of Uranus. Yet despite such disagreements, you stay together because you like to challenge and goad each other. The problem is that unless the relationship has some compensating factors, this way of life could eventually become tiresome and cause you to part company. People can stand only so many bruises, even intellectual ones. It would be better to direct the energy outward, rather than have it working between you.

Composite Mercury Trine Composite Uranus

Mercury trine Uranus in the composite chart promises an intellectually alive relationship that will have a strong effect upon both of you in your ways of looking at the world. One of the main purposes of this relationship is to cause you to look out at the world from new points of view and with less rigid preconceptions. While this aspect does not in itself indicate whether the relationship will be a long-term one, it does indicate that you both will derive something of value from it. It is always good to have one's point of view challenged, and the challenge this aspect offers will not wipe you out mentally but will be a pleasant mental excitement.

Like some of the other Mercury-Uranus aspects, this one is especially useful in a business or professional association in which the two of you have to find a new and different solution to some problem. Mercury and Uranus jointly rule inventions and discoveries.

But even in a personal relationship this aspect can be useful in solving problems. Instead of trying the old familiar tried-and-true methods of problem-solving, which often do not work, you will find new methods that might be quite a bit more successful, especially because they relate to your individual needs. At any rate, you can expect that your relationship will be mentally stimulating.

Composite Mercury Opposition Composite Uranus

Mercury opposition Uranus in a composite chart creates an extremely restless mental environment for the two of you. Do not expect this relationship to be a peaceful place where you can retire from the challenges of the outside world. Your relationship will constantly challenge you and prevent you from falling into set patterns of thought. And it will not do this in a very gentle way.

There is much potential for growth with this aspect, if you both are willing to expand your views enough to encompass the new experiences this relationship will bring. Some people actually enjoy the incessant mental stimulation, although most will not admit it. They may complain about the lack of peace and quiet, but in fact very few people get into a Uranus relationship of this sort unless they want it that way. You should acknowledge this fact about yourselves in order to get the best out of the relationship.

In this combination with Mercury, the Uranus influence may make you enjoy goading each other into responding to outrageous comments, just to see what will happen. This is the "joker" attribute, which both Uranus and Mercury possess, and the opposition aspect brings it out most strikingly. The point is not to take each other too seriously, for if you do, you may hurt each other unnecessarily without intending to.

Composite Mercury Conjunct Composite Neptune

Mercury conjunct Neptune in the composite chart is a strange combination of planetary influences. Mercury represents the principles of the rational mind—precision, orderliness, and logic—while Neptune represents the mystical and spiritual principles of the universe, with all their paradox and illogic. The effects of Neptune on Mercury are twofold. On the one hand, it can totally neutralize the logic of Mercury, leaving only confusion, self-deception, and unclear thinking. On the other hand, it can bring to the intellectual perceptiveness of Mercury a higher knowledge of the universe, with which Neptune is ultimately connected.

The first effect brings chaos, the second great sensitivity. Unfortunately, it is not possible to predict with certainty which potential will be brought out in a relationship; the two possibilities are equally accessible to you.

It will not be easy for you to determine precisely what you are to each other. Self-delusion is one of the great risks of a Mercury-Neptune combination. Usually it takes the form of overidealization, of confusing what you would like with what actually is. When you eventually confront reality and discover the facts of the matter, you may be extremely disappointed.

The best way to approach the situation is to live in the present in your relationship. Do not anticipate and idealize. If you keep your antennae up and become aware of what is happening, the positive effects of this aspect will be brought out. Neptune can bring you to an understanding of the truth only if you keep your attention on the present situation; living in a dream world of future anticipation will only lead to disappointment.

A business or professional relationship with this aspect should be avoided whenever possible. Such relationships demand straightforwardness and honesty, or at least a clear head and a definite sense of where you are with respect to each other. Possible exceptions are creative or artistic associations in which imaginative creativity is very important to the success of the relationship.

Composite Mercury Sextile Composite Neptune

Mercury sextile Neptune in a composite chart indicates that the two of you are seeking some intellectual or mental ideal within this relationship. At its best this aspect can bring about instantaneous nonverbal communication between you, a direct intuitive understanding of each other's mind. At its least productive, this aspect can mean that one or both of you is overidealizing the relationship rather than experiencing it as a reality. Even though the reality may not be that bad in itself, it is not taken for what it is.

However, this is not a particularly difficult aspect to handle; even in the most overly idealized fantasy, there is likely to be enough real communication between you to prevent crushing disappointment when the fantasy vanishes.

Idealism will always be a strong element in this relationship, even if you keep your feet on the ground about most things. There is nothing wrong with your idealism, because sometimes just believing in an ideal can help make it happen. This is a positive result that you can look forward to with this aspect.

Composite Mercury Square Composite Neptune

With Mercury square Neptune in the composite chart, the two of you must keep yourselves firmly in touch with reality. Otherwise the effects of the Mercury-Neptune square will probably be quite devastating.

To begin with, this square makes it very likely that unconscious forces will have a great but hidden role in shaping your experience of this relationship, so that to an unusual extent you will see what you want to see rather than the truth. It can even get to the point that instead of experiencing the other person as he or she really is, you experience some image you have in your mind.

The second effect of this aspect is to cause extreme confusion about the purposes and goals of your relationship. For example, an association that should be concerned with business might get mixed up with personal matters, or vice versa. Or a friendship may be hurt by efforts to make it a love relationship.

Another problem that can result from this aspect is unclear or willfully false communication between you: in other words, lying. The lies may be intentional or unintentional, to yourselves, each other, or people outside the relationship. Needless to say, when you eventually confront reality, it can be quite destructive.

If the two of you succeed in keeping your realities sorted out, you will be able to enjoy the benefits of this combination, which are acute sensitivity and awareness of each other's being and the ability to communicate without words. Otherwise, this could be a very disappointing relationship.

Composite Mercury Trine Composite Neptune

Mercury trine Neptune in a composite chart provides for a highly developed sensitivity toward each other and the ability to communicate nonverbally and intuitively. The two of you will have to say less to each other than most couples do, for your minds seem to operate in an instinctive harmony. You know what the other feels even if you are apart.

In addition, you are idealistic about your relationship, so that it appears to you more beautiful than others think it is. This is not a romantic idealism, but idealism based on intellectual and mental harmony. You may be realistic about each other's foibles, but you share an ideal of how things ought to be, which is one of the factors that keeps you together. The experience of this relationship may stimulate your poetic tendencies. Both of you will look at the world with heightened sensitivity and awareness. The only warning that is necessary with this configuration is to keep in mind the truth as it is at the moment. Do not confuse your ideals with present reality, but keep them in mind as a goal to work toward. If you do this, the effects of this aspect will be very beneficial in the long run.

Composite Mercury Opposition Composite Neptune

Oppositions affect relationships more strongly than other aspects, and the opposition between Mercury and Neptune can present many problems if you are not conscious of its effects. This combination in a composite chart can produce very unrealistic ideas about your relationship.

The unreality can take several forms. One of the most common effects is that one of you does not tell the other the truth. This happens to some extent in every relationship, but here it can be really destructive, because it causes one person to live in a fantasy about the other. When the truth ultimately becomes apparent, the deluded partner is bitterly disappointed and unhappy. Obviously, to overcome the worst effects of this aspect, you must at least try to tell each other the truth.

But even with the best of intentions, you may still honestly delude each other, so you will have to adopt an uncompromising standard of truth and reality in all your dealings with each other. That is the main challenge of this aspect. If you cannot bring yourselves to do that, do not be upset by the little surprises that tell you that your relationship is not what you thought it was. With this aspect in your composite chart you can't afford to lose track of reality and indulge your fantasies without restraint. Every time you do so in this relationship, you are likely to be disappointed.

Composite Mercury Conjunct Composite Pluto

Mercury conjunct Pluto in a composite chart combines the mental and intellectual functions of Mercury with the powerful transforming qualities of Pluto. These planets together indicate that this relationship is likely to have a strong effect on the way you both think. Within your relationship you will analyze aspects of yourselves and how you work together that in previous relationships you simply would not have bothered with. This aspect is an indication of acute psychological awareness, which is very helpful in a relationship if it is not overdone to the point that little issues are distorted and magnified out of all proportion.

But there is a more difficult side to this Pluto-Mercury combination that you must watch for carefully. It can give rise to mental power struggles between you; that is, one of you tries to totally dominate the thoughts and opinions of the other. It is not possible to tell from this aspect alone which person is the dominating one. Actually both people often do it to each other, with one being dominant in an obvious, overt way, while the other uses passive, more subtle techniques, such as maneuvering into a position of being the apparent victim in order to gain sympathy from outsiders. Either party may use either tactic at various times. This is not an inevitable result of this aspect, but you should recognize the possibility and avoid it.

Another possible effect of this aspect is that its energy may be turned outward. When this happens, the two of you may find that you are able to influence other people's opinions and ideas. This aspect would be especially useful in the composite chart of people who have to influence public opinion, such as those in advertising, public relations, or politics. Here the influence of this aspect is a powerful tool that can be used for either good or bad, whatever is intended.

Composite Mercury Sextile Composite Pluto

Mercury sextile Pluto in the composite chart provides the two of you with deep psychological insight and a grasp of the normally hidden forces that operate within a relationship. Mercury rules the rational mind, while Pluto has to do with hidden transforming forces. The sextile gives a rational understanding of these hidden forces, so that the two of you can actually deal with them on a rational level, instead of simply feeling their effects and not knowing how to handle them.

At the same time, and partly because of this quality, this relationship will change your ways of thinking about life; through it you will experience different aspects of human psychology that you may not have encountered before and therefore have not understood. This experience is not likely to damage either of you, and you will probably derive great benefit from the new understandings.

This aspect is an indication that the two of you will forge an intellectual bond that will bind you together in a creative way for some time. Even at the worst, this aspect will enable you both to benefit from the relationship, even though you may not recognize it immediately.

Composite Mercury Square Composite Pluto

The square of composite Mercury and Pluto poses some challenges to any relationship, the greatest of which is learning to tolerate each other's ideas. Somewhat like the conjunction, but with fewer easing factors, this aspect implies intellectual power struggles as each of you tries to impose your own thinking upon the other. But one of you may very well weaken or destroy the relationship by forcing the other to make a fight for freedom in order to escape the tyranny of the Mercury-Pluto effect.

If you are aware of this problem, however, there is another effect of this planetary combination that can be used favorably. If you can enlarge your own views enough to encompass your partner's, you will have the capacity to truly understand that point of view and include that perception of the truth in your own perception.

Here again, as with the conjunction, the energy may be turned outward, so that the two of you are always trying to influence other people's opinions. Here also there is a danger that you could provoke a damaging response; other people, instinctively fearing domination, might fight back against your ideas. Here again the remedy is to enlarge your own point of view sufficiently to encompass the views of others and make those ideas part of your own understanding.

Composite Mercury Trine Composite Pluto

Mercury trine Pluto in a composite chart can grant the two of you a deep and subtle understanding of what your relationship is about, which can be very useful. Your relationship will not founder because of a lack of insight, although it could falter if you don't acknowledge your insight. The Mercury-Pluto trine grants understanding even of the hidden psychological forces that are normally not accessible to people involved with each other.

This relationship will strongly affect your way of expressing yourselves to others as well as your ways of self-understanding. You will encounter new aspects of your own inner lives that you were not aware of, and you will be enriched by these understandings if you truly acknowledge them and do not resist them.

The awakened awareness that should come about through this aspect will also stimulate your interest in exploring new dimensions of the world around you, as well as the world within. And this interest will greatly enlarge your views of the world.

Composite Mercury Opposition Composite Pluto

The opposition of composite Mercury and Pluto will create very intense conflicts between you if you make no effort to enlarge your consciousness of this relationship.

A typical situation is that during an argument one of you will start to psychoanalyze the other and will present a very plausible case, supposedly in the interest of bringing out some foible and examining it objectively. However, what is really happening is that at each turn the truth is subtly distorted so that the one being analyzed becomes the loser in the battle. The so-called analyst also tries to force the other into his or her own ways of thinking.

The process is all the more devastating in that the truth, slightly amended, is used as the weapon, which makes it even harder to fight. Finally, however, a crisis point will be reached, and the victim of this procedure will strike back and make a break for freedom, even though this seems to violate "common sense" as the other partner sees it.

However, since at least one of you thoroughly understands the truth, it is a pity not to use it to create more understanding instead of using it to dominate. This in fact is the way to handle the negative consequences of this aspect. Use your understanding of the truth to get at more truth, not to win over your partner. And the same goes for your dealings as a couple with people outside of the relationship, since this aspect also gives the two of you power to influence others.

Composite Mercury Conjunct Composite Ascendant

The conjunction of composite Mercury and Ascendant signifies a relationship in which communication and shared ideas are very important. You like to talk with each other, and communication between you is clearer than it is with many couples. Your ideas stimulate each other.

By the same token, this conjunction also improves communication with others outside of the relationship. Therefore this is a good aspect in the composite chart of persons who are working together in communications or in any kind of commerce, especially involving transportation of goods.

Fortunately, you are not likely to fall into rigid patterns of behavior in this relationship. Mercury is a restless planet, which means that you are always looking for new challenges and experiences. The two of you will seek as many varied experiences as possible, but you will tend not to go into any of them very deeply.

Shallowness is the most negative characteristic of Mercury, although it is not a terribly serious defect. You will not do things thoroughly; although you may cover a lot of ground in your experiences together, you often only skim the surface. In this way you lose much of the richness that is encountered only when you live your life in depth. This is particularly true at the emotional level. Do not let superficiality deprive the two of you of deep emotional experiences together.

Composite Mercury Sextile Composite Ascendant

The sextile of composite Mercury and Ascendant is a sign that the two of you are likely to get around, physically and/or mentally. Mercury is the planet of travel, and the sextile is traditionally associated with the third house, which also rules travel, so travel is very heavily emphasized in this relationship. The point must be made, however, that travel is not necessarily limited to its literal meaning. It can also mean mental journeys, encounters with new ideas and ways of thinking.

The two of you exhibit a restlessness of thought that makes it very unlikely that you wili settle into any rigid mental patterns. At the same time, however, there is a danger that your restlessness will make it difficult to settle down into a stable relationship. Fortunately, with this aspect, restlessness is not likely to weaken the relationship, only to make it less predictable.

The two of you have very strong ideas about what you want in this relationship, and you like to talk about these ideas. Because you are very clear about what you want, you are able to plan out the best course of action for attaining it.

Friends are important to both of you, but they must be stimulating people. You do not like to have dull people around. You enjoy lively banter with others because it stimulates your own thinking processes. It appeals to your need for new experiences, particularly on the intellectual level.

In a personal relationship, this aspect may emphasize intellectual exchange of ideas at the expense of intimate emotional communication. Try not to intellectualize your feelings; instead, allow yourselves to experience your feelings simply as feelings.

Otherwise, communication between you is better than average, and this aspect will help considerably in any kind of relationship.

Composite Mercury Square Composite Ascendant

The square of composite Mercury and Ascendant is a relatively easy square to handle. It signifies that the two of you discuss what overall purposes this relationship will serve in your lives. But you keep these discussions to yourselves more than other couples might. As with all aspects of composite Ascendant and Mercury, communication between you is quite good. Just be careful not to get so wrapped up in yourselves that you neglect communication with others. While you are a unique pair, so is every couple, and the experience of others can help you too.

The square between composite Mercury and Ascendant indicates that you are unusually concerned about what you are doing together. You are very involved with analyzing your objectives. But do not overintellectualize, and try not to let analysis become a substitute for simply experiencing life as it is. Avoid spending too much time conceptualizing the meaning of your relationship. The analytical side of Mercury can be quite destructive in a personal relationship, because the all-important emotional experience becomes secondary to intellectual analysis, which is a substitute for real understanding.

Composite Mercury Trine Composite Ascendant

The trine of composite Mercury and Ascendant is a very good aspect in any kind of relationship. It has the good effect of increasing self-understanding and mutual understanding between the two of you, and it allows you to communicate meaningfully. You can easily express the important feelings about your relationship that people often have trouble saying to each other. You both know how to say the right words at the right time. Insofar as it is possible to express the deep inner feelings that arise in a personal relationship, you are able to do so.

At the same time, this relationship will have a broadening effect on the two of you. By coming together you will be exposed to many new experiences, and you both will benefit through greater understanding and awareness of the world around you. You will become more tolerant of the differences between you as well as between yourselves and others. You will come to see that such differences are only challenges to your understanding and not real threats to your way of life, which is how many people regard such differences.

It may well be that intellectual concerns such as education and philosophy will become important in this relationship. In these areas your basic mental and intellectual affinity will enable you to achieve much together. Even if this is not a working or professional relationship in any way, shared interests will play a very important part in bringing you together and keeping you together.

Composite Mercury Opposition Composite Ascendant

The opposition of composite Mercury and Ascendant should not be thought of as an opposition in the usual sense. It is better to think of it as a conjunction of composite Mercury and Descendant. This aspect has two very different manifestations, both of which are derived from the same principle. In this relationship, your minds are engaged with each other in a very strong and intimate way.

On the one hand, this aspect may take the form of a very deep and significant intellectual union between you. You seem to think almost like one person, sharing the same ideas and thinking in a complementary way. This means that the two of you can communicate with others as a team and be more effective than you could as individuals.

On the other hand, the opposition of composite Mercury and Ascendant can take the form of vigorous intellectual disagreement and conflict between you. It is not just that you disagree, but that you actually derive something very vital from disagreeing. Others may think that you are destroying each other, but really you are engaging in a contest. Each of you is dependent upon the other for stimulation, even if you make a great pretense of being angry and fed up with each other.

It is not often recognized that opponents make up the same kind of intimate one-to-one union as partners in the ordinary sense. You may be opponents or you may be peaceful partners. In either case you depend on each other to reinforce your ways of thinking and dealing with the world, either by positively reinforcing them or by using each other's ideas as a negative reference point to argue against. In either case you both would find it difficult to operate without the other. If you have taken the "opponent" path, especially, you need to recognize this.

Chapter Eight

Venus

The Meaning of Venus in the Composite Chart

Venus is obviously important in any kind of relationship, because it rules both love and the ability to form relationships, particularly those based on emotion. If Venus is badly placed, you may have a long-term relationship, but it will not have much love. On the other hand, if Venus is strong and well placed, but other relationship indications are not too good, the two of you may be drawn to each other very strongly even though you are not really compatible. This creates a very stormy, short-lived relationship.

In its deepest meaning, Venus represents the principle in the universe that draws two entities together by natural and spontaneous inner forces, much the way positive and negative charges attract each other. No external compulsion is needed. But the power of Venus attracts only if the two entities have fully defined themselves as individuals within the universe. In human terms, this means that you have to be yourself in order to love someone else. If you live according to other people's ideas of what you ought to be, without regard for your own inner impulses, you will not really be a whole person enough to love another.

The position of Venus in the composite chart indicates how far this relationship will allow both of you to express yourselves through love. It also describes what part of your environment you most desire to bring into this experience. It is not necessary to have a good Venus in order to make a relationship survive, but a good Venus will make the relationship worth having.

Composite Venus in the First House

Composite Venus in the first house signifies a relationship that is based on love and affection. It is not necessarily based on sex, although this position is certainly good for any sexual relationship. The ultimate meaning of Venus is attraction based on the ways in which you are different rather than the ways in which you are similar. This makes for a relationship of complements, which form a whole that is stronger and more lasting than either of the parts.

Composite Venus in the first house means that the two of you form such a partnership. You were strongly attracted to each other when you first met, even if you did not immediately know the reason why, and as you learn more and more about each other, you remain strongly attracted.

The emotions aroused by Venus are quiet in their expression, friendly rather than wildly passionate. But they are intense in their own way and much longer lasting than some more intense emotions. This kind of affection will sustain a relationship for a long time. This placement enables you to forgive each other for the occasional hurts that arise in every relationship.

In some cases a first-house Venus may indicate that the two of you have come together for a creative purpose. This could be anything from working at an artistic craft together to farming or simply raising children. Somehow this relationship will manifest the creative drives of Venus more than most.

Composite Venus in the Second House

Composite Venus in the second house indicates a love of beautiful things and a desire to have them as personal possessions. In a personal relationship in which you own property together, it simply means that you enjoy owning beautiful or artistic objects. This reflects the fact that the two of you place a high value on beauty and art. Even if you do not own property together, for example if you are just friends, there will still be this emphasis on the value of beautiful things. Venus also emphasizes comfort. As a couple you will like surroundings that are soft, comfortable, and warm as well as beautiful.

Incidentally, in any kind of relationship, Venus in the second house is a good indication that you will have these things as well as the money to pay for them. It can be an indication of wealth, or at the very least, of having whatever you need.

In a business or professional relationship, this position suggests financial success, especially in fields related to entertainment, art, or pleasure and beauty.

Composite Venus in the Third House

Venus in the third house of the composite chart signifies that together you have an intellectual concern with beauty that you may not have been aware of as individuals. You think about the beautiful in life, and you try to surround yourselves with beauty as much as possible in your home and where you work. Or you like to go places where you can find beauty. Similarly, you are fond of discussing beautiful things, such as painting, poetry, or music, and you may stimulate each other to take an interest in the arts.

Venus in the third house also means that you are in touch with your feelings, that you can discuss your relationship and verbalize what you feel. In fact, you may possibly be more inclined to talk about love and friendship than to do anything about them. There is the danger that you will deal with love on a superficial, intellectual level and not fully experience it on a deep emotional level. At any rate, do not try to subordinate your emotions to your intellect. Nevertheless, the ability to verbalize your emotions that this placement of Venus provides should prove valuable in the long run.

Composite Venus in the Fourth House

The effects of Venus in the fourth house of the composite chart are felt in the most intimate and inward areas of your relationship. On the psychological level you have a great concern for beauty in your most personal surroundings, and this in turn is reflected in your desire to make your home or other property that you own together as tasteful, beautiful, and comfortable as possible. Even if you don't have much money, you will probably succeed in creating an elegant home.

If you do not own a home together, the effects of the fourth-house Venus will be less evident. But this is an angular house, so the planet that is in it has greater importance than it would otherwise have. A fourth-house Venus simply indicates that in this relationship the principles of love and beauty are strong and prominent, although they are expressed most clearly in your intimate personal lives rather than in the lives you share with the outside world. This placement is usually an excellent indication for an intimate love relationship.

Composite Venus in the Fifth House

Composite Venus in the fifth house is one of the stronger indications that this will be a relationship of love or, at the very least, friendship. The fifth house is the house of love affairs, self-expression, and children. Venus, of course, is the planet of love, affection, and beauty and therefore has a natural affinity for this position. It denotes a relationship between two people who really enjoy being together and who make each other feel good. You will share a great love of pleasure, of going out and doing things together, especially attending amusements, theater, and other forms of entertainment.

The fifth-house Venus is a light-hearted position. Perhaps its only real flaw, which is not too difficult to overcome, is that it does not provide the energy needed for a long-term, serious day-to-day relationship, such as marriage. With this position you may be reluctant to face the difficult and sometimes unpleasant work of building up a stable relationship, which isn't as much fun as the good times you enjoy together. However, if you can overcome this lack of seriousness, a fifth-house Venus guarantees that this will be a pleasant and loving relationship for both of you.

If you are married, you will love your children very much and will develop a warm relationship with them.

Composite Venus in the Sixth House

The sixth house of the composite chart is not the easiest place for Venus to express itself. This is the house of work, duty, responsibility, and service, which does not square easily with Venus's love of beauty, grace, ease, and pleasure. The sixth is to some extent a house of self-repression, while Venus is a planet of self-expression.

Within this relationship your concern for love and affection is kept subordinate to what you may consider to be more important or more practical matters. For example, in a marriage, this position of Venus would tend to make the two of you stay together "for the sake of the children" or perhaps to continue some business or work project you have become involved in together.

Venus in the sixth does not indicate a lack of affection between you; it simply means that love is not the highest priority keeping you together. Just remember, however, that no personal relationship can survive for purely utilitarian motives. The lighter, self-expressive feelings must be allowed to come out too, if only to allow the relationship to survive.

One other outcome of this position should be mentioned. Your love for each other may be partly predicated on a feeling that you can do something fairly specific for each other, something that your partner needs to have done, beyond making him or her feel better.

Composite Venus in the Seventh House

Composite Venus in the seventh house is a good indication that this is a personal relationship based to a considerable extent on affection. There may be other reasons for this relationship, but love is certainly one of the most important. This position of Venus does not guarantee a successful relationship, but it does help. After the Sun and Moon positions, this is one of the most important elements in the chart of a love relationship.

You will have a strong sense of shared emotion and feeling and a great need to share your experiences. You will think of yourselves as a unit, a couple, rather than as two single individuals. You will want to be together and do things together as much as possible.

The only danger that you should watch for with this position is that you may tend to be too accommodating; that is, you will try to agree with each other even when one of you has a legitimate grievance. Instead of expressing it, you will remain quiet for the sake of preserving the peace and harmony of the relationship. The problem is, if you do this too often, eventually the friendly atmosphere wears thin, and all kinds of resentments boil out, with no way to control them. Do not let your desire for peace and harmony prevent you from confronting important issues. Speak your mind—it can't seriously disturb a good relationship.

Composite Venus in the Eighth House

With composite Venus in the eighth house, the love and affection between you will have an intensity that is often lacking in the other houses. This position does not guarantee that you will have a love relationship, however; it simply indicates emotional intensity concerning love.

Traditionally the eighth house is the house of death, although that does not always literally mean physical death. The eighth house has as much to do with the creation of something new as with the destruction of something old. So Venus in the eighth house represents the mingling of love and death, or more accurately, love and regeneration.

In a love relationship, the expression of love will be quite intense, with a powerful quality that will transform both of you in some fundamental way. You will experience love as a regenerative experience that makes you over into a new person. A sexual relationship particularly will have this intensity. Your love will not be light and gay but something very serious that involves both of you at all levels of mind, body, and soul.

On quite a different level, the eighth house can also refer to joint finances and property. Venus promises material prosperity within this relationship. It is often said that Venus rules money, and although some people have questioned that, Venus does produce an ability to attract money, especially in the second and eighth houses. This is an especially good placement if the two of you ever require financial help from others.

Composite Venus in the Ninth House

With composite Venus in the ninth house, love and affection tend to be intellectual issues that are discussed and pondered over rather than felt. The ninth house of the composite chart represents the overall life-view shared by the two of you—your collective attitudes and the nature of your intellectual exchange. Consequently there is a danger that you may overintellectualize your feelings in this relationship. Love is a more distant experience rather than something felt and shared intimately.

However, in compensation, you both examine the nature of your feelings and are more capable than most people of understanding what you mean to each other. You are somewhat less likely to behave in an unconscious and inappropriate manner toward each other. You can communicate at a very high level concerning your relationship.

Love may become a philosophical ideal in this relationship, much as it was in the medieval code of chivalry. You tend to think in intellectual terms and to devote considerable attention to bringing about your ideals.

The experience of this relationship may also make both of you see more clearly and become more aware of the world around you. Venus in the ninth house can signify love as an agent of consciousness expansion. One or both of you will be exposed to a broader range of experience because of this relationship.

Composite Venus in the Tenth House

The tenth house of the composite chart is an angular house, and therefore the effect of Venus is emphasized. Your experience of love within this relationship will very strongly affect the lives of both of you.

The tenth house rules the purposes for which the relationship exists, the nature of its individuality, and its role in the larger society. On the psychological level, this relationship will aid both of you in discovering what you want to do with your lives. Loving each other should reinforce you and give you greater confidence in yourselves.

Partly because of this mutual reinforcement, you are likely to be very openly affectionate in the company of other people. They will regard you as a loving couple, or if you are friends, as having a very close friendship. This is a relationship that stands openly before the world and does not hide from the view of others.

At the same time, this relationship will teach you about the nature of love and how you relate to others on an intimate personal level. The only way you can learn what living with another person means is by doing so. That is one of the purposes of this relationship.

On a very different plane, the tenth-house Venus may also mean that you have come together for some purpose connected with the arts, entertainment, or luxuries. This may be either amateur or professional.

Composite Venus in the Eleventh House

Composite Venus in the eleventh house is one of the best placements for an intimate personal relationship. The eleventh is the house of friendship, and at the very least, Venus here will help to make you friends. However, the emotional depth of this relationship is not limited to friendship. This position can also be a sign of a deep love affair. In some ways it is better than a fifth-house Venus, because along with "being in love" you also love each other. That is, you have a strong abiding affection for each other along with that well-known, often short-lived feeling of intoxication.

The eleventh house is also the house of hopes and wishes, and Venus here is a good indication that the two of you have harmonious ideals. Because you both are seeking the same things, being together will help you find them. It can also mean that you idealize either the feeling of love or your relationship, which can be a problem if either of you is prone to unrealistic attitudes about feelings. But if both of you are reasonably realistic about yourselves, you will experience this relationship as something beautiful and ideal, because the experience is based on truth.

The eleventh-house composite Venus is one of the best signs for a balanced and harmonious relationship of any kind.

Composite Venus in the Twelfth House

Composite Venus is one of the least difficult planets to have in the twelfth house. There are problems associated with it, but there are strong points as well.

This placement signifies that while you may have strong feelings of affection for each other, you may not be demonstrative about them. Other people may not even be aware of how you feel about each other. The twelfth-house Venus can be a sign of a secret relationship.

This is also the house of your own unconscious, of those areas of your lives and experience that you have repressed from your conscious mind. With Venus in the twelfth, your relationship may be influenced to a considerable degree by unconscious factors in both of you. It may be difficult to understand the dynamics of this relationship, and you may do things for no apparent reason. This can be either good or bad, of course, depending on what you do. In any case, you should try to understand what lies behind your relationship, if only to gain greater control over yourselves.

On the clearly positive side, this placement can help both of you overcome your ego-drives within the relationship. It enables each of you to give way to the other when that is desirable. You are able to think of yourselves as a unit and to subordinate your personal interests to your interests as a couple. This ability can eliminate many problems that will arise.

Composite Venus Conjunct Composite Mars

With Venus conjunct Mars in the composite chart you will find that feelings run high between you. This is a passionately intense relationship that is likely to be based at least partly on sexual drives, even if you are of the same sex. This is not to say that it will be a homosexual relationship, but that something of the emotional intensity that arises in relationships between the sexes will be present in your relationship also.

If this is a sexual relationship, it will be intense, with a strong need for physical expression; it is very unlikely to be platonic. Venus and Mars are the feminine and masculine symbols respectively of sexuality. When they are conjunct, it means that the feminine and masculine principles are working together.

All the emotional reactions between you are heightened considerably by this conjunction. Anger, sadness, and above all, love, are more intense. It is very difficult for people who have this aspect in their composite chart to remain indifferent to each other. Even if you should become enemies, which could happen, you would be intense enemies. The strong attraction between you prevents you from being detached in any way about each other.

Composite Venus Sextile Composite Mars

Venus sextile Mars is a good aspect to have in the composite chart, for it indicates a good balance in your relationship between your drive to express yourself fully as an individual (Mars) and your need for relationships with others (Venus). Often these two needs are in conflict, and the fulfillment of one results in the denial of the other. For example, some people can relate to another only by suppressing themselves, and some can express themselves only by trying to dominate the other instead of relating on an equal basis. With the Venus-Mars sextile, however, you have the ability to express yourselves by means of the relationship rather than in spite of it. This is most helpful in any relationship.

This aspect produces its greatest benefits in a personal relationship between the sexes, however. It relates especially to sexual self-expression, for sex is the form of self-expression that requires a relationship with another person. And Venus and Mars are sexual planets. This aspect in the chart of a love relationship helps to ensure sexual compatibility and makes physical love-making easy and pleasurable.

Even in friendship, where sex is not an issue, the Venus-Mars sextile indicates a complementary balance of energy between you, which helps keep the relationship going.

Composite Venus Square Composite Mars

Venus square Mars in a composite chart has potential for both good and bad. In a sexual relationship it can make physical love-making better and more satisfying than usual. It often makes people of opposite sex feel irresistibly attracted to each other. But it does not guarantee that the relationship will be easy and peaceful. The problem this combination presents is that sex can easily become a device for one person to dominate the other. It is very important that this does not happen, because such domination can make great difficulty in a relationship that has much potential for mutual satisfaction.

In other relationships, the main challenge of this aspect is that you will find it hard to strike a balance between your individual egos and your desire to relate to each other. Competitiveness may sometimes interfere with cooperation. You will arouse in each other strong feelings that will sometimes be difficult to cope with—feelings of anger, sadness, happiness, or whatever.

It is possible that one of you will assume a dominant Mars role, while the other assumes a more passive Venus role. This is perfectly all right if both of you are satisfied with the situation, but be sure that you really are. It would be better for each of you to alternate the dominant and passive roles. That would express the symbolism of the aspect in a benevolent and constructive way.

Composite Venus Trine Composite Mars

Venus trine Mars is one of the better aspects to have in a composite chart. Much like the sextile, it means that there is a balance between your individual ego drives and your need for the relationship; that is, you can get along together without feeling that either of you is losing your individuality. In fact, you will find that this relationship helps both of you to express yourselves more fully—unlike many relationships, which act as barriers to self-expression.

This aspect fulfills itself most clearly in relationships between the sexes, for the sexuality of the two planets is then expressed easily. The trine of Venus and Mars strengthens the need for physical sexual expression and makes it satisfying. You both will be greatly fulfilled by sex, and you will work together to make it even better. There won't be the differences of timing and style that make many sexual relationships difficult. You truly complement each other.

Complementarity is one of the benefits of this aspect for any kind of relationship. Each of you is strong where the other is weak, so together you will be stronger than you are alone.

Composite Venus Opposition Composite Mars

Venus opposition Mars in a composite chart creates great magnetism between two people, especially if they are of opposite sexes. Even if you are of the same sex, there is likely to be a kind of magnetism, which if examined closely would be found to have a somewhat sexual quality. You each might feel that the other has some tremendously important quality that you lack.

This aspect often creates a strong bond between people, but it does not guarantee that the relationship will be smooth. For one thing, it can create expectations that are very hard to live up to, so there is a constant sense of striving rather than just letting things be. At the same time, getting what you think your partner has may become such an ego-issue that you are not willing to cooperate in making the relationship work. Unless you are very careful, you may find yourselves trying to get something out of each other, rather than creating something with each other.

In a sexual relationship, what you are trying to get from each other is sexual fulfillment, for Venus-Mars in opposition is a strongly sexual aspect. But this tendency to regard sex as something to be gotten from the other will become a barrier to getting it unless you force yourselves out of that thought pattern. If you both recognize that sexual fulfillment is something you will get out of the relationship by working together, then you will get what you want and it will be good. With this aspect, physical sex is a very important factor in a relationship, even more so than it ordinarily is. If you can keep in mind the need for true cooperation, you should be able to find what you seek.

Composite Venus Conjunct Composite Jupiter

Venus conjunct Jupiter is one of the best aspects to have in a composite chart. No matter what the purpose of the relationship, this aspect will help fulfill it. If this is a professional association, the Venus-Jupiter conjunction will help bring material success.

Both of you will feel that this relationship reinforces you and makes life easier to bear. You will feel happier and more optimistic, which will help make events go well for you, although others are likely to think that you are lucky. Of course, luck often comes from having a positive attitude.

In a personal relationship with this aspect, love and affection are abundant and easily expressed. Your feelings of warmth exist independently of anything you do for each other; you love each other for what you are, not for what you would like each other to be or do, an unusually ideal situation. Each of you accepts your partner's flaws to a remarkable extent and is tolerant of the little things that many people find hard to take. You are willing to give each other room to be whatever you want, and your experience of each other is not hindered by too-great expectations.

No relationship is perfect, of course, and things can go wrong even with this aspect. But its presence in a composite chart will help the relationship to grow in a positive way and will help both of you to grow within it.

Composite Venus Sextile Composite Jupiter

The sextile of composite Venus and Jupiter indicates an affectionate relationship. It is especially good in the chart of a friendship, love affair, or marriage. It is a sign that the two of you genuinely like each other and feel positive about yourselves and each other. Jupiter is the planet of growth and Venus is the planet of love, so the combination can be read as growth through love. The intensity of feeling signified by this aspect may range anywhere from friendship to a very intense love affair, but it is not an especially sexual love. It is love as a positive feeling of warmth between the two of you, with no other motivation for existence.

On another level, the sextile of Venus and Jupiter opens up opportunity. The two of you are able to do the right things at the right time in such a way that events work out well for you, both materially and emotionally. To others this may appear to be luck, but actually you are creating a favorable environment for happenings that are nice and pleasant. These cannot happen unless you give them a place to exist. In other words, you must feel the optimism that allows you to recognize opportunities when they arise. The sextile of Venus and Jupiter signifies that together you have that kind of optimism.

Composite Venus Square Composite Jupiter

The square of Venus and Jupiter in the composite chart is one of the easiest squares to deal with. Jupiter and Venus are so compatible that it is almost impossible for their influences to be combined in a negative way. The square is an active aspect; that is, it signifies actions that are taken. In the case of Venus and Jupiter, it suggests that together you will actively seek out pleasure and ease in order to enjoy yourselves and each other's company. You will be fond of beautiful and elegant surroundings and will go to great lengths to acquire them. The only potentially negative attribute of this combination is that elegance, ease, and pleasure can become greater priorities in your relationship than other, more important elements.

Another difficulty that sometimes occurs with this combination is that its very great energy brings together two people who are unsuited to each other. The Venus-Jupiter square has an undiscriminating quality and does not in itself tell whether your relationship is appropriate or not. All it signifies is that there is likely to be a great attraction between you.

Nevertheless, you can expect an affectionate and loving relationship, no matter what the original reasons for your coming together. And this affection will hold you together even in times of difficulty.

Composite Venus Trine Composite Jupiter

Venus trine Jupiter in the composite chart is one of the aspects that really helps to make a relationship successful, particularly a personal one. In fact, a professional association is very likely to become personal as well. The Venus-Jupiter trine is a strong indication of a warm, affectionate feeling between you.

In particular, this relationship will have a strong idealistic force that will make you optimistic about yourselves and each other. And this optimism will help bring about the ideal state of affairs that you expect. You will find that the relationship will help both of you grow as individuals, for it continually brings out your best qualities. There is a feeling of ease and peacefulness with this aspect. Neither of you seems to make unreasonable demands upon the other, but that can sometimes present another problem. If one of you must make some really important changes, the other may be reluctant to raise the issue for fear of disturbing the peaceful atmosphere.

Nevertheless, this is a relationship in which you will feel that you can relax and be yourself with your partner. This relationship ought to be successful and rewarding for both of you, whatever the reasons for your coming together.

Composite Venus Opposition Composite Jupiter

This Venus-Jupiter aspect is one of the easiest oppositions, for it creates a strong attraction between the two of you that makes a good relationship all the more likely. The only difficulty to watch for is that sometimes you may not get exactly what you expect from the relationship or from the other person. However, what you do get should be perfectly satisfactory, so that is not a great problem.

A personal relationship benefits the most from this aspect, for it signifies feelings of warmth and affection between two people. But even a professional association will have the same good feelings, which will make your relationship more personal. In this case, however, a situation can arise in which the personal feelings conflict with the original purpose of the relationship. At that point you may have to decide which is more important to you, the personal relationship or the professional.

Even when you disagree or when, as may happen, you get into a friendly, kidding kind of competitiveness, you will retain your basically good feelings for each other. You won't let disagreements spoil your relationship.

The most important point about this aspect is that it does create a strong attraction between you. Because of the active nature of the opposition, one or both of you will very probably take the initiative in starting this relationship so that it will grow and be of benefit to both of you.

Composite Venus Conjunct Composite Saturn

Venus conjunct Saturn in the composite chart can present problems for a relationship, particularly a personal one. In professional associations it is not so difficult.

Saturn represents the principle of reality, at least as most people see it. As a planetary power it represses the warm and self-expressive nature of Venus and can make a relationship very cold. Even if there are strong feelings between you, the expression of those feelings is somehow always subordinated to more practical considerations. One of you may feel that despite your affection for one another, this is not the right time or the right place for your being together. Perhaps it would foul up a personal relationship that one of you has with someone else. This aspect particularly can prevent a sexual relationship from ever being consummated, not for lack of feeling, but because of the considerations just mentioned.

This aspect can have another, quite different effect. Your affection may be expressed, and a sexual relationship may be consummated, but in a very cool and restrained manner. There is little of the spontaneity and flamboyance that is supposed to characterize a love affair. Nevertheless, the feeling is genuine, and Saturn's slowing effect may make the relationship steady and enduring rather than an affair that burns itself out, as some do. It may turn a potential love affair into a platonic relationship. The same cooling and steadying effects will also be seen in a friendship.

There is no reason to assume that this aspect will deny a satisfactory relationship, but it will slow it down and keep it cool. The two of you must ultimately decide what you want from this relationship. If you want a cool, steady, and reliable bond, this is it. But if you want an exciting and romantic affair, you won't find it with this aspect.

Composite Venus Sextile Composite Saturn

Venus sextile Saturn in a composite chart will have a certain restraining effect upon a relationship, ranging from a lasting sense of distance between you to a restrained but otherwise very affectionate bond. A love relationship with this aspect may be more durable than most, but both of you would approach it with a sense of duty as well as enjoyment. If this is a marriage, this aspect might make you stay together for the sake of the children or some such reason, when other couples would have split up.

If there is affection between you, it is quiet and without fanfare; in fact, you may not show it overtly at all. However, that should not be allowed to happen, since you seldom really know each other's feelings unless you express them in a clear-cut way. With this aspect particularly you should not rely on your partner receiving your message by intuition.

Nevertheless, you can have a very positive relationship, as long as you take the trouble to let each other know that you are still there in spirit and haven't drifted off into some world of your own.

In a business or professional relationship this aspect favors such endeavors as commercial art and practical design work of all types.

Composite Venus Square Composite Saturn

Venus square Saturn can be a most troublesome aspect in a composite chart, depending to a great extent on what you expect of the relationship. It can prevent a love relationship that is otherwise good from ever being physically consummated. Things seem to get in the way—either circumstances are not favorable or one of you blows hot while the other blows cold. In a relationship with more problems, this aspect may be the final indication that it cannot be satisfactory from any point of view.

In the first case, the relationship can be a very happy one, even though it may not be everything you would like it to be. If you can restructure your expectations, there may be sufficient reason to enter into it. In fact, whenever this aspect occurs in a composite chart it is best to proceed without any expectations, taking whatever comes as it happens. Expectations simply provide a structure to hang your disappointments on when reality does not live up to what you want. This can be a most satisfactory relationship if you do not saddle it with too many demands about what it must be in order to work. If you are willing to take whatever you get, it can be all right.

Composite Venus Trine Composite Saturn

The trine of Venus and Saturn in the composite chart can affect you in either of two ways. On the plus side, it creates a steady feeling between you that changes very little from day to day. While you may not be the most unrestrained and demonstrative couple, your feelings for each other are real and reliable. This is true of either a friendship or a love affair.

In a professional relationship this trine can actually be quite beneficial. Saturn rules business, and the combination of Venus and Saturn by a trine literally means a business relationship. There is a balance in your association between the function of self-expression—this is something you both do because it suits you—and the function of accomplishing some specific purpose together. And this sort of balance also applies to other kinds of relationships. You can work together and enjoy life together, which is a very decided plus.

On the debit side, this aspect can cause you to be caught up in repetitious patterns. The other side of the steadiness of feeling is a tendency to get into a rut, so that the relationship becomes dull and routine. With a Venus-Saturn trine, whatever you get into together is hard to get out of. If you find this happening, you must try to get out of the pattern you have created and discover a new point of view about yourselves and your relationship.

Often it is a good idea to separate for a while—take separate vacations, for example, and get away from each other so that you can see things differently. Don't worry that this will bring the relationship to an end. Chances are, the factors that brought you together in the first place will bring you back again. And if not, that will be all right, too.

This aspect can hold two people together very well. Your relationship may not be one of the most exciting, but at least you can count on it in a positive way.

Composite Venus Opposition Composite Saturn

The opposition of Venus and Saturn in the composite chart means that there is a significant barrier to the expression of feelings between you. This does not make a relationship impossible, but it does make it difficult. Maybe you just do not like each other, but if you do, you find it difficult to say so for some reason. Perhaps one or both of you has inhibitions, or you are simply too shy. Or perhaps some external circumstance has created this barrier. For example, if this is potentially a sexual relationship, one of you may have another commitment that makes it difficult to acknowledge your feelings to your partner.

It can also be the case that you have strong emotions about each other, but at different times, so that whenever one of you is interested, the other is not. A sexual relationship with this aspect in the chart is usually not consummated, and if it is, there is likely to be some other serious defect in your way.

A relationship with this aspect is most likely to be successful if the two people do not really want to be terribly close. That is fine, but be aware of that fact and do not try to make the relationship into something it cannot be. It is very important for you both to be willing to take whatever comes. Do not saddle your relationship with all manner of expectations; it may become very good or it may amount to nothing at all. Certainly there will be some restrictions on it, but if you go along with an open mind, you will get whatever good it has to offer. If not, you will get only that side of the relationship that seems difficult.

Composite Venus Conjunct Composite Uranus

With Venus conjunct Uranus in the composite chart, you will have to keep certain points in mind in order to get the most out of your relationship.

If this is a sexual relationship, it is very likely that your feelings for each other arose suddenly. This is not an affection built up over a long period of time; in fact, it happens almost immediately. Even a friendship with this aspect develops quickly.

But no matter how intense the feeling, recognize that any attempt to hold onto this relationship and make it long-lasting is probably doomed to failure. It is not inevitable that this will be a short-term affair, but if you want it to last you must give each other lots of room to move. The more freedom you give yourselves and each other, the better the relationship will be. If you try to limit each other, you will probably destroy whatever good could come from your association. You both must be very open to strong feelings for others as well as to all sorts of feelings within yourselves.

A relationship like this shakes your established thought patterns and gives you both the opportunity to find something new in yourselves. It can and probably will be exciting, but it won't proceed according to the script you have in your mind. And if the moment comes when it must end, let it go, for you won't be able to keep it. Possibly it won't end like that, but that chance cannot be a factor in your considerations. This relationship may very well change your life. Give yourselves the freedom to go where it takes you.

Composite Venus Sextile Composite Uranus

The sextile of Venus and Uranus in the composite chart indicates a relationship that is very free and open in its expression. You each have freedom to be yourselves, and you will not consider your partner to be your property. Probably you will reach some unconventional arrangement with each other, an arrangement that others may think very unusual. And it will be, but it will express what you want, no matter what others think.

At the same time, this relationship will change your thinking, for the experience of it will cause both of you to regard the world in a new light. This in itself will make you reluctant to follow any particular set of rules except those that you set up for yourselves. Even the usual categories, such as friendships or love affairs (regardless of your sex), will not be followed in the usual way at all. If it is a love affair it will also be a friendship.

Let yourselves flow with the tide of events in this relationship. If you let it establish its own patterns, you should find it quite good.

Composite Venus Square Composite Uranus

With the square of Venus and Uranus in the composite chart you can confidently expect the unexpected. A relationship can flare up and then die with incredible speed when this aspect is present. Any effort to make such a relationship fulfill narrow expectations is doomed to failure. Indeed, from the normal point of view, it is extremely unstable. It would be best for the two of you not to count on this relationship for anything in particular. Not that it will have no value for you, but it is not likely to be what you expect.

If you are looking for a quiet, reliable, long-term association, this is probably not it, unless you really can enjoy and appreciate an unstructured relationship with almost no rules. If you can give yourselves room for such an experience, by all means do so, but remember that you will be constantly challenged.

A relationship with this aspect is destroyed usually because one of the people tries to hold on to something within it. This makes the other person feel trapped and rebellious about the restrictions. But such a relationship does not need to have a long-term purpose; it can be an affair that goes almost as soon as it begins. And when it goes, you must let it.

Often a relationship like this has something very unusual about it and may even fly in the face of social convention. Many extramarital affairs have this aspect or a similar one. In a way, the relationship lives because of this forbidden quality. If you break off your old relationships in favor of one such as this, you will discover that making it legitimate has taken away the "zing" of unconventionality. The two of you lose interest in each other, and the affair dies. A friendship with this aspect survives to the extent that it provides each of you with an escape from the ordinary routine.

In its own terms, a relationship with this aspect is usually successful in one way or another. But if you want it to be long-lasting, you must operate from a very unstructured and open position with a minimum of restrictions.

Composite Venus Trine Composite Uranus

The trine of Venus and Uranus can be very beneficial in the composite chart of any kind of personal relationship, as long as you both are willing to strike out against the conventional paths and find a path of your own. For this relationship has a flavor that others would consider unusual, even eccentric. Something about being together makes you both impatient about doing things in a totally ordinary way.

A sexual relationship with this aspect is likely to be very open; that is, both partners may permit each other to have other relationships with the opposite sex. Or it may simply be that both partners are willing to grant each other much more freedom of movement than usual. There are countless other ways of being unusual as a couple. The point is that if you don't want to follow the customary script for your relationship—love affair, friendship, marriage, or whatever—then you don't have to.

There is a good quality to your relationship that will be brought out only if you do things your own way. Uranus is the planet of freedom and unconventionality, but it can also mean instability if forced to follow conventional modes of expression, because it is the planet of rebellion.

At the very least this aspect will allow you to experience a relationship that is different from any you may have known before. Allow yourself this experience, and it will be good.

Composite Venus Opposition Composite Uranus

The energies of the opposition of composite Venus and Uranus are quite difficult to handle. Normally this aspect creates a very exciting relationship that lasts only for a short time. Typically, it will have tremendous ups and downs that give the participants very little peace or quiet. This is particularly true of love relationships. Other personal relationships are less affected, although they will be very disruptive at times. The degree of disruption is usually related directly to the intimacy of the affair.

The two of you may be very different in class, age, culture, or some such factor. And usually the unusualness of the attraction is what keeps it going. Consequently, any attempt to make the relationship normal or ordinary will cause it to die.

This relationship may flare up quickly and then suddenly die out. The two of you should not count on anything in particular if this aspect is present. Not that you cannot derive any benefit from your relationship, but it is best to take it as it comes and not try to live in the future. A marriage with this aspect in the chart will be difficult, unless both of you are willing to give each other a lot of freedom.

A friendship with this configuration is often more successful, because the roles are less ritualized and you have more freedom within the relationship. Uranus has a way of jarring people out of their ruts, which can be a powerful force in a friendship.

Whatever the nature of your relationship, let it take the course that it wants to take.

Composite Venus Conjunct Composite Neptune

With the conjunction of Venus and Neptune in a composite chart, your affection for each other can become idealized to the point of unreality, unless you are careful. This combination of Venus and Neptune can be a beautiful illusion, or it can be the perfect mystical ideal union, which obviously is an ideal that is not easily achieved.

A love relationship with this aspect usually starts out in a burst of romantic fervor, for the Venus-Neptune aspects are the most romantic of all astrological configurations. Unfortunately, however, such a relationship usually doesn't take place between two real individuals but between two fantasies that people form about each other. Be sure that your love is for a real person and not for some imaginary ideal that your partner represents to you. The effect of Neptune can be to make your disappointment more intense when dull reality replaces the beautiful illusion.

If in fact you both come close to each other's ideal, you will have a beautiful relationship, the kind that inspires song and verse. But be honest with yourselves; such ideal situations are rather rare.

Neptune is a nonphysical planet and therefore may turn an affair that would otherwise be sexual into a platonic relationship. The physical aspect of sex somehow does not come up to the spiritual idealism of Neptune. Often this aspect will bring the deepest love but no sex. Even a friendship will have this idealistic quality, but in that case the physical aspect is less of a problem.

The important reminder with this aspect is to be realistic.

Composite Venus Sextile Composite Neptune

Like all composite Venus-Neptune aspects, the sextile increases the idealistic and romantic tendencies of a relationship. A friendship becomes more than an ordinary encounter, for each of you idealizes the other in some almost magical way. In fact, this aspect favors friendship more than a love affair, because like the other Venus-Neptune combinations, it inclines toward a nonsexual relationship. Neptune operates on the nonphysical, nonmaterial plane and denies physical manifestations, including sex.

Nevertheless, this aspect does not mean that a would-be sexual relationship will be unsuccessful. It simply means that it will have a strongly spiritual tone in addition to its sexual and physical dimensions. This can be a very beautiful relationship for both of you, if you keep your feet on the ground, at least a little bit. It should open your eyes to the sublime aspects of the world around you and make you more receptive to beauty. Through this relationship you will also experience the beauty that lies within you. At its best, this can be a bond between true soul-mates who are matched spiritually as well as physically.

Composite Venus Square Composite Neptune

The square of composite Venus and Neptune requires that the two of you be quite wary about the true nature of this relationship. If you are not careful and unless you evaluate yourselves thoroughly, you could experience great disappointment. With this particular Venus-Neptune aspect, you may believe that you have met the ideal of your life, especially in a romantic sense. The love of your life is here! Everything may seem perfect and ideal, but there may come a time, rather suddenly, when it all turns out to be quite different from what you had imagined.

Neptune is the planet both of illusion and the ideal, and under its influence you are likely to find it very difficult to tell which is which. This relationship may be fact be a very good one from which you will derive much value, although even at best you will probably idealize it. But even a really good relationship may at the same time be a complete illusion. Without knowing it, the two of you may not be able to see each other for what you are at all. You must ascertain whether each of you is for real; that is, are you relating to each other or to some idealized fantasy? Is the spiritual element that you see in each other and in your relationship real or not?

You must examine this situation very closely, for you cannot afford to live in a fool's paradise. Your relationship may be either very good or very unreal, and you must find out which it is.

Composite Venus Trine Composite Neptune

The trine of composite Venus and Neptune indicates a highly idealized relationship. If this is a love affair, it is a very romantic one; if it is a friendship, you probably idealize each other's attributes. In either case, something about this relationship stimulates your spiritual side, so that you see each other as well as the world around you in a more idealized way. This relationship may also stimulate great creativity in one of you, enabling you to write poetry or music. However, it is more likely that it will only stimulate a desire to be creative, rather than actually give you the ability.

Venus and Neptune together mean the beautiful illusion. In a trine, however, the word "ideal" might be more appropriate than "illusion." Even so, you must try to stay in touch with the everyday world; any relationship, no matter how ideal, has to work out some everyday details that may not quite come up to the beautiful ideal. With this aspect, the two of you may even reject physical sex as being too earthly and material. Like many other configurations of Neptune, this aspect is often characterized by a platonic relationship. If there is physical sex, it is highly idealized.

The effects of this aspect are not really bad, although others may think that the two of you are a little bit crazy. Your relationship should actually be quite beautiful and pleasant, but in order for it to exist successfully in the material world, you cannot spend all your time in the ideal world of your dreams.

Composite Venus Opposition Composite Neptune

The opposition of Neptune and Venus in the composite chart requires that you take great care when you enter into this relationship, whether it is a love affair, friendship, marriage, or whatever. In any of these, your feelings for each other will be very refined and idealized. At least in the initial stages, this relationship will seem to have a perfection that you have never found with anyone else. And there may be a spirituality between you that you have never before encountered. Often one of you will look upon the other as a spiritual leader who can act as a guide out of the confusion of ordinary life into some new, higher spiritual realm.

But the question arises, who are you really in love with? In any love relationship you project elements of your own inner self upon your partner; that is, you experience those characteristics as being outside of yourself. But what you see in the other is often only a reflection of yourself, so you are your own lover. In a successful relationship, the other person corresponds to the projected image closely enough to make the illusion work. But in some relationships there is little or no correspondence between the image and the real person. Consequently, when this truth is recognized, great disappointment sets in. Unfortunately, the Venus-Neptune opposition is particularly subject to this kind of disappointment, because the ideals are too high to begin with, so the letdown is even greater.

Do not try to find Salvation with your friend or lover. Be satisfied with a human being in this relationship and look elsewhere for your god. Few people can measure up to such expectations, so accept the reality of the other person. You may find a far more beautiful reality than you would have imagined to be possible.

Composite Venus Conjunct Composite Pluto

Venus conjunct Pluto in the composite chart signifies the power of love as a transforming agent. In this relationship, whether it is a friendship or a love affair, you are seeking something more than love in the ordinary sense. In other words, you are hoping to find a very intense experience that will change and transform you, hopefully forever, but at least as long as the relationship lasts. Consequently, everything about your being together becomes extremely important; nothing is treated lightly.

In a sexual relationship, physical lovemaking is approached with an intensity that can make the experience very powerful and beautiful. On the other hand, it can exaggerate the importance of sex so much that the whole relationship hinges on the success of each instance of lovemaking.

At any rate this is not likely to be a casual relationship. You will be intensely involved with each other. Unfortunately, however, the intensity can sometimes take a peculiar and undesirable form. Love can be transformed into a power struggle if one or both of you tries to use the relationship as a tool for manipulating the other. The victim is powerless to do anything about it, and a strange love-hate tension is set up. Sometimes one of the partners feels degraded by the other but at the same time is held by a curious fascination. When such a situation finally explodes, it can be disastrous.

Obviously, from what has been said, this is not a relationship to play with. You must enter into it with serious intentions of making something good of it. You will both have great power over each other, so use it well.

Composite Venus Sextile Composite Pluto

Venus sextile Pluto in the composite chart is an intensely transforming aspect, but it works in an undemanding way. The basic significance of this aspect is that your relationship will change the ways you think about the world, as well as changing your personal objectives. You both will be changed by the relationship, but you may not be aware of the process as it is happening. The only thing you will notice is that your feelings will have a depth that is not often found in a relationship.

Even a friendship with this aspect will have a greater sense of emotional involvement than usual. Most friendships, especially between men, have a casual quality with no particular awareness of love, just a friendly easiness. With this aspect, however, your emotions will be evident, even in a friendship.

In a sexual relationship the qualities of this aspect become especially evident. The whole relationship, and particularly the physical part of it, becomes a way of transcending the ordinariness of life. But it is not an escape, for your awareness is heightened rather than diminished. The emotions you feel will make the ordinary seem extraordinary, and the everyday concerns will be of great importance.

Do not treat this relationship lightly, but do not be afraid of it either. It can be particularly rewarding.

Composite Venus Square Composite Pluto

The Venus-Pluto square in the composite chart means the power of love or the power in love. This is not a relationship to be treated lightly, for powerful forces are at work here. Some very unusual and difficult emotional patterns can arise in which one of you is fascinated by the other and comes under his or her complete control. Even if the dominated one is aware of what is happening, there seems to be nothing he or she can do about it. The feelings can become a mixture of love and hate.

Usually the effect is not that intense, but still there are problems. Even in a more usual relationship one of you may use the love you share as a device for manipulating and controlling the other. This often has disastrous consequences if the dominated partner tries to break free. When such a relationship breaks up, it leaves feelings of bitterness that are greater than those in any other breakup.

There can be many good things about this relationship. Your emotional involvement is intense, and you are very deeply concerned about each other. In a sexual relationship there is a strong emphasis on physical lovemaking. If you can avoid the kinds of games described above, you can have a rich and rewarding relationship. Try not to play around with each other's feelings. Although you will find it difficult to leave well enough alone, you must learn to do so or face the consequences of bad feelings and mutual recriminations.

Composite Venus Trine Composite Pluto

Like all composite Venus-Pluto aspects, the trine produces extremely intense feelings in any kind of relationship. But with this aspect it is perhaps easier to control the energies and still keep the strong points of such a relationship.

In a love relationship between the sexes, you will find it easy to demonstrate your feelings for each other. You will enjoy loving and being loved. The experience will transform you and make your world and your perception of it into something new. You may not be able to see how your life has changed, but there will be change. Most likely, it is your point of view about life that will change, which can be a very important change. Your point of view determines how you respond to the world.

With a Venus-Pluto trine, love has an almost psychotherapeutic effect on you both. Even a friendship with this aspect has a transforming quality.

Sexual love is very important in this relationship. In a marriage, children may assume a greater than usual significance. They are seen as a tie to the future, which somehow ensures that the two of you will never die. Parents usually have this notion, unconsciously, of immortality through their children, but in this case you are likely to be very aware of it.

The Venus-Pluto trine confers an intense quality that can bind two people together and give the relationship more than ordinary importance.

Composite Venus Opposition Composite Pluto

With the opposition of Venus and Pluto in the composite chart you will have to be very careful. Your relationship has a peculiar intensity that makes both of you experience and display strange, usually unconscious feelings. Somehow this relationship dredges up all kinds of deeply buried emotions that you may not really want to cope with. At its best, this power can cause you both to become new and more authentic people than you have been. But at its worst you will just play around with each other's feelings, and what comes of playing around will make both of you feel quite bad about yourselves.

This is not a trivial relationship. If you are lovers, your feelings for each other, both good and bad, are very strong. If you are friends, your friendship is very deep and moving. Even if you are enemies, which is a possibility with this aspect, you will affect each other profoundly and quite probably in a positive way, although that will not necessarily be obvious at the time.

Whatever your relationship, with such intense emotions you should not trifle with each other, for you can help or hurt each other tremendously. Typically, one of you may play God or psychotherapist and use the insights that you gain to threaten or manipulate your partner. But it isn't a good idea to fall in love with your psychoanalyst, or to be a psychoanalyst to your lover. Instead, try to just experience your love. The feelings between you can be powerful forces for good or bad, so use each other wisely.

Composite Venus Conjunct Composite Ascendant

The conjunction of composite Venus and Ascendant is a particularly good aspect for any kind of personal relationship, especially a love affair or marriage. It signifies that the two of you are extremely complementary in many respects and that as a couple you are a whole that is stronger than the two parts.

Love and emotion are very strong in this relationship. Even a casual relationship will become loving. A professional or business association with this aspect will also be a friendship, without the difficult personal entanglements that can sometimes destroy a professional relationship. In any kind of relationship, the two of you can cooperate, and each makes up for what the other lacks.

People around you will be aware of the way you feel about each other, and this fact will improve your relationships with others. A loving couple makes other people feel good, and they will enjoy being around you.

Under some circumstances, the conjunction of Venus and the composite Ascendant can attract money and other kinds of property. In all, this is an excellent indication for any relationship.

Composite Venus Sextile Composite Ascendant

The sextile of composite Venus and Ascendant is an excellent aspect for a personal relationship. First of all, it is a sign of loving friendship, whether you are lovers or simply friends. It is easy for each of you to indicate your feelings to the other, without the hesitancy or shyness about revealing emotions that can make a relationship difficult from time to time. You always feel comfortable and easy with each other.

When stressful times occur, you both are primarily concerned about the survival of your relationship, so you willingly make the necessary compromises to ensure it. The only problem to watch for is that the energy of Venus may be so accommodating that one partner will give way when he or she should take a stand in order to save self-esteem and respect. Fortunately, however, you both are inclined to do this, so at least it is not always the same person who gives way. Even so, don't allow your desire for a smooth relationship to make you hold back tensions and energies that should be expressed, even if they cause some trouble. This problem becomes more severe if there are other indications of trouble in the chart.

This relationship may possibly become associated with some artistic or aesthetic activity involving music or the arts or a branch of the entertainment industry. Certainly the two of you will be attracted to such activities, especially if you had an interest in them before.

Composite Venus Square Composite Ascendant

The square of composite Venus and Ascendant is not a difficult square. On the contrary, it is a very beneficial aspect in a composite chart. This Venus-Ascendant aspect is a sign of a deeply loving relationship.

This combination will manifest itself particularly in your home. If this is a relationship in which you have a home together, it will be an expression of your feelings for each other. It will be a place where the two of you can retire from the outside world, not as an escape but as a refuge where you can prepare yourselves for the next day. You will do everything you can to make your home pleasant and comfortable, with beautiful art and decor, comfortable furniture, and good food. And these comforts are not simply an indulgence, but an honest expression of your desires to make each other feel as comfortable as possible.

Sometimes the energy of this square operates outside the home as well. Instead of expressing itself in your personal world, your home, this energy may be expressed through your social and public lives. Instead of keeping your love to yourselves, you may make your relationship very public and open, so that others will sit up and take notice of two people who feel strongly about each other.

In a professional relationship this aspect can mean that you are engaged in an occupation related to art and beauty or the entertainment industry.

In a relationship that has no clearly identifiable home, this aspect means that the two of you feel that your love for each other comes from a strong similarity in your pasts. Many elements of your lives before you met have given you something in common, and this binds you together.

Composite Venus Trine Composite Ascendant

The trine of composite Venus and Ascendant is one of the best aspects to have in a composite chart, especially for a love relationship or marriage. It indicates that the two of you enjoy each other and that your love is founded on the ability to be yourselves in each other's company. Each of you accepts your partner for what he or she is, without making endless demands that the other change in ways that are impossible. You both understand that the other is what he or she is, not in a spirit of resignation but of joy.

Because of this attitude, you are tolerant of each other's faults, and you let each other alone instead of causing conflict. It is not just that you have good feelings for each other, but that the way you feel about each other broadens your understanding of life in general.

On another level, you enjoy having good times together. You like to get out and attend the theater, nightclubs, and other amusements. If you have come together for business or professional reasons, you would succeed quite well in professions relating to these fields. In an individual, this aspect may be a sign of artistic ability, and in a relationship it may mean that the two of you are somehow involved with the arts.

Under any circumstances this aspect should help to make your relationship pleasant and worth having.

Composite Venus Opposition Composite Ascendant

The opposition of composite Venus and Ascendant signifies the possibility of a partnership of real love, one of the best to have in the composite chart of a love relationship or marriage. It can pull a relationship through the worst situations that can occur.

Regardless of why you have come together, this aspect will produce a love relationship between you. The two of you feel that you complement each other in some definite but indefinable way and that together you are stronger than you would be separately. This is not merely appearance, for at its ultimate level, Venus signifies the attraction between two people who are truly complementary. That is to say, your differences do not create barriers between you but allow you to work together in life. Each one has what the other lacks and needs. Venus on the composite Descendant is a strong indication that the two of you form such a complementary team.

Chapter Nine

Mars

The Meaning of Mars in the Composite Chart

The basic principle of Mars is the ego-drive, the energy by which you sustain your sense of being an individual, both toward the world and toward other people. You inevitably build up your notions of yourself through the ways in which you interact with others. Without some kind of active inner energy, you would not be able to withstand encounters with others at all and would be forced to drop out of life altogether. And indeed this does happen to some people.

In a relationship, people try to establish some kind of positive connection with each other, but ego-drives often get in the way. If you have a sound sense of yourself, as signified by a well-placed Mars, you will have little difficulty getting along with others. But if Mars is badly placed, your sense of your own being is deficient, and you will get into conflicts that make it impossible to relate to others. A conflict between two people arises whenever one challenges a weakness in the other's sense of individuality—in other words, the ego.

In a composite chart, Mars signifies your ability to create an environment within the relationship for both of you to express yourselves fully without threatening each other and provoking destructive conflicts. Some—perhaps quite a lot of—conflict in a relationship is inevitable, and conflict per se should not be suppressed. But your ego drives must be basically compatible within the relationship, or nothing can be accomplished.

In a sexual relationship, Mars also rules the sex drive. A successful sexual relationship requires that both Venus, the ability to relate, and Mars, the ego-drive, be in good condition. There is a large ego component in a successful sexual relationship. If the relationship does not express each of you, it will not work. A poorly aspected Mars in a composite signifies deficient ego-drives, which will affect your ability to get along with each other, and in a sexual relationship, it will affect the quality of physical sex.

Composite Mars in the First House

Composite Mars in the first house demands that this relationship be a complete expression of both of you. This should be the case with any relationship, but it is even more important in this instance. It would be best if you could find something that you both like to do together, and the more physically active the better. There is a lot of energy in your relationship that must be expended somehow.

If you can find a common purpose, all of your energy will be focused on that instead of on each other. You will be able to accomplish a tremendous amount of work together, and in the process you will enjoy each other. There is no way around the fact that this relationship demands activity.

Unfortunately, if you do not handle these energies properly, Mars can signify fighting and conflict. It is not that you necessarily dislike each other, although that could be the case, but that the relationship doesn't give any relevance to the matters that are really important to each of you individually. There are you, the other person, and your relationship, all of which seem to have very little in common.

Keeping this problem in mind, this can be an excellent placement for any relationship that is specifically aimed at accomplishing a job or task, such as a professional association.

Composite Mars in the Second House

Mars in the second house of the composite chart indicates a relationship in which your mutual ego-expression revolves around acquiring things, but not necessarily holding on to them. The second house is the house of one's resources, both material and psychological.

There is a tendency to be reckless with resources, such as spending money too quickly or taking chances with possessions. It is as if the two of you glory in being able to do whatever you want with what you own. The problem is that you both have to agree on what to do with your mutual possessions. If you cannot agree, there could be serious disputes over property, possessions, and finances. Even if the relationship is otherwise satisfactory, the way you handle money and possessions could be a serious threat to harmony between you. It is very important that you come to some understanding about this issue as early as possible.

Even if you do agree, you should be careful about what you do with your resources. Otherwise you may find that the resources you need to accomplish something have disappeared.

Mars in the composite chart relates to joint ego-expression. The second-house position means that this will be achieved through property, possessions, and money. Plan very carefully how to achieve what you want, and be very sure to do something with what you have, for that is what the position signifies.

The second house can also signify values in an intellectual sense. Whatever your value systems are, be sure that you have a conscious understanding of them, or they could become an issue that divides you.

Composite Mars in the Third House

Mars in the third house of the composite chart indicates several areas of expression in a relationship. First of all, the third house rules the lower mind, that is, the mind in its routine day-to-day functioning. If the two of you are not getting along well with each other, this placement of Mars signifies arguing and disputes and general intellectual disagreement. The problem is that each of you may identify with your own ideas and opinions so strongly that you regard a challenge to your beliefs as a challenge to your innermost self. Habits and other ingrained behavior patterns could also become an issue for dispute in this relationship. You must straighten out within yourselves and with each other what is going on inside you. In other words, you have to have great self-awareness.

The third house also rules the immediate environment and relatives. If your relationship is working out well, this simply means that the two of you will be actively and vigorously involved with your immediate family and relatives. If events take a negative turn, however, you may be constantly at odds with your immediate environment—continual disputes with relatives, for example. Again it is necessary that you both watch out for unconscious habits of thought.

Composite Mars in the Fourth House

The fourth house rules the innermost bases of life—your own inner foundation, the home, the unconscious mind, your parents and in-laws. Mars in the fourth house of the composite chart is most noticeable if its energy is not working smoothly. If the Mars energy is working smoothly, you will hardly be aware of it. The two of you will work together with a natural rapport and an inherent smoothness.

However, if the Mars energy is not working smoothly, there will be a number of difficulties to work out. To begin with, the sources of your ego conflicts are buried deep within the relationship, so it will be difficult to root them out and bring them into the open. The causes of conflict will be in matters that you take so much for granted that you are not even aware of them. For this reason you must question even your most fundamental assumptions to discover how you are subverting your relationship.

The effects of this energy will be apparent in the most basic aspects of your lives. If you live together, the energy could manifest itself as arguments in and about the home. You might have differing concepts of what a home ought to be, which could be a serious source of conflict. Or if you are married, your parents might be the immediate occasion for battle. But neither home nor parents is really the problem. The basic difficulty is that your unconscious ideas and notions on various subjects become clear to you only when they are challenged. It will take a very deep inquiry into yourselves to get at these problems.

Composite Mars in the Fifth House

The fifth house is a very compatible position for Mars in a composite chart, but the needs it generates must be met. It is a position of great self-expression, so there must be ample opportunity for self-expression in this relationship. You must give each other plenty of room to be yourselves with a minimum of interference. If you impose all manner of limitations on each other, there will be considerable conflict. Mars is related to ego energies, which create no problem if expressed. If they are not expressed, however, they can create many difficulties.

It would be excellent for the two of you to be as active as possible together, with a common set of goals toward which you bend your energies. In that way the energy that might become a source of conflict can bind the two of you together.

In a sexual relationship this position can be extremely beneficial, provided that you follow the advice given above. The fifth is the house of love affairs, while Mars, along with Venus, rules sexual energy. In a sexual relationship with this position, if you don't work well together on a sexual level, there is not likely to be harmony on any other level. The energy that should be used in sex instead becomes the source of very divisive ego conflict.

Composite Mars in the Sixth House

With composite Mars in the sixth house, you will have a sense of work to be done together. The sixth is the house of work, and in a composite chart it signifies the duties and responsibilities that the two of you must fulfill through this relationship.

The difficulty with this position, as with all planets in the sixth house of the composite chart, is that your sense of duty will often overwhelm the feelings of joy and pleasure that should be present in a relationship. The two of you may begin to regard the relationship as a burden, a set of tasks, rather than something to be enjoyed for its own sake. This is a deadening point of view and is particularly difficult in a sexual relationship.

This position is least problematical in a business or professional association in which work is the sole object. But even here the two of you must enjoy being together, so that your work becomes a form of self-expression as well as a duty. The sixth house emphasizes the needful aspect of work rather than the self-expressive aspect.

If the two of you do not feel that you are accomplishing something fairly concrete by being together, this will be a disruptive problem. Enjoying each other or feeling that you are both growing through your relationship is not usually enough to satisfy the demands of this placement of Mars. There is work to be done.

Composite Mars in the Seventh House

Mars in the seventh house of the composite chart can indicate that the two of you have a great sense of common purpose. On the other hand, it can mean a total conflict of purpose to the point that you are clearly enemies rather than friends or lovers. Either you will feel that your energies are infinitely better expressed by being together rather than apart, or you will be in an extreme state of conflict with each other. Which way your relationship will work depends to a great extent upon finding a way to express yourselves together, discovering something that you can do together. The seventh is the house of partners and of open enemies. Even at the very worst you will know exactly where you stand with each other.

It is also possible, of course, for these two effects to occur together. This creates a love-hate relationship in which your feelings toward each other oscillate rapidly between loving and hating.

The presence of Mars in this house indicates that the ego-energies within this relationship are very strong. In this situation it is not always easy for one of you to accede to the other's wishes. Here the martyr game that characterizes so many relationships—with one of you always conceding grudgingly to the other—will not work.

This position requires that the two of you be on an equal footing. Any attempt to place yourself over your partner will make a very tense situation. Give each other plenty of room to find fulfillment within the relationship and also to find something that you can work for together. Then this position of Mars will be a help rather than a hindrance.

Composite Mars in the Eighth House

Composite Mars in the eighth house indicates that in this relationship the two of you express your egos in a way that forces you to look for new insights into the nature of your ways of living. The eighth house of the horoscope is very complex. It is the house of transformation and of the psychological energies that underlie any major changes within the self. As each of you encounters the other, you will be challenged, not necessarily in a destructive way, but in a way that will make growth necessary.

The eighth house also represents regeneration, and Mars in this house can create a great deal of sexual energy for regeneration of the self through the creation of another person. In this relationship, sex will be very important and may even become a vehicle for transforming both of you.

This is the house of joint resources, which makes it very important to a relationship. In some cases there may be conflict between you about money or property. To avoid this problem you both must learn to back down and make sure that petty expressions of the ego are not getting in the way of the relationship. Try not to become too involved with your possessions. If you identify with them too strongly, they will become a source of problems.

Composite Mars in the Ninth House

Composite Mars in the ninth, the house of the higher mind and long journeys, indicates a strong involvement with ideas, beliefs, and philosophies of life in this relationship. That is, your beliefs are very important to each of you, and being together makes them even more so. If your ideas and attitudes toward life are compatible, you will work very hard together to protect them, and you will try to convince others of the rightness of what you are doing.

If your attitudes are not compatible, you will waste a lot of energy trying to convince each other of them, causing much conflict in the process. The universe is actually large enough to encompass both sets of ideas, as well as the beliefs of those whom you disagree with. But the two of you probably do not realize this, feeling that if other people's beliefs are true, yours cannot be, and vice versa. You are likely to react to opposition almost as if your lives were in danger. Be careful of this and try to expand your views so that they can encompass those of other people.

This placement of Mars may also indicate that the two of you will do some work together that involves traveling over long distances. Or it can mean working together in some academic or intellectual field.

Composite Mars in the Tenth House

Mars in the tenth house of the composite chart means that the energy of Mars must be successfully expressed through this relationship, or there is likely to be trouble. The tenth is the house of the ego's most complete expression, symbolizing what you must do in order to evolve in life. In a composite chart, the tenth house has to do with how well each of you can express your life purpose within the relationship. With Mars in this house, the issue of ego-drives will be even more important than in most relationships.

You must allow each other plenty of room to follow your own paths. It would not be a good idea for one of you to sacrifice your goals in life in order to allow your partner to pursue his or her objectives. Eventually that course of action would become a sore point that could disrupt the relationship. Each of you must be allowed to do your own thing while you are together. Obviously it will be helpful if you have similar ideas about what you wish to do with your lives. Whatever your ambitions, they will be an issue in this relationship.

If you can agree on this issue, the energy of the tenth-house Mars will serve you in good stead. You will approach business or any other joint activity very aggressively and energetically. The results should be excellent. However, take care not to let these energies get out of hand, because they could generate a great deal of opposition from others that would be harmful to your best interests.

Composite Mars in the Eleventh House

Composite Mars in the eleventh house indicates that the two of you will enjoy working with other people in groups. It is an indication that you will derive more satisfaction from your work and energies if you feel that what you are doing is part of a greater whole. Together you will identify with various group projects, movements, and other situations in which the individual ego is subordinated to group expression. It is easier for both of you to completely express your personal energies through your relationship this way.

This position may also indicate that you will try to dominate your friends or associates, which will make matters rather difficult for the two of you. No matter where Mars is located in the chart, you must be careful how you handle its energies so that they do not cause strife and arguments with others.

The eleventh house is also the house of your ideals and hopes in life. Mars in this position indicates that the two of you will work very hard to attain whatever you want out of life. Consequently it is very important that you have similar or at least complementary goals in life. Otherwise, disagreements on this issue are likely to be a great source of conflict.

Composite Mars in the Twelfth House

Composite Mars in the twelfth house makes it absolutely imperative that the two of you understand exactly what you want from this relationship and each other. You must arrive at a conscious understanding and agreement. In most relationships, agreements are made tacitly, not formally stated or written down. But for the two of you it might be very profitable to write out an agreement. By doing so you may discover that you have included all kinds of demands that you never thought you would ask for. If you don't make the demands explicit, you can be sure that every time one of them is broken it will cause a conflict, even though neither of you will understand exactly why.

The literal meaning of Mars in the twelfth house might be stated as unconscious forms of ego expression. The twelfth house is not really unconscious, but it often indicates signals that you are sending out into the world very strongly but not acknowledging. Whether or not you acknowledge them, you will have to live with the consequences.

It is just the same with a relationship; the twelfth-house Mars signifies that you are putting into the relationship sources of conflict that could weaken it badly. Even worse, it would be very unclear why the problems exist. If you do not make an effort to find out what you really expect of each other, it will be difficult to ascertain why you are having conflicts. You may find that if you verbalize your wants, they will be full of contradictions, double-binds, and contract arrangements that can't be fulfilled. Only if you take the trouble to examine your expectations closely will it be possible to understand what you really want from each other and whether your needs can be met.

Composite Mars Conjunct Composite Jupiter

The conjunction of Mars and Jupiter in the composite chart denotes a relationship that has a great deal of energy, either physical or psychological. You like to be active and to do things together. Some couples may work this energy out by participating in sports together, and others may do so by sharing work. One thing is clear: whatever you do together will be successful. This is an aspect of luck, or at least that is how others will see it. What actually happens is that the two of you have a good sense of timing in your activities together, so you get the best possible results. Also, you approach whatever you do together with optimism and the expectation of success, which aids you in accomplishing your objectives.

The Mars-Jupiter conjunction creates a relationship that favors ego-expression; that is, you can do what you really want to do, and you each can be the kind of person you really want to be. This aspect also helps to ensure that the end results of your efforts will be good for all concerned.

In a sexual relationship, this aspect helps to make the physical expression of your love good and satisfying. Sexual expression acts as a solid basis for the whole relationship, and yet it does not remain the only positive quality. Your success in that area becomes the foundation for an overall success that others may well envy. It seems as though everything you do together works out for the best.

Composite Mars Sextile Composite Jupiter

Mars sextile Jupiter in the composite chart is a good indication that your ego drives are harmoniously related within the relationship. That is, each of you can do what you want and be what you want without getting in the way of your relationship. In fact, this aspect usually signifies that being together helps you both to be yourselves and do what you want.

The symbolism of the Mars-Jupiter combination is fortunate action. You work well together, think well together, and have the happy facility of wanting the same things at the same time or of seeking objectives that you can pursue together. And all these activities cement your relationship. If you are friends, this aspect will help you to be good friends. If you are lovers, you will also be friends, which is quite unusual in a love affair.

This aspect confers a rare quality of optimism on a relationship. You expect things to work, and that expectation somehow makes it happen. As a couple you will set high goals for yourselves, and they will be within your grasp. Sometimes the effort you expend, although real, will not even be apparent. It simply comes so easily that you are not aware of the effort at the time. This aspect can be instrumental in making a relationship successful, regardless of its purpose.

Composite Mars Square Composite Jupiter

Unlike most squares, the square of Mars and Jupiter in the composite chart is not all that hard to deal with. It gives the two of you a great deal of energy and makes you fond of doing things together. In fact, it is essential that you accustom yourselves to working together, for there is an underlying element of friendly competition between you that you have to understand if your relationship is to work out positively.

In the early stages, you may be irritated by each other's friendly kidding and goading, until you realize that it is harmless. As you become more familiar with your style as a couple, you will find that you make each other put out more effort and get more done than you could separately. The ego conflicts that arise somehow become the source of more energy.

On the other hand, if you do not try to work together and share your activities, this energy will still be present. But then it is likely to become a disruptive element and a source of bickering and conflict. It may not seriously undermine your feelings for each other, but it will be an unnecessary irritant. The more you work together, the more usefully this energy will be expended. The two of you cannot afford to stare lovingly into each other's eyes, or if you are friends, to sit around and meditate together. This relationship requires action.

Composite Mars Trine Composite Jupiter

Mars trine Jupiter is one of the best trines to have in a composite chart, for it indicates that there is harmony between you. You like to be together and to do things together, which contributes to a greater understanding of yourselves and each other. This is a growth relationship. Both of you will find that you can be yourselves in each other's presence without apology or explanation. When one of you is down, your partner cheers you up, and happiness permeates everything you do together.

Your optimism and exuberance extend to your activities, as if you had a Midas touch that turns everything to gold. This is not really luck, although others will think it is, but a sense of timing and a knowledge of your own abilities that develops as you learn about yourselves from each other. You do not expect things to go wrong, and they do not.

In a marriage, this aspect will help make child raising a positive experience. You are very likely to have children, and you will cherish them as the fruits of your relationship. In fact, this aspect makes any fruits of a relationship turn out well, no matter what they are.

Composite Mars Opposition Composite Jupiter

This aspect between Mars and Jupiter in the composite chart is one of the easiest oppositions to work with. It does create within a relationship a great deal of energy that must be given some kind of outlet. If the energy is bottled up, it can create problems.

To use the energy of this aspect, it is necessary for the two of you to be active together. Whenever practical you must do things jointly and pool your resources. If you do, you will find that together you can perform tasks that you could never do as separate individuals. You arouse physical energy in each other.

But if you do not find an outlet by working together, the energy can create a competitiveness that will tend to break up rather than cement the relationship. Mars-Jupiter energy is very physical, and often is best expressed in athletic activities, such as playing together in sports. Also, sports provide an expression for the naturally competitive nature of the aspect. You will spur each other on to action in a light-hearted and friendly way. You may tease and make fun of each other, but this competitiveness will not become destructive unless you try to suppress it.

If you work together cooperatively, the best of this aspect's energies will be brought out in your relationship.

Composite Mars Conjunct Composite Saturn

The conjunction of Mars and Saturn in a composite chart can be quite difficult to deal with, especially in a personal relationship. The basic principle of these planets together is blocked action. In a relationship, the symptoms of this are feelings of frustration and futility by one or both of you. Something about being together simply does not allow you to express yourselves freely.

Mars rules the ego drives, the energies by which a person establishes who he or she is in the world. But in a Mars-Saturn relationship each of you is constantly getting in the way of the other's ego drives. There may be cutting remarks, sarcasm, digs, and other tactics, but never an honest confrontation that would clear the air and release the negative energies that build up in a relationship.

Another result of this aspect in a sexual relationship is that one of you is always "hot" while the other is "cold." One feels loving while the other feels distant. A long-term relationship can survive this problem, but you will have to learn to live with the situation of being out of phase with each other.

With this aspect, what is most difficult to do is the very thing that must be done. You must let each other be and give each other room to breathe. It is particularly important to avoid unconstructive criticism, especially the kind that masquerades as being constructive. And you must be tolerant of each other's ups and downs, even if you cannot gear your own moods to coincide with them. Be prepared for these mood changes, and do not take them too personally.

Composite Mars Sextile Composite Saturn

The sextile between Mars and Saturn in the composite chart is not very easy to deal with. But it does have some strengths, particularly in a professional relationship in which some particularly exacting and painstaking work must be performed.

In a personal relationship there is a great danger that the two of you will get locked into behavioral ruts that are difficult to get out of. Every time one of you acts in a certain way, the other can be counted on to react in a certain, set manner that never changes. This aspect signifies habits, and as far as relationships are concerned, not very positive ones. Often the habits have very little to do with you as individuals; you probably behave quite differently with other people. But there is something in this relationship that makes you both behave strangely. Neither of you permits the other to be himself or herself. These little negative rituals develop so that you can handle being together on a daily basis.

The only way to deal with this aspect successfully is for both of you to become conscious of what you do that triggers your partner's responses. It is possible to solve this problem, for this aspect is by no means fatal to a relationship. All it takes is effort. Fortunately, one of the beneficial effects of this aspect is that you will have quite a bit of patience in dealing with each other.

Composite Mars Square Composite Saturn

Even in an otherwise favorable composite chart, the square of Mars and Saturn is quite difficult, for it indicates that the two of you are working at cross purposes. At its worst, this aspect will make you get in each other's way to such an insufferable degree that you cannot get along at all. At best, there will be friction because one of you is always in a different state of mind from the other. But this aspect does not often give rise to open warfare. Usually it produces negative feelings that seethe below the surface without ever coming out into the open. Occasionally your feelings will go past the boiling point, however, and there will be a big explosion of angry words between you.

With this aspect in your composite chart, you obviously have work to do. First of all, you must open the channels of communication between you. You will tend to hide your anger even when it is not good to do so. Learn to let it out and get it over with. It is better to blow off steam more often and less intensely than to hold back your anger for a long time. Say exactly what is on your mind and try not to express irritation in little cutting remarks.

In a sexual relationship, this aspect often creates differences of timing. One of you will always be in a different mood from the other, and both of you will insist on what you want when you want it. Obviously someone has to give, and that will be difficult in this case. But if you each can decide, at least occasionally, to give in without a fuss, it will improve your relationship immeasurably.

Composite Mars Trine Composite Saturn

The trine of composite Mars and Saturn is not one of the easier trines to deal with. It tends to lock the two of you into patterns of self-expression that continue to operate even when most inappropriate. Like the sextile, this aspect indicates habits in a relationship. You tend to develop set ways of thinking that are very difficult to get away from, and therefore you find it hard to see matters as they really are.

You both must learn to be more flexible in your thinking about the relationship and avoid responding to each other in automatic ways. However much you are tempted to respond as you have in the past, try to look at your partner as if you had never seen him or her before. You will find that each new situation, which you have been handling in the same old set way, is actually quite different and should be dealt with in a very distinct manner. Apply this idea to yourselves also. Watch your behavior and try to avoid doing the same things you have always done before. Only by looking at yourselves will you be able to do this.

In any personal relationship, but especially in a sexual one, it is important to give each other room to be what you are. If you can accept each other only on certain conditions, you should get out of the relationship. If you can each grant freedom of self-expression to the other, many of the ill effects of this aspect will be overcome.

Composite Mars Opposition Composite Saturn

The opposition of Mars and Saturn in the composite chart indicates a severe conflict between your life styles. It presents quite a few obstacles for your relationship to overcome. Most commonly the conflict takes the form of one-sidedness, so that one of you has all the emotions. Or the two of you may alternate your roles. One of you will like the other very much, while that person is feeling "cool," and then the cool one will suddenly turn on, just when the first partner turns off. Even more important in a sexual relationship, this aspect indicates differences in rhythm and timing.

A relationship may go on for some time with one partner being very affectionate and the other responding only with increasing demands, giving very little in return. In such a case, communication will be very poor between you, for both of you are afraid that your partner will reject you or not let you be what you are. Because of these fears, important issues that you ought to face directly are not faced at all. When the situation gets tense, as happens in any relationship, but especially here, stony silence reigns. Neither of you will say anything, as if every word were too painful to utter. Yet both of you are seething with frustration and anguish, unable to give it any vent.

The obvious cures for this problem are for both of you to let each other be and allow any difficulties that arise between you to be expressed openly. Do not hold it in. It is better to blow up occasionally than to blow out. Give each other room and confine your criticism to real issues. In any relationship some ego conflict is inevitable, but here there will be more than usual. You must allow for this conflict and expect it, but when it comes, don't take it as seriously as you may be inclined to.

Composite Mars Conjunct Composite Uranus

The conjunction of Mars and Uranus in the composite chart signifies totally unexpected and strange occurrences, so this relationship will not be an ordinary one. It may be that your relationship exists partly to express rebellion against established modes and patterns in the outside world; the two of you have come together to defy the world. Of course that is an extreme case, but even a more commonplace relationship, no matter what its purpose, will develop in an unusual way.

If the relationship does not have this quality of defiance, there may be many ups and downs and unexpected changes within it. This is not the ideal aspect for a stable, reliable association. You may have come together under unexpected circumstances or at a most inconvenient time. If this is a sexual relationship, one of you may have another commitment, which will be severely disrupted by this new encounter.

Clearly, with this aspect in your composite chart, the two of you must deal with your relationship in a very flexible manner. As with most Uranus combinations, you will have to take what you get. Let the relationship take its own course and don't saddle it with a lot of expectations. If you are not free to go wherever its natural energies take you, perhaps you should avoid it altogether. This relationship could be quite dangerous emotionally, particularly if you are involved in another that would be incompatible with this one.

Composite Mars Sextile Composite Uranus

The sextile of Mars and Uranus in the composite chart indicates that certain elements of this relationship will change your lives, not necessarily in great cosmic ways but nevertheless meaningfully. Through this experience you will find that your old ways of doing things are constantly challenged and forced to change. The results will not be shattering, however, but challenging and interesting. Regardless of the purpose of this relationship, you will also be friends, and together you will be eager to set off in new directions.

Sometimes of course, the newness of it all may be a bit frightening. Some elements of this relationship simply do not follow the ordinary script, but don't worry about that. If you go along with the natural flow of this relationship, it should work out satisfactorily.

At its best, this aspect will give the two of you new opportunities that you can take advantage of only if you are willing to strike out onto new paths. This relationship will not only prod you out of your rut, but will also help you understand why you should be prodded.

No matter how strange, unpredictable, or chaotic this relationship may seem, this aspect will give it a new dimension and make it rewarding to follow through to its conclusion.

Composite Mars Square Composite Uranus

You have the square of Mars and Uranus in your composite chart. To a great extent the virtues and flaws of any aspect in a composite chart depend upon your objectives. A personal relationship with this aspect is most likely to be successful if you have few expectations for it, because if it does not live up to what you expect, you may consider it a failure. With the square of Mars and Uranus in your composite chart, the two of you are especially impatient of objectives that "must" be attained. This relationship will take its own course, and expectations will not rest easily on it.

This is not an especially good aspect if you are planning to be married or hope to establish some other type of permanent bond. Nor is it very good for a business relationship, for example, in which there are definite objectives to be gained. Such a relationship is not impossible, but you must allow a great deal of room for the unexpected and for sudden change. The more you restrict a relationship with this aspect, the more likely it is to cause problems. Almost certainly there is something here that goes against social convention. If that fact restricts either of you, it will be even more difficult.

On the positive side, one thing is certain. If you are looking for a stimulating relationship that will bring something new into your world, this is it. Just give yourselves room to move.

Composite Mars Trine Composite Uranus

The trine of Mars and Uranus in the composite chart is a symbol that through this relationship you both will strike out and find new paths for self-expression. You will be unconventional and you won't do what others expect you to, but that will not bother you very much, for you will be doing what you want.

This relationship will affect your whole view of the world and make you see it from a new perspective. Your old ways of looking at things will be transformed, and this new perspective will lead you to new kinds of action.

A love relationship with this aspect is very strongly affected, because it will be more open than most. Possessiveness should be avoided, and you must give each other a great deal of freedom to be yourselves. If one of you feels confined, you will become very restless, which will make the relationship unstable. You cannot expect this to be a quiet, stable, predictable relationship, and you won't know what to expect at times. But it can be very stimulating, whatever its purpose. It would be a pity not to let this encounter show you what it can do.

Composite Mars Opposition Composite Uranus

The opposition of Mars and Uranus in the composite chart requires the two of you to have a great deal of flexibility—far more than most people have, unfortunately. With this aspect it is very difficult to let things be. Usually you get into a very competitive situation in which you are constantly trying to goad each other. It is almost as if you were trying to make your partner explode. Each person's self-expression becomes a challenge to the other.

Sometimes the relationship itself takes such an unusual turn that you will find it very difficult to pursue in ordinary society. Other people often cannot tolerate such an "impossible" relationship because it is such a challenge to their way of looking at life. Something about the way you act together does defy society at large.

Obviously a relationship with this aspect should find a social setting that is extremely tolerant of the unusual. At the same time the two of you must also be unusually tolerant of the unusual. Trouble is often caused if you try to make this relationship into something ordinary, which is neither desirable or possible. The pressures that make it what it is are so strong that they must be expressed. Otherwise the relationship will become so explosive that it cannot survive. If you want it to survive, do not try to change it. If you cannot take this encounter as it is, you should get out completely.

Composite Mars Conjunct Composite Neptune

The conjunction of Mars and Neptune in a composite chart is not an easy aspect, for it signifies the union of two planetary forces that are not readily combined. The problem is that on the level of mundane reality, where most of us operate most of the time, Neptune is confusing, weakening, and debilitating. Mars is the planet of one's own strength, and in a composite chart it symbolizes the ability of the relationship to contribute to each person's ego-expression. With these planets in conjunction, the two of you will find it difficult to derive positive reinforcement from each other.

Often this aspect creates a relationship in which you both feel inferior, unsuccessful, and debilitated. You may feel that as individuals you are becoming weaker than you were before. One of you may become so weak as to be totally dependent on the other. Your feelings of hostility do not usually come out into the open but are expressed by making your partner feel guilty or by depriving him or her of self-esteem.

On a higher plane, however, Neptune brings spiritual self-awareness. This planet is quite destructive to ordinary awareness, but if the two of you can go beyond your attachment to the everyday world and receive Neptune's message, you may discover a whole new way of dealing with the world. This is the only way to handle this aspect. You must be in a state of consciousness in which you can detach yourself from your ego-drives in dealing with each other. This does not mean you should suppress your ego-drives; instead, they should be truly unimportant. If you merely suppress them, you will act like a martyr all the time. And martyred behavior is one of the subversive tactics of aggression that this aspect sometimes signifies.

Composite Mars Sextile Composite Neptune

The sextile of Mars and Neptune in the composite chart often denotes that the two of you have come together for some idealistic task or purpose. It is an aspect of friendship, but not ordinary friendship, for you are together not simply to enjoy each other's company but to accomplish something. It is not very likely that this will be work in the usual physical sense; it is more likely to be spiritual or psychological work. The real task of such a relationship is to alter each other's conception and experience of reality through what you do together. You will handle your lives differently because you have known each other. The alteration can be either good or bad, so it is up to you to ensure that it is good.

The challenge of this aspect is to keep your intentions clear with regard to each other. As with all Neptune aspects, there is a great danger that you will become confused and act wrongly from that confusion. Unlike the hard aspects of Mars and Neptune—the conjunction, square, and opposition—the sextile does not usually indicate that you willfully create confusion or deception. But if you do not make a concerted effort to understand what you are doing with each other, your aims and purposes can become confused.

In its highest manifestation, this aspect indicates that you will be spiritually transformed by your association with each other. Even if events seem strange or confusing, do not fight them. Simply try to understand and accept them until the purpose of the relationship becomes clear.

Composite Mars Square Composite Neptune

Mars square Neptune in the composite chart can be quite difficult. It indicates that your intentions and the way you interact weaken each other's effectiveness. Usually one of you acts in such a way as to confuse or delude the other, but also you may have a negative reinforcing effect on each other. It is quite likely that you will act upon each other in turn.

The problem is that you each view the other's successful self-expression as a threat. One of you may fear that the other will dominate and extinguish your individuality. But this is fear more than actual fact. Also, the relationship may present both of you with issues that you do not know how to face at this time.

The only way to deal with this aspect is to stop playing ego games, which is easier said than done, because such games are usually played out unconsciously. Neither partner is aware of what is going on.

In an extreme case you may be consciously deceitful toward each other. In a marriage, this might be done through infidelity; in a friendship, it might be actions that intentionally go against your friend's interests.

If this is the only area of difficulty between you, the relationship can still be quite rewarding. But if this is one of many problems, it might be best to break the relationship off. If it has already begun and you wish to continue it, the only defense is to be completely honest with each other and at the same time reasonably gentle in your honesty.

Composite Mars Trine Composite Neptune

The trine of Mars and Neptune in the composite chart can indicate a relationship that is motivated by the desire to attain an ideal, or it can mean simply that you are unclear about what is to be done. Lack of clarity about your aims can lead each of you to act in ways that are likely to be misunderstood by the other, or even to work inadvertently against each other or the relationship. It is therefore necessary to be unusually clear about what you are doing together.

It is often the case that the two of you are seeking a spiritual goal. However, you must not let your search for the spiritual ideal obscure your practical needs in a relationship, regardless of what kind of relationship it is.

At its most successful, this aspect can help you attain your ideals, if the two of you are very aware. You may find that being together furthers your highest form of self-expression and that you gain new insights into the world through your experiences together. At its least successful, this aspect may cause you to have cloudy objectives, so that neither of you will concentrate enough on the practical problems of making the relationship work. You will have to work out which way it will go between you.

Composite Mars Opposition Composite Neptune

Mars opposition Neptune in the composite chart indicates the need for great clarity and total honesty between the two of you. In this relationship the actions and words that with other couples pass for little white lies have effects out of all proportion to the intentions behind them. And if the intentions are destructive, the consequences will be even worse. For at its worst, this aspect is a symbol of mutual weakening; that is, unless you both try to modify your behavior, you will cause each other to become confused, unclear, and uncertain about almost everything you have built up between you. This weakening effect will spill over into other areas and make both of you less effective in your own lives.

At its most extreme, this aspect indicates a relationship in which one of you deceives and works surreptitiously against the best interests of your partner, who goes on believing that everything is all right. On the other hand, the two of you may simply react upon each other in such a way as to weaken self-confidence on both sides and make it harder to assert yourselves. Sometimes this aspect indicates a drug or liquor problem that is somehow reinforced by the relationship.

If you really want to get out of the difficulties caused by this aspect, there is only one way to do it. But be sure that you really do want to solve this problem, for the negative effects of this combination often come about because two people want to be caught up in this kind of relationship.

Part of the nature of Mars is that you feel you must always be right and that it is not necessary to condemn yourself if you are wrong. That is what is really meant by asserting yourself. Neptune is basically antithetical to Mars, for it relates to a level of existence in which there is no need or opportunity to protect one's ego game. Asserting yourself merely creates the resistance that is manifested as the "bad" effects of the Mars-Neptune combination.

To deal with this aspect, you must become more concerned with knowing the truth about what is going on in your relationship, regardless of whether it may seem to you "right" or "wrong." You need to know the truth, but being "right" is only something you think you need in order to feel better. It will not help solve your problems. If you recognize this principle in your relationship, you will go a long way toward mitigating the effects of this aspect.

Composite Mars Conjunct Composite Pluto

The conjunction of Mars and Pluto is a very powerful aspect to have in the composite chart, for it indicates a strong power drive within the relationship that may express itself in many ways. Recognize that any of the manifestations are possible in a particular relationship and that it is up to you to create the one you want.

The two of you may have come together to accomplish a particular task involving a great deal of effort in order to change certain conditions in your lives or in the lives of those around you. This is an aspect of powerful transformation, which can be either creative or destructive. Together you have the power to transform anything you aim at in your lives. Since it is certain that you will direct this power at something, you should be conscious of it, so that you can choose what you will transform.

If you are not conscious of this energy, it may come out as a power struggle between the two of you, with one trying to dominate the other. "I would like you much more if..." is a common phrase with this aspect. It is possible to transform each other creatively, but that is not likely to happen unless you try to transform out of love, not egotism. This aspect is not egotistical in itself, but such powerful energies are often subverted to purely egotistical ends, because that is where one's energy usually is, no matter how altruistic or spiritual you think you are.

The ego brings out the worst energies of Pluto, so it is best not to put them to the service of the ego. These energies are too great for the ego to handle. Nevertheless, this is precisely what the Mars-Pluto combination signifies. In order to soften the effects of this combination, you must love and accept each other, or you will probably do each other a great deal of injury.

The other way to use these energies productively was mentioned above. You can project it outside of yourselves onto the world and work together to make changes in conditions around you. But even here it is very important that you do so from a position of love and tolerance. Otherwise you will provoke such opposition from others that you may be defeated by outside forces.

Composite Mars Sextile Composite Pluto

The sextile of composite Pluto and Mars gives the two of you the potential for transforming yourselves through the relationship you create. You will arouse each other's sense of will and purpose in a complementary rather than a competitive way, and this will allow you to express your powers as individuals without getting in each other's way.

At the same time, you each will find that through interacting you will gain greater understanding of how the other works, and this experience will enable you to change.

While this aspect furthers your individual ego-expression, it also allows you to cooperate in gaining whatever you wish to gain together. You are able to work hard together, for you call forth energies in each other that you may not have known you had. The two of you will attack each problem and task competently, because you will thoroughly analyze its nature before you begin. And you will bring all your creative energies to bear upon the task as well.

The greatest task that you face together may be the creative transformation of yourselves. But you will bring the same creative energies to this project that you bring to any other, thereby ensuring that this relationship will be profitable to both of you in many ways.

Composite Mars Square Composite Pluto

The square of Mars and Pluto in a composite chart requires some care and consideration within a relationship. Ego forces run high between you, because something about your interaction makes you constantly challenge each other. That also means that you each invest a great deal of energy in being right at the other's expense. Consequently this aspect can create the most intense competition between two people, even to the extent of both physical and psychological battles. When the energies of this aspect operate unconsciously within a relationship, they can lead to considerable violence. Obviously it is very important to be conscious of them.

The two of you have very different aims in life, and if you choose to get in each other's way, you will certainly succeed in doing so. You will be able to get along with each other only by recognizing that there is plenty of room in the world for each of you to do what you want. Not only is there plenty of room in the world, but if you are willing you can also find room within your relationship for your separate aims. But both of you must be willing to make an effort, or you can't complain when the relationship blows up in your faces. This aspect does not make for getting along easily and spontaneously; you have to make it happen.

Composite Mars Trine Composite Pluto

The trine of Mars and Pluto in the composite chart is an indication of much powerful energy within the relationship, which can change both of your lives if you choose to let it. First of all, if you have to do any kind of work together, you will be able to cooperate and get the job done. As a couple, you may find that you have more perseverance than you have as individuals. Also, something about the way you interact makes you both more desirous of changing conditions around you and affecting your world. In some relationships this may take the form of stimulating business or professional ambitions.

In a sexual relationship this aspect is favorable to strong expression of your physical drives. Direct physical expression of your love will be very important to you both; you are not likely to be of the quiet, ethereal, and romantic school of lovemaking. However, along with the physical expression is the need for your love relationship to be a transcendental experience in which you are transported out of ordinary reality by the intensity of your feelings.

Whatever kind of relationship you have, it will probably transform both of you. One expression of this will be a mutual interest in the study of various forms of healing and regeneration—particularly yoga, because it concerns the physical body—and psychotherapy.

Composite Mars Opposition Composite Pluto

With the opposition of Mars and Pluto in the composite chart it will be difficult for the two of you to avoid conflict and power struggles in any kind of relationship. In extreme cases there could be physical violence.

The reasons for the extreme effects of this aspect are as follows. Mars has a great deal to do with the ego-drive, whereby one becomes a fully self-expressive individual. Pluto, being one of the outer planets beyond Saturn, has to do with factors in the universe that are outside of normal consciousness but that have a strong conditioning effect upon it. Pluto represents the energy of intense and fundamental transformations. When Mars and Pluto are opposed, this energy is combined inharmoniously with the ego-drives. Or to put it in less philosophical terms, a cosmic power is subjected to purely personal and selfish drives. While one should not necessarily equate ego-drives with personal and selfish aims, that is how it most commonly works out.

In order to deal with this energy constructively, it is necessary to reverse the roles of Pluto and Mars, so that the ego-drives are transformed by the cosmic power of Pluto. Unless you both do this, the experience will be very unpleasant. You must let this relationship change and transform you without resistance. Do not worry that your partner is getting away with something, for that will only create conflict and power struggles, which can be quite intense. Give up trying to make an impact on each other, but agree that you will let each other have an impact. That is, don't make it happen; let it happen.

Composite Mars Conjunct Composite Ascendant

The conjunction of composite Mars and Ascendant can be a source of either strength or difficulty. It signifies a relationship in which ego energies run high, so it is very important that the two of you get along well. Unfortunately, by itself this aspect does not tell whether or not you will get along.

If there are other difficulties between you, this aspect is an indication that the two of you will have some fairly spectacular disagreements. You both are too busy being individuals with your own points of view to really relate to each other. Probably you will irritate each other instead of making each other feel good. And neither of you can take an irritating situation lying down; you are very vocal about it, which is one source of the problem. If the energy of this aspect works out in this difficult way, the two of you must first settle whether or not you want to have a relationship. If may not have occurred to you to ask that question, but ask it anyway!

If other indications are favorable, composite Mars on the Ascendant can be very useful for your relationship. It means almost the opposite of what has been said above, implying that you reinforce each other's egos.

Together you make a very strong combination, which other people may see as formidable opposition. Needless to say, this is an excellent indication for any relationship in which there is work to be done. Mars is the planet of energy, and the conjunction of Mars and composite Ascendant means that you arouse energy in each other, which helps to get the work done. And you work well as a team, which is also helpful.

As you can see, this aspect is two-sided. To some extent it is in your power to determine which manifestation you will encounter. If you can subordinate your very strong egos to the relationship, you will be a very strong team. Otherwise you will not have much of anything.

Composite Mars Sextile Composite Ascendant

The sextile of composite Mars and composite Ascendant makes it likely that the two of you will be known as a very active couple in every way. Mars is the planet of energy, and the sextile to composite Ascendant means that this relationship will stimulate energies in both of you—energy for work, for play, and for anything else you may want to do together. You are also active in a psychological sense, for you each have the capacity to jog the other out of lazy patterns and routines that you have developed separately. There is always something to be done, and the two of you are willing to work, both as a couple and with other people.

The energy that you arouse in each other might be competitive energy in another couple, but you manage to work together as a team and not waste energy with needless competition. This aspect signifies cooperation.

At the same time, you stimulate each other's thinking. You both will become more active mentally and more willing to encounter new experiences that you can grapple with intellectually.

The energy that you stimulate in each other is transmitted to others around you, so that they too find your company stimulating. Things get done when the two of you are around.

Obviously this aspect is at its best in situations where work must be done, and it is especially good in a professional relationship.

Composite Mars Square Composite Ascendant

The square of composite Mars and Ascendant can be very difficult. It signifies that the pursuit of egoistic goals is likely to come between the two of you. Something about this relationship makes you each acutely aware of your own ego energies and how this relationship will further or inhibit them. Unfortunately, if you operate on an unconscious level with each other, you will find that the relationship does get in the way of your ego energies; that is, it will be difficult for you to "do your own thing" in each other's presence.

You may argue constantly about seemingly trivial matters, which actually represent deeper psychological pressures that you are not expressing to each other. These pressures are very likely to be expressed as disagreements about your home together (if you have one) or about your overall objectives in life. The latter is a more truthful expression of the real problem. Disagreements about your home or other aspects of your inner personal life are only side issues.

The main point is what the two of you are doing together. There may be perfectly valid reasons for this relationship, and being together may be a very good experience for both of you. However, you must ask the question anyway, because the naturally competitive energies of Mars may make you think you are completely incompatible, even if you actually have a deep need to be together. This relationship calls for a great deal of self-awareness.

Composite Mars Trine Composite Ascendant

The trine of composite Mars and Ascendant is a good sign that you are able to express yourselves to each other without having to make compromises. This is a relationship in which the two of you are able to be yourselves and express your egos fully and without reserve in each other's presence. There is enough room in your life for your partner, and neither of you has to pretend that you are something other than what you are. Also, you work well as a team. Together you reinforce and complement each other, so that you can be individuals and work as a unit at the same time.

This relationship will arouse in the two of you a great deal of physical energy that must find some form of expression. You should not sit around when you are together; instead you should be doing something. Being active together is the finest expression of the energies that you call forth in each other. If this is a business or professional relationship or if you have other work to do, the energies of Mars will be especially favorable. Work that you do together seems to require little or no self-sacrifice. For the two of you, such work is the most perfect kind of self-expression. This relationship signifies that as a couple you will achieve a more perfect self-expression than either of you could experience in relationships with others.

Composite Mars Opposition Composite Ascendant

The opposition of composite Mars and Ascendant is equivalent to a conjunction of Mars and the composite Descendant. This aspect has two distinct possibilities, either of which you may experience in your own relationship. This can be a very perfect union of your individual energies in a creative working relationship, or it can be an endless contest between you, as if you were together only to challenge and goad each other.

In any case, you can be sure that the two of you form an intimate unit. The only question is whether the union is a destructive or a creative one. One point is clear; it is vital that you direct your energies toward accomplishing a task or purpose outside of the relationship. If you are not engaged in some activity together, the energies of Mars are likely to become disruptive rather than creative. If not expressed outwardly, the energies will turn inward, into the relationship.

Even if you succeed in turning the Mars force outward, you may have to deal with another danger if you are not careful. You may experience hostility from people outside your relationship. In part this is because of the strong energies that you put into the world, often without understanding them. If the two of you find that others are opposed to you either as a couple or as individuals, you should consider carefully what you may be contributing to the problem. Of course, it may be that others are hostile simply because you are honestly being yourselves. In that case, you can't do much about it. But if you are actively contributing to the hostility, maybe the situation can be changed.

Chapter Ten

Jupiter

The Meaning of Jupiter in the Composite Chart

Jupiter in the composite chart signifies the areas that will provide a solid basis for growth through the relationship. A strong Jupiter helps to ensure that whatever the course of the relationship and whatever may happen to it, you both will be aware of how much you have been helped by being together.

The house position of Jupiter designates what aspect of your relationship will be emphasized as a growth area. The two of you will be able to depend on that area for sustenance together, and unlike other aspects of your relationship, it will not be the cause of conflict and difficulty.

Nevertheless, what Jupiter brings to a relationship should not be taken totally for granted. There is always a danger that you may overextend yourselves in the area in which Jupiter is significant, which can convert it into a source of difficulty. If the energy of Jupiter is flowing easily, it is unlikely to cause trouble. But if the energy is flowing with difficulty, there may be problems, usually brought on by doing something to excess. In any case, Jupiter is not usually a major source of trouble in a chart and can usually be counted on to bring benevolent results.

Composite Jupiter in the First House

Composite Jupiter in the first house is a generally good placement for any kind of relationship. Jupiter is the planet of growth and development, and the first-house position signifies that this relationship will help the two of you to become better and more fulfilled individuals.

But in addition to these general indications, this placement may have a more particular significance. Jupiter is the planet of law, ethics, ideals, religion, and philosophy. The first-house position of this planet indicates that one or more of these areas is important to your relationship. At the very least you can expect that together you will be intensely idealistic in some way. This position also creates a kind of optimism that will help you succeed in your expectations. As a couple you put out energies that make it possible to meet idealistic expectations, even if others see them as excessively high.

This relationship should be optimistic, happy, and productive for the two of you. Even if it breaks up, you will not have great feelings of bitterness, because you both know that you have gotten a great deal out of it. You will have grown and increased in your awareness of life, which is more than many couples can claim.

Composite Jupiter in the Second House

Jupiter in the second house of the composite chart is excellent for all matters relating to property and possessions within the relationship. It does not necessarily indicate that the two of you will be wealthy, but it does indicate that you will have enough of whatever you want. In other words, resources are not likely to be a source of insecurity with you. Business associations are especially favored by this position of Jupiter.

The only problem to watch out for is that Jupiter here can make people excessively materialistic, both individually and in a relationship. This can cause the two of you to sacrifice matters that are important to your happiness in order to gain wealth.

One of the fortunate attributes of this position is that making money and gaining property are not areas of anxiety, so you can feel detached from these issues and can express yourselves through material generosity to others.

There may be a danger that you will be careless about money and unwise in its use. However, this will not happen because of unluckiness but because you like to take chances. If you take the time to stop and think, you will know what to do in a situation. Make caution and success in handling money more important than the excitement of gambling.

Composite Jupiter in the Third House

Composite Jupiter in the third house indicates that this relationship will broaden and expand your consciousness in your everyday life. The third house is the house of the mind in its routine day-to-day functioning, your automatic and unconscious actions. This part of your mind is laden with routine habits and ways of thinking that can prevent you from taking full advantage of opportunities that arise. This relationship will help to change those habits in a very pleasant and helpful way. Jupiter does not usually bring about change through upsets.

Narrow habits of thought and rigid ways of thinking will be expanded by your experience of this relationship. It will open new ways of dealing with everyday matters, so that your handling of them should improve. You may find that together you will become more interested in philosophy and other mind-expanding disciplines. A third-house composite Jupiter is a sign of a relationship that will broaden your consciousness.

Composite Jupiter in the Fourth House

Jupiter in the fourth house of the composite chart indicates that if this is a marriage or love relationship, the home is very important as a center of security and comfort. In concrete terms, both of you will be happiest in a large home where you can entertain extensively and have lots of company. In such a setting you would be extremely generous and hospitable, and yet you would always have enough for anyone who came along. This position of Jupiter symbolizes protecting and nurturing people through sharing.

In psychological terms, this relationship will reinforce both of you and give you a feeling of security and safety as you approach the outside world. You may not understand exactly how this happens, but rest assured that you do help each other in this way. Whatever difficulties the two of you may encounter in the world, you will be able to turn to each other for sustenance. This is an extremely supportive relationship.

If you own land or real estate together, Jupiter in the fourth signifies that you may have such property in abundance and that it is likely to be a major source of wealth.

Composite Jupiter in the Fifth House

Composite Jupiter in the fifth house is a generally positive indication for the success of any kind of relationship, but especially for friendship or a love relationship. The basic meaning of this placement is that being together will alow both of you to grow and become happier human beings, simply by being yourselves. It is a position of benevolent self-expression. You should be able to relax and enjoy each other's company to the fullest, and each of you will feel that the other supports you for what you are. You will express your affection for each other warmly and easily. There will be a minimum of negative challenges and efforts to tear your partner down, even when you are having difficulties.

At the same time, you both will be quite idealistic about this relationship, feeling that you should maintain the highest standards of ethics with each other. Honor will be a significant issue, and you will not relate in such a way as to diminish each other's importance.

It is possible that this relationship may have come about because of a mutual interest in religion, philosophy, metaphysics, or the law. But whatever your initial reasons for coming together, you should have a more than ordinarily satisfactory relationship.

Composite Jupiter in the Sixth House

Composite Jupiter in the sixth house indicates a relationship in which serving others has become an ideal. You both feel obligated to help humanity, and you will take on this obligation willingly and with dignity. This is probably not a burden imposed on you from without; but if it is, you accept it gladly.

In a business or professional relationship, this placement of Jupiter means that the two of you will do whatever is necessary to make the relationship successful, without feeling put upon. For this reason you are likely to be successful, regardless of your objective.

In any relationship, this placement signifies that you are unusually willing to help and be of service to each other. Needless to say, this can only help you.

One factor should be kept in mind, however. The symbolism of Jupiter demands that whatever is given be given freely. If one of you tries to impose on the other more duties than that partner is willing to take on, there may be considerable trouble. The one who is restricted will feel that all freedom has been destroyed, and he or she will begin to look elsewhere for freedom of self-expression. Otherwise, this placement should be a source of strength for both of you.

Composite Jupiter in the Seventh House

Jupiter in the seventh house of a composite chart is very favorable for most relationships. It means that the two of you are likely to feel that being together is your most important means of growth. You feel that you both can grow faster through the relationship than without it. In fact you probably idealize your relationship, but not to the extent that it becomes impossible to live up to the ideal.

Even though you idealize being together, you are not totally possessive; you know enough to give each other room to breathe. In fact, the only possible problem with this placement is that under certain conditions one of you may demand more freedom than the other is willing to give. However, in such a situation, if the restrictive partner can give the other that freedom in some particular instance, it will work out all right.

Normally this placement of Jupiter will be very favorable. You may demand high standards of behavior from each other, but you are also likely to get what you demand in that regard.

Composite Jupiter in the Eighth House

Jupiter in the eighth house of the composite chart, the house of major transformations in life and of joint property, signifies that both of these areas will be areas of growth. In this relationship you will never cease to grow and change. Both of you will experience continual transformation through the experience of being together. Even if you grow apart, as can happen to any couple, you will part without much difficulty, knowing that the relationship has been good, even if not permanent.

This placement of Jupiter may also have the effect of making you quite successful in your dealings with property and resources in general, so long as you work together. This is a very good placement in the chart of a business or professional relationship, particularly one that must rely on outside financing to any extent.

If this is a marriage, you may receive bequests or other financial assistance from others. At any rate, you should have little trouble borrowing money jointly whenever you need it.

In a sexual relationship, this placement helps to ensure that sex is a source of reinforcement for both of you, even if there are problems at times.

This placement will neither make or break a relationship, but it can help smooth over bad times by making it easier to meet your material needs.

Composite Jupiter in the Ninth House

Jupiter in the ninth house of the composite chart is in many ways "at home." That is, this is the house most naturally suited to the meaning of Jupiter. The ninth is the house of higher consciousness, expanded awareness, philosophy, and one's overall philosophy of life, as well as of long journeys. These are also the concerns of Jupiter.

This placement indicates a relationship that will expand your awareness in many ways by presenting you with new perspectives and new experiences. It may be that at some time you will travel extensively together. However, it is far more likely that the influence will come out as strong intellectual interests in common. At the same time you will evolve a world-view in which honor and ethics play a very important part. Your ideals will be very strong, and you are likely to work hard together to change conditions to what you think they should ideally be.

Most important in terms of your immediate experience is that this will be a growth relationship. Regardless of what happens, you both will become more complete human beings than you were before. While Jupiter in the ninth house is no guarantee that a relationship will be long-lasting, it does mean that it will have great value for both of you.

In particular, this position favors any association that deals with intellectual or educational concerns.

Composite Jupiter in the Tenth House

Jupiter in the tenth house of the composite chart has a number of possible effects, depending on the nature of your association.

In a personal relationship it indicates a strong concern with goals and status. The relationship will revolve around some sense of purpose, which may range from very mundane to very high-minded. In a marriage, for example, you both may have an inordinate concern for getting ahead in society—in other words, social climbing. Or it can indicate that the two of you will have a high social status without any effort on your part.

There will also be an emphasis on integrity and honesty. At least you will consider these values important. However, in some charts there will be a more negative effect from Jupiter, resulting in an attitude of haughtiness and arrogance toward others that will not serve you well. It can also create an attitude of hypocrisy, a pretense that somehow you are morally better than you really are. Jupiter makes you aware of moral issues even when you cannot live up to its moral criteria.

In a professional relationship this placement of Jupiter can be a very strong indication of success, particularly in fields pertaining to law, religion, philosophy, higher education, or foreign interests. In almost any other field of endeavor this is also a good indication of success. In addition, this placement indicates that the work you do together will be carried out with a high degree of integrity and honesty, which will help immeasurably in your eventual success. Your achievements will not be the result of accident or luck.

Composite Jupiter in the Eleventh House

Jupiter in the eleventh house of the composite chart is an excellent placement for any relationship. It indicates that there are good feelings between you and that you will give each other opportunities to grow and become more evolved human beings. You stimulate each other's idealism greatly, and you will work very hard to realize your ideals. The eleventh is the house of your ideals and hopes or, in a composite chart, the ideals that the two of you share.

Since the eleventh house represents friendship, Jupiter here is an especially good indication of warm friendly feelings between you. The relationship will have excellent overall consequences for both of you. A love affair or marriage with this position will be in excellent condition. Not only are there good feelings between you, but you are likely to be lucky in a material way. This is because you are very optimistic in each other's company, which generates the kind of positive thinking that helps bring good fortune. As a couple you will have good friends among the people you know, and circumstances in your environment will be favorable to your relationship.

Composite Jupiter in the Twelfth House

Jupiter in the twelfth house of the composite chart has to do with several areas of your relationship. The twelfth house rules the forces that are working unconsciously and their influence on the success or failure of the relationship. It also rules the actions that each of you may take that can affect your future as a couple. These are usually unconscious actions or actions that you refuse to acknowledge unless you are forced to.

Fortunately, Jupiter in this house is an indication that unconscious actions are less of a problem than in most relationships. You are not destroying your relationship in the manner that so many are destroyed. Although you may have troubles at times, at least you can bring your problems out into the open. In fact, one effect of Jupiter is that the two of you are able to get at problems that most couples keep buried. Such problems can cause great difficulty in a relationship precisely because they are unacknowledged.

The twelfth house is also the house of secret enemies, that is, people whom you inadvertently alienate simply by being yourselves. But the presence of Jupiter also helps prevent this from being a problem. It makes you conscious of your actions so that you don't alienate people in the first place. Quite a few of the problems that can occur in a relationship are alleviated by this placement of Jupiter.

Composite Jupiter Conjunct Composite Saturn

The conjunction of Jupiter and Saturn in the composite chart may have more than one effect. On the one hand, it can make a relationship very unstable and changeable. In this case the two of you seem unable to go forward or backward on any issue, so that you constantly vacillate between the alternative possibilities. Or you cannot figure out whether or not you are happy in the relationship or whether it is working toward the objectives you have set for it. Your uncertainty makes the two of you have tremendous ups and downs. This conjunction will have these negative effects on any relationship that is not in very good shape. Flaws induced by other aspects are maximized by this one, for it tends to emphasize instability.

On the other hand, in a reasonably stable relationship, these two planets can achieve an equilibrium. The outgoing, expansive quality of Jupiter can be checked by the carefulness and caution of Saturn, so that you become cautiously optimistic in your dealings with each other. You make plans for your future very carefully and never overextend yourselves, always being aware that things may not turn out quite as expected.

At the same time, since the idealism of Jupiter is tempered by the pragmatism of Saturn, you accept each other as you are and do not make too many additional demands. You may not think that this relationship is perfect, but on the other hand you don't really believe such perfection exists, so you do not demand it.

By itself, this is not an aspect that can make or break a relationship. It will strengthen a good one and make a weak one more unstable.

Composite Jupiter Sextile Composite Saturn

Jupiter sextile Saturn in the composite chart represents an excellent balance between practical and idealistic concerns in your relationship. Your expectations of each other are balanced and realistic, yet neither of you feels forced to compromise your goals in order to get along with each other.

The same kind of balance is reflected in the way you approach long-range planning together. Here again you set realistic goals and work patiently to attain them, moving neither too quickly nor too slowly.

When you have problems with each other, you manage to avoid flying off the handle. Unlike so many couples, you don't act hastily, which only makes things worse. Your inclination is to wait patiently for the correct moment and then cool things off with discussion and calmness.

As friends, you will find that your relationship brings out the strongest points in both of you. The balance that this aspect represents enables you to make up for each other's excesses. This is especially fortunate if either of you by yourself is very impulsive or inconsiderate. In this relationship you will find yourself proceeding much more moderately, without feeling held back by your partner.

Composite Jupiter Square Composite Saturn

The square of Jupiter and Saturn in the composite chart indicates that the two of you have some difficulty in reaching a balance between optimism and idealism on the one hand, practicality and/or pessimism on the other. Most likely this will manifest itself as great swings of feeling and mood when you are together. Sometimes you will be very positive and optimistic about your relationship, while at other times you will doubt that you can ever make it work. Most couples go through this process to some extent, but in your case it will be worse than in most relationships. Serious ups and downs are likely to be a major threat to the stability of this relationship.

One of the factors behind this problem may be that one of you sees the other as a wet blanket who continually dampens enthusiasm and spontaneous self-expression. It may not always be the same one who has this effect; instead you may alternate roles. Nevertheless, the result is that there are oscillations of mood.

You both must try to be more patient with each other, for impatience is also one of the problems created by this aspect. Whenever your mood begins to change for the worse, you should sit down together and try to find out what is causing this situation. Although your temperaments may not be perfectly matched, this shouldn't be allowed to spoil the relationship.

Composite Jupiter Trine Composite Saturn

The trine of Jupiter and Saturn in the composite chart gives your relationship a steady quality that is quite enviable. You go on from day to day, avoiding most extremes of mood. You can depend on each other always being there. Both of you have the ability to accept each other for what you are and tolerate each other's foibles. The demands you make of each other are enough so that you work to satisfy them, but not so great as to be impossible to satisfy.

As a couple, your expectations are well tempered by your understanding of the way things are. You are very patient with each other and willing to give your problems time to work themselves out. Since you do not act impulsively, you avoid some of the difficulties that other couples experience when they act on the impulse of a bad mood and damage their relationship.

When you have to plan together for the future, you are equally careful without being overcautious. You act only after weighing all the factors, and you usually act at the right time, for your sense of timing together is excellent.

Regardless of the original goals of your relationship, if you take advantage of these abilities, you should be better able to ride out the difficult times than many other couples.

Composite Jupiter Opposition Composite Saturn

The opposition of Jupiter and Saturn in a composite chart means that the two of you must find an equilibrium. You have a natural tendency to swing back and forth between moods of opposite extremes, such as deep pessimism and great optimism. As a couple, your desire to go out into the world, to be more positive and assertive, is always at war with your sense of caution and a need to be careful. You want to keep all the loopholes in your life plugged against circumstances that might take advantage of you.

It is often the case that two conflicting tendencies are represented by each of you separately, one of you taking the expansive role while the other is more cautious. You find it difficult to be patient with each other because the tension between you, which has to be expressed somehow, usually emerges as impatience and excessive criticism.

Needless to say, the two of you must learn to be patient in dealing with each other. You have to give each other room without trying to limit freedom of self-expression. If each of you can express your mood swings without constantly running into resistance from your partner, the two of you should be able to coexist in some degree of harmony and avoid unnecessary ups and downs.

Composite Jupiter Conjunct Composite Uranus

A relationship with the conjunction of Jupiter and Uranus in the composite chart may experience various effects.

First of all, in this relationship you will have to give each other a great deal of breathing room. That may not necessarily be a problem, however, because you probably came together in the first place because you sensed some quality of freedom and lack of inhibition in each other. This is definitely not a relationship for people who want to cling to each other.

This aspect represents not only freedom, but also new discovery. Pursuing new kinds of self-expression and new ideas in life will be a major factor in this relationship. Give yourselves and each other the room to experience these discoveries and don't get tied down by convention and established ways of doing things. You have the capacity to make new discoveries in life and to give others the benefit of your experience.

All of this pertains to professional relationships as well as to personal ones. Whatever your reasons for being together, the more freedom you have to discover new paths without restriction, the more capacity you will have for creativity and satisfaction. Any attempt to make this relationship conform to the pictures in your mind will limit it unnecessarily and at the same time make it very unstable. If one of you is denied the freedom that this aspect requires, he or she will be forced to find it outside of the relationship.

Composite Jupiter Sextile Composite Uranus

With the sextile of Jupiter and Uranus in the composite chart, this relationship will be different in a new, free, and innovative way. Together you will strike out in new directions, not following the conventional patterns of your type of relationship.

For, example, in a love affair with this aspect, both of you will be freer and more individualistic than is usually the case. There will be little of the tendency to cling to each other that makes many relationships fail for lack of room to breathe. With this aspect, a love relationship is also much more likely to tolerate the expression of love and affection for others.

There is a strong idealistic element in this relationship that encourages your hopes for making things come true that have never been but that could be. The two of you feel that there is no reason why these things should not be. You find it easy to view life in a new way and to act differently from others. Even the setting of this relationship is not likely to be an ordinary one. Your ability to see the opportunities presented by new ways of thinking attracts people who are sympathetic to your causes, and you will find an appropriate environment for yourselves.

This aspect is especially beneficial to any relationship that requires innovation and inventiveness. It encourages the development of you both as individuals because of the individual freedom it confers.

Composite Jupiter Square Composite Uranus

The square of Jupiter and Uranus in the composite chart means that in this relationship you must give each other a lot of room. It is not a favorable aspect if one of you wants to "possess" the other in some way and limit his or her freedom. If you try to do this, your partner will break away in order to avoid being confined. This relationship makes it necessary for both of you to be free from excessive restriction by each other.

Even at its best, this relationship is likely to have a certain quality that makes it very unusual and atypical. Other people will not be able to categorize you easily as lovers, friends, partners, or whatever. Your relationship will not have the usual trappings of its type.

Even under the most favorable circumstances, this will not be the most stable and predictable relationship. It will follow its own course, which may involve considerable ups and downs.

Try to give each other freedom and let the relationship develop in its own way. If you do, you may find that in return for giving up absolute reliability, predictability, possessiveness, and so forth, you will gain an experience that is quite unique and stimulating. But in order to experience this, you both must be willing to give up many of your expectations about how your relationship ought to run.

Composite Jupiter Trine Composite Uranus

This aspect indicates a relationship that will achieve its own unique self-expression. Like the other Jupiter-Uranus combinations, this one indicates that your relationship will not follow any established patterns. Nevertheless, there is nothing here that you should fear. This can be a very creative relationship, as long as you are willing to let it run its own course.

This aspect signifies new and creative ways of doing things. It expresses hope and confidence in a bright and different future, with fresh ideas and ways of looking at the world. Whatever the reasons for your coming together, you both will be exposed to new ideas and concepts, which will prevent you from getting into any kind of rut.

A love relationship with this aspect will not follow the established script in many ways. For example, you will give each other a great deal more freedom than most people would. You may even come to an agreement that will permit other relationships outside of this, as long as there is an honest commitment between you. There will be a great emphasis on honesty, which you will be able to maintain because you don't confine each other. In other words, you will give each other enough freedom of movement so that you won't have to be "unfaithful". And you will be friends as well as lovers, which is a very good thing in a love relationship.

Composite Jupiter Opposition Composite Uranus

The opposition of Jupiter and Uranus in the composite chart may make it difficult for you to have a stable relationship, regardless of your reasons for being together. This aspect creates a situation in which individual freedom and independence may be more important to each of you than the goals of the relationship. Therefore you must give each other plenty of room in order to minimize tension and avoid having one of you feel the need to break away.

A sexual relationship or a marriage would be most affected by this aspect, because such a relationship is inherently the most limiting of your freedom. In order to survive as a couple, you will have to arrive at very unusual accommodations with each other. The important point here is that you must not be afraid to make any agreement that will enable the relationship to survive, even if the terms of the agreement are rather strange. The more you try to force yourselves into standard patterns, the more you will feel confined. One might find this aspect in an open marriage, for example, in which two partners agree to allow relationships with others.

Other personal relationships are less affected by the energy of this aspect, but even so you should avoid being narrowly possessive of each other, for that presents a major threat to the survival of the partnership.

If you can allow this relationship to take its natural course, you may find it quite rewarding. If you cannot, it might be best to stay away from each other.

Composite Jupiter Conjunct Composite Neptune

The conjunction of Jupiter and Neptune in the composite chart indicates that your primary concerns are not of this world. This will be a somewhat unusual relationship, with a strong spiritual component. The two of you may feel that you have come together to find out about your innermost soul. This belief is not necessarily a delusion, but you should try to keep in touch with reality. Even though you may believe that the mundane world is not your concern, ignoring such matters can have a seriously negative effect on your relationship. On the other hand, do not ignore your sense of spiritual communion. At its highest level of manifestation, this aspect can bring about a great and positive learning experience.

This aspect can also have a completely different effect. The principle of combined Jupiter-Neptune also rules gambling, not only in the literal Las Vegas sense, but also in the more general sense of taking risks. It produces a sense of well-being that may make the two of you feel that you cannot lose. Unfortunately, if you trust this energy so blindly, you can indeed lose. Be optimistic and positive but not foolish. Keep your sense of reality and don't let the joyful idealism of this relationship take away your understanding of what is real. This advice is especially important in any relationship that involves making money.

Let the effects of this aspect add spice to your world, but do not let them obscure your vision.

Composite Jupiter Sextile Composite Neptune

The sextile of Jupiter and Neptune in the composite chart is an indication of an idealistic relationship. The idealism is not likely to be destructive but will give the two of you a spiritual quality that can carry you out of the mundane world into your own world of beauty. This aspect indicates deep friendship, even in a sexual relationship. But in such a relationship it can cause difficulties because it tends to make a love affair platonic. Its energies are so removed from the physical world that they don't combine easily with physical sexuality. When the combination is made, however, physical sex acquires a spiritual dimension that can be quite extraordinary.

In dealing with everyday practical matters, this aspect can present certain problems, but they are not insuperable. The two of you must learn not to indulge in contempt for mundane reality. Remember the concerns of the world around you, even though this relationship enables you to escape from it. It is beautiful to be transported above the ordinary world, but stay down here anyway, for there is much to be done.

Composite Jupiter Square Composite Neptune

The square of Jupiter and Neptune in a composite chart makes it very important that you know where you are with respect to each other and that you don't indulge excessively in idealistic fantasies. Keep matters straight between you. One writer has described this combination as "false or seeming happiness," with the clear warning that just when your relationship seems most beautiful, its illusory nature becomes clear, and there is great disappointment. The danger of this happening is greatest in a love affair, which is so vulnerable to illusions.

However, you should not be constantly suspicious of what appears to be a happy relationship. This aspect simply indicates that you should acknowledge the truth when it appears. It is not that the energy of this aspect obscures reality but that you are unwilling to face it, even when you know in your heart what it is. The problem is not really "illusion" in the sense used above. It is reluctance to handle things that are unpleasant and reluctance to deal with the real world.

Your happiness will not be false with this aspect; if you have a sense of happiness, it is real. But try to recognize whether you really feel it. If you are aware of lurking problems and unacknowledged fears, then deal with them, for they will not go away by themselves.

But remember that even the square between these planets has an optimistic quality, which will enable you to handle the difficult periods, once you decide to deal with them.

Composite Jupiter Trine Composite Neptune

Like all Jupiter-Neptune aspects, the trine is idealistic, and here the spiritual side of the combination is brought out most strongly. You feel that you have come together to learn. There may even be a conscious teacher-student relationship between you that holds you together. However, in the best manifestation of this aspect, you will alternate roles; the same partner will not always play the same role. But that cannot be done consciously; it must just happen.

Even in a love affair, this spiritual component will be evident, which may cause the relationship to be platonic rather than physical. But even in a sexual relationship, sex will be experienced in a very spiritual way.

You both will be very optimistic about your lives together, although other people may not see why you should be. They may think you are living in a fool's paradise and not dealing with the real world at all. There may be some truth in that view. You will have to strike a balance between everyday matters and your idealism. Try to stay in touch with reality, even though this relationship allows you to have experiences that are quite removed from the ordinary physical world and that help you appreciate this world. Most people are too wrapped up in their own lives to see what is just beyond the range of their vision that would give them so much more to live for. These things you should learn through this relationship.

Composite Jupiter Opposition Composite Neptune

With the opposition of Jupiter and Neptune in your composite chart, you must ask yourselves whether you really know what your relationship is about. You are very likely to idealize each other and your relationship rather than dealing with the facts as they are. This aspect does not indicate that the facts are anything to be afraid of, but you are reluctant to face them anyway. It may be that you don't find the truth interesting enough to be concerned about, but you ought to. Otherwise it is possible to build up a false sense of security and well-being, and when your illusions come tumbling down, as they often do in such a situation, you will be very disillusioned.

Disillusion and disappointment are not inevitable with this aspect, but if you do not deal with the truth, they are much more likely. Do not play games with each other, for you will only deceive and hurt each other when you do. And again, avoid idealizing each other. Your partner is a real person with real faults and strengths, which you must learn to accept. Idealism has its place, and the naturally idealistic quality of your relationship will not be destroyed by truth, even though you fear that. Your optimism and idealism will carry you both through difficult times, if you know yourselves and what you have together. If you do not have this understanding, you will only be disappointed.

Composite Jupiter Conjunct Composite Pluto

Jupiter conjunct Pluto in the composite chart indicates that you have come together in order to accomplish something. Jupiter and Pluto combined in this manner are symbolic of a strong drive to succeed and to accomplish important objectives. It can also mean a strong power drive.

Your relationship may have many different goals—love and affection, security, friendship, or whatever—but in any case it exists to do something. This is one of the best aspects for any kind of business relationship, because the two of you are able to work well together and accomplish a great deal of work. It is a strong indication of success and of financial gain, if that is an objective.

Remember, however, that as with any strong Pluto energy, you must use your tactics carefully and avoid all kinds of ruthless behavior. Otherwise you will provoke opposition to your efforts, which could conceivably stop the two of you from accomplishing what you want.

In a love relationship this energy is expressed as an exuberant desire to make changes, to grow, and to expand your world. You will seek to transform each other, and you will be transformed very greatly by this experience. But the nature of this combination is such that your transformations will not make the relationship difficult. The growth you help each other achieve will be positive, as you will recognize from the very beginning.

Composite Jupiter Sextile Composite Pluto

The sextile of Jupiter and Pluto in the composite chart is an aspect of growth and opportunity. It will enable both of you to take advantage of situations and help you accomplish what you are trying to do.

Whatever the nature of your relationship, you will have a friendship that will make you feel more confident and able to pursue your objectives in life. At the same time, this relationship will broaden your insight and allow you to see more clearly the opportunities available to you. And that in turn will lead you to become increasingly interested in learning more about yourselves so that you can further expand your opportunities.

You will probably find that your inner growth will attract others who are trying to grow, with whom you can discover even more that you are searching for.

But understand one thing. This is an aspect not so much of luck as of growth. It ensures that the two of you will have the kind of positive attitude that helps create circumstances you can take advantage of. In other words, although the two of you may appear to be lucky, you have actually created your own opportunities through the relationship you have made together.

Composite Jupiter Square Composite Pluto

The square of Jupiter and Pluto in the composite chart can make it difficult for the two of you to get along, because you see each other's success as a threat to your own. The result is a typical Pluto power struggle, rather than the cooperative relationship you would ideally like to have. Success of one sort or another is a very large issue in this relationship. The Jupiter-Pluto energy represents will and power to grow and expand, to succeed and to get things done. This energy cannot exist passively without trying to affect the world in some way.

This is true for your relationship to each other and to the world outside. You find it difficult to leave things alone, which creates the danger that one of you will turn against the other or that the world will fight back against you both.

You must learn to moderate your ambitions and your will. What you want to accomplish together is not wrong, but you do not have the patience to go about it gradually. This creates a feeling of pressure in other people or in each other, if the energy of this aspect is channeled into your relationship. It is this feeling of pressure that creates problems. If you can learn to be more subtle, you will be better able to get what you want from each other and from the world at large.

Composite Jupiter Trine Composite Pluto

The trine of composite Jupiter and Pluto is an excellent aspect for any relationship in which you have to work together on some task or bring about changes in the world around you. This is a success aspect. It confers luck, not through fate but through the excellent sense of timing that results when two people complement each other's abilities. This is also an aspect of foresight. The two of you can see developments that may later affect you while they are still in the early stages, before they reach the point at which nothing can be done.

You complement each other's ambitions in a very creative way. Together you want to make changes in your world, and through your relationship you will gain strength and ability that will enable you to get whatever you seek.

Even if you have difficult times with each other, the energy of this aspect will enable you to pull yourselves back together. This aspect can contribute greatly to the overall stability of a relationship.

Composite Jupiter Opposition Composite Pluto

The opposition of Jupiter and Pluto in the composite chart indicates a great need for the two of you to suppress your individual ego-drives somewhat. If you do not, your relationship will be nothing but competition and constant efforts to control each other. Something about this relationship stimulates your drives to control and to dominate. The best solution would be to cooperate and turn that energy outward. However, even here you must be careful, because strong Pluto energies tend to arouse opposition from others, so you might spend all your time fighting other people and accomplishing very little.

In extreme cases, the energy of this aspect can create trouble with authorities, even legal difficulties. How this happens may not be clear, but you can be sure that the energies are coming from the two of you and the way you operate together.

Your one recourse is to control these drives within yourselves and to work in a more subtle manner, either on each other or on others. If the energies of this aspect are kept under some reasonable control, they can be quite useful, because they give you the drive and ability to accomplish what you want. The problem is simply to keep the energies down below the point where they cause more trouble than they can solve.

Composite Jupiter Conjunct Composite Ascendant

The conjunction of composite Jupiter and Ascendant is a very good aspect for any kind of relationship. No matter what eventually happens between you, this will be a growth relationship. Because of it, both of you will be better off in some important way than you were before. When Jupiter, the principle of growth, is strong in a composite chart, it helps to ensure a positive relationship. In a business or professional association, this aspect indicates financial success. In a personal relationship, it allows the two of you to feel good about each other and about yourselves as a couple.

With this aspect you will not be sidetracked by trivial matters. You both will look at the relationship from a broad perspective. Because you understand that being together is more important than winning points against each other, as so many other couples do, you don't let petty irritations get the better of you. Consequently, you are much more tolerant of each other than most couples.

You will find that being together broadens your range of experience, and together you will discover new aspects of the world that will help you grow as human beings. Even if the relationship is not an enduring one, each of you will recognize the important role it has played in your personal development. You will be glad, therefore, that you have had this experience.

In many cases, this aspect may signify that you have come together because of some shared intellectual interest. Jupiter often particularly signifies a very deep and profound kind of growth on an intellectual level.

Composite Jupiter Sextile Composite Ascendant

The sextile of composite Jupiter and Ascendant is a good indication that this relationship will enable both of you to grow in whatever way you want. In any relationship it is a good aspect for mental and spiritual prosperity, as well as for material prosperity. Relations between you are easy and lacking in stress, because you each understand that your partner accepts you as you are and is concerned about you. Whatever else you may be to each other, you will be friends as well.

This relationship will stimulate your ideals and also give you the necessary optimism about yourselves and each other that will help you attain your goals. Consequently, your ideals about yourselves and this relationship are not unrealistic, and you will be able to work toward them. The two of you broaden each other's scope in such a way that when an opportunity comes up, you recognize and take advantage of it. But this is not done in an exploitative way; rather, when you see an opportunity, you know how to use it.

In this relationship you will not be troubled by the routine habits of thought that often get in the way of a relationship by causing two people to irritate each other unconsciously. You have the capacity to take these habits at their real value, which is usually not very great. This helps immeasurably to smooth over the potential rough places in any relationship.

Composite Jupiter Square Composite Ascendant

Normally, the square of composite Jupiter and Ascendant is a good aspect. It helps to make a relationship work so that the two of you can further each other's chosen path in life rather than get in the way of it. This is accomplished in two ways.

On the one hand, the two of you have some understanding of what you are doing with your lives, at least as it concerns each other. In addition, you also know how to work together so that you support and further each other's plans. Because of these factors, this aspect is often a help in a business or professional relationship.

On the other hand, this aspect makes it easy for you to reinforce each other in your intimate personal lives. You are emotionally supportive and try to help each other through difficult times, including periods of emotional problems. You each have the capacity to make your partner feel good about himself or herself.

However, problems can sometimes arise, and if they do, many of the good effects of the Ascendant-Jupiter square are then reversed. Instead of supporting each other's egos and aiding each other in your life courses, one of you takes advantage of the other, who may have to play second fiddle to the first partner's ego-trip. In a normal chart, the negative manifestations of this square are not too likely to occur. However, it is enough of a danger to be worth mentioning.

Composite Jupiter Trine Composite Ascendant

The trine of composite Jupiter and Ascendant is an excellent aspect for any kind of relationship. It is a sign that the two of you are able to create from yourselves a higher-level being, the relationship itself. And you are willing to give this relationship everything necessary to make it a positive experience for both of you.

With this aspect in your composite chart, the two of you recognize that the petty irritations and upsets that exist in any relationship are not important enough to warrant upsetting what is otherwise a very good situation. You are positive about each other and about being together, and each of you tries to make the other feel better about himself or herself. Any irritating characteristics that annoy you or your partner are corrected through constructive growth rather than criticism.

You are concerned with each other's growth, and as a consequence the relationship is characterized by growth. No matter what happens between you in the long run, you will recognize that this has been a good experience for both of you.

New experiences and opportunities will be opened up by your being together. Jupiter is a planet of expanded consciousness, and whenever it is strong in a composite chart, as it is here, the relationship will help develop your awareness of the world.

This aspect can also manifest itself on the material level, in that the positive energies it signifies will attract good things, both material and spiritual, as you need them.

Composite Jupiter Opposition Composite Ascendant

The opposition of composite Jupiter with Ascendant should not be thought of as an ordinary opposition but as a conjunction of composite Descendant with Jupiter. Instead of being difficult, as many oppositions are, this is a very positive and easy aspect in a composite chart.

This aspect signifies that the two of you have come together as a team for mutual growth. This growth can happen in either or both of two distinct ways.

The first manifestation of the Jupiter energy is on the psychological and spiritual level. Here the position of Jupiter on composite Descendant signifies that you will nurture and support each other through all kinds of adversity and that you will share in the high points of each other's lives as well. This aspect also helps to ensure more high points in the relationship than there might otherwise have been. You are not overly critical of each other, and any criticisms that you do have are given and received in a constructive spirit. Both of you will grow in awareness and understanding of yourselves and the world. No matter what happens to the relationship, you both will see it as a positive experience.

The second level of manifestation is material. This aspect signifies that your relationship is likely to be quite prosperous. This is the result of the same energies as described above. The optimism and positive attitude engendered by this aspect attract whatever material things you may need. And you will get pretty much what you feel you may need.

Chapter Eleven
Saturn

The Meaning of Saturn in the Composite Chart

Saturn is always a very complicated symbol. It has many meanings, some of which are difficult to deal with. To begin with, it often represents those areas of the relationship that are likely to be a source of insecurity. It is this attribute that can make Saturn very hard to handle, because it signifies fears, which can generate a negative energy that makes the worst come true. You must learn to relax about those areas of the relationship that are most influenced by Saturn.

Saturn also refers to limitations on the relationship, which are often more apparent than real. Saturn is an inhibitor, representing the aspects of reality that limit our efforts to expand and grow. As a consequence, through the resistance of Saturn, everything in both the material and psychological world is forced to assume a definite form. The position of Saturn in the composite chart will tell a great deal about what areas of the relationship are most likely to be structured and even rigidified, if the influence is unchecked.

Saturn is not always difficult, however. Very often it indicates a lasting relationship that will endure. Much of the time you will respond to Saturn simply by accepting the reality it imposes and not expecting that which is impossible. This prevents the frustrated idealism that makes so many love relationships difficult. In such instances Saturn replaces flamboyance with reliability.

At other times, however, Saturn's influence will make a relationship nearly impossible. When this happens, it is a reality that must be accepted. Properly handled, the experience of Saturn can be one of the most significant ways in which you learn how you will act in certain situations together. But it must be acknowledged that this process is not always particularly pleasant.

Composite Saturn in the First House

Saturn in the first house of a composite chart can be quite troublesome to a relationship, although not necessarily deadly. Under proper circumstances, it can be very beneficial, for it can bind the two of you together in an enduring association. The effect depends on how the energies are handled.

Under any circumstances, Saturn in the first puts a clamp on how much the two of you can project yourselves into the world; that is, its effect is to make a relationship very self-contained. Others will not know what is going on emotionally between you. If you are having difficulties, you will tend to keep them hidden from others. Even if you are getting along very well and are quite happy, it will not be immediately obvious. You will always present a quiet, reserved appearance that does not tell much about what you are really feeling.

At its worst, Saturn in the first house can create barriers between you that will make it very difficult to communicate with each other either verbally or nonverbally. The effect can be that of a wall between you. In general this is not the best placement for Saturn in a composite chart. But if you do have this placement, the best solution—once you have decided to enter the relationship—is to eliminate as many barriers as possible and to communicate about everything. Make yourselves as much a part of each other as possible.

Composite Saturn in the Second House

Saturn in the second house of the composite chart usually gives a relationship a great sense of material insecurity. In the old books, a second-house Saturn in the chart of an individual was considered an indication of poverty. But many millionaires have had a second-house Saturn; in fact, it is this placement that caused them to amass a fortune in the first place. They were so afraid of poverty that they nearly killed themselves in an effort to avoid it.

This is also true in a composite chart. Money is a source of concern to the two of you and therefore it is also a possible source of problems, even if you have enough money. You may be so cautious in your handling of financial matters that you don't allow yourselves to enjoy life. Similarly, the fear of losing money may lead to all kinds of arguments concerning it, so that money becomes a very divisive issue between you.

Of course, this placement of Saturn can result in the two of you not having enough material resources. But in that case it is your negative attitudes that actually drive away opportunities to make money or secure the resources you seek. You may be so conservative that you don't even see the obvious opportunities to do something about your problems. You hang onto the orthodox ways of doing things because they are familiar, even though they have served you poorly in the past.

While you will always be careful with material resources, you must learn to be open-minded toward new opportunities and proceed with a positive point of view. That will help considerably.

Composite Saturn in the Third House

Saturn in the third house of the composite chart indicates that the two of you must be careful not to fall into set patterns of thought in this relationship. This applies to the ways in which you think as a couple as well as to the ways you think about each other. For example, it can indicate that there is a real barrier to communication between you, because each of you is so locked into certain ways of thinking and communicating that you cannot loosen up and listen to what your partner is saying. Remember that it is always necessary to talk in the other person's language; no matter how successfully you can communicate in your own language, it will do no good unless your partner understands you.

Unfortunately, a communications gap is precisely the problem that Saturn in the third house is likely to create. You must abandon any tendency to believe that your way of thinking is superior to your partner's, because that will only make communication more difficult.

Saturn in the third house also makes the two of you fond of structuring your immediate environment, a tendency that arises from the mental habits just discussed. Mental orderliness is reflected in the way you organize your world. You dislike disorder and will do everything in your powers to prevent it.

In a personal relationship, Saturn in the third can also give difficulty with relatives. Here again, the best solution is to alter your ways of thinking and try to communicate in the same terms as the people you are talking to.

Composite Saturn in the Fourth House

Composite Saturn in the fourth house will have its most serious consequences in a marriage or a love relationship in which you intend to live together. Saturn in this position designates an inner incompatibility that makes living together very difficult. Not that it will be impossible, but this will be the area in which there are the greatest difficulties.

Even when the influence of Saturn is under control, it will have effects. Your home life will be characterized by austerity; that is, you will keep your home very simple, uncluttered, and neat. There is nothing wrong with this, as long as it is not an outward reflection of an inward coldness.

In any kind of relationship with Saturn in the fourth house, there will be a feeling of distance between you, as if you were unable to touch each other at some very deep inner level. If you are consciously experiencing problems, you will have to dig very deeply to find the answers. They are not superficial problems, and a superficial solution cannot deal with them. Both of you will have to get past your deep-seated inner fears in order to confide in your partner with complete trustfulness. For this reason, it is probably a good idea to get to know each other gradually. Do not be in a hurry. Under favorable conditions, Saturn can make a relationship quite enduring.

Composite Saturn in the Fifth House

Saturn in the fifth house of the composite chart will make it rather difficult to get a love relationship or a marriage off the ground. The fifth is the house of fun and lightness, amusements and self-expression. It is also the house of love affairs. Obviously, Saturn is not very much at home here; its heaviness and severity are not particularly compatible with the fifth house. This placement tends to restrict the lighthearted sense of joy that a love relationship should have, subordinating joy to considerations of duty and responsibility.

Any relationship with Saturn in this house will be surrounded by feelings of obligation and necessity. You seem to feel that under different circumstances there would be no relationship between you, but since matters are the way they are, you will make the best of it. This much can be said in your favor; you will really try to make the best of it, because you are realistic about life. This is not an idealistic romance. You probably take life much too seriously, which in the long run tends to magnify problems out of all proportion to their real importance.

In a marriage with this house placement, the foregoing discussion suggests that you may have difficulty in freely expressing your love for each other. But this is also the house of children, and Saturn here may deny children or at least create problems in having them. It would be a very good idea for the two of you to plan on having no more than one or two children. If you concentrate on that one or two, the best manifestations of this placement can become apparent.

Composite Saturn in the Sixth House

Saturn in the sixth house of the composite chart has both strengths and weaknesses. This is the house of duty, responsibility, and work. In this capacity it is an excellent house for Saturn, which is concerned with many of these same values. Whatever your purpose in being together, you should be able to live up to the duties and responsibilities required of you. Obviously this is a good placement for any kind of professional relationship, because your work will get done.

In some cases, there may be a tendency for your sense of duty and obligation to overwhelm the other areas of your relationship, transforming it into drudgery, an obligation taken on unwillingly, rather than a spontaneously joyful and demonstrative affair. It will be a work relationship in the bad sense as well as the good. If this is your situation, you must find some way of making matters lighter between you. Otherwise the relationship does not stand a chance in the long run.

At its worst, a sixth-house Saturn relationship can make both of you feel enslaved by the other or by the very nature of the relationship. If it ever gets to that point, the only solution is to break the connection for a while, until you can regain your sense of perspective about each other.

Composite Saturn in the Seventh House

Saturn, the planet of separation and repression, in the seventh, the house of marriage, might seem to be absolutely fatal to such a relationship, but it is not. Saturn here is quite compatible with any kind of relationship, although it does create certain problems.

On the one hand, it can bind the two of you together, because it signifies that together you will have to face certain difficulties and responsibilities. By itself it does not signify that love is the bond that holds you together, although that may be the case for other reasons. The binding forces of Saturn are requirements that must be met in the real world. You are tied to each other by duties, obligations, and responsibilities, in addition to any feelings of affection that you may have. In fact, the seventh-house Saturn can tie two people together even when they want to split up.

But this placement can also signify that under some circumstances there will be no relationship at all between you. However, if Saturn in the seventh house is really operating at a malefic level, it is highly unlikely that the two of you will want to come together in the first place. If you have settled that you want to have a relationship, you have already proved that Saturn is not operating at the malefic level in your composite chart.

Composite Saturn in the Eighth House

Saturn in the eighth house of the composite chart pertains both to joint property and resources and to major personal transformations and regenerations.

To deal with the first area, the effects of Saturn in the eighth house can be similar to its effects in the second, in that you may feel very insecure about the physical resources you share. You may have fears of not having enough money, for example. And as in the second house, this insecurity may actually cause the two of you to concentrate on money to such an extent that you become wealthy. Insecurity is the real problem here, rather than any lack of money. However, you might conceivably have trouble with other people's money—banks, finance companies, and such. It would probably be well to avoid these if you can.

Turning to the area of regeneration symbolized by the eighth house, Saturn here can indicate that the two of you will resist the deep transformations that must take place in any relationship. The eighth house is the house of death, both real and metaphorical; in other words, it signifies very important and fundamental changes, such that your lives will not be the same as they were before.

But the two of you are likely to be afraid of such changes and will try to build up structures in your lives that will prevent change of any sort. It is not good to do this, however, because the transformations of the eighth house are very difficult to resist, and resisting them only makes them more catastrophic when they do occur. You should not face life from a rigid position. Relax and let yourselves be open to any changes that may occur. They will probably be for the better.

Composite Saturn in the Ninth House

Saturn in the ninth house of the composite chart can be very useful. It signifies a very careful and cautious approach to life. The two of you will plan very carefully for your future, so you are not likely to be caught off guard by unpleasant surprises from the outside world. Together you have a strong sense of reality—not that you are incapable of idealism, but you keep it well under control. Your approach to the real world is very structured.

But the two of you should be on guard against certain negative effects of this position. If Saturn's effects in this house are allowed to become too strong, they can lead to such narrowness and excessive caution that you will overlook the real opportunities that come your way.

This placement may also signify that each of you is solidly entrenched in your position in life and can't be easily moved from it, especially in matters concerning each other. Be very careful that with Saturn in this house you don't get to the point of being unable to deal with each other's point of view. Like the third house, the ninth is a house of communication, but if Saturn is too strong, communication between you will be totally lost. For any relationship, that is a bad sign.

You must avoid narrowness of thinking, either about each other or about other people, because it can ultimately destroy any relationship.

Composite Saturn in the Tenth House

In many ways Saturn is in its own house here. Composite Saturn in the tenth means that the nature and goals of this relationship are very important to the two of you. You will be strongly conscious of your objectives and will work very hard to reach them. This placement is perhaps more favorable to a professional relationship than to a personal one, but in either case it will not hurt.

Together you will work very hard to get ahead on your own terms, whatever they may be. You both will feel that it is necessary to work hard, although that feeling may be exaggerated.

Sometimes Saturn in this position can make you believe that the world is bearing down on you. Whether or not this is actually true, you will have to work quite hard together to get where you want to be. Success will not come easily, but it will come if you work diligently and do not take shortcuts. The success of this relationship, whatever its purpose, depends upon doing your work carefully and meticulously. The presence of Saturn guarantees that if you do not do your work thoroughly and lay a strong foundation for future action, you will have trouble later on.

On the other hand, if you follow this advice, a tenth-house Saturn will make it possible to reach your objectives with great success. This is not a bad position for Saturn, but it requires you to exercise a great deal of responsibility.

Composite Saturn in the Eleventh House

Saturn in the eleventh house of the composite chart is in one of the houses of relationships, since the eleventh represents friendship. This can refer to your feelings of friendship for each other as well as to friends that you have as a couple.

In the first instance, Saturn in this house does not make friendship between you impossible, but it does somewhat cool your expression of it; you may still have a very enduring relationship. You may be quite reserved with each other, but that may be just as well, for it will permit your relationship to last longer. An eleventh-house Saturn can indicate a very long-lasting friendship.

The eleventh is also the house of one's ideals, hopes, and wishes. In some cases, Saturn can signify that the two of you have very different ideals and that you don't usually react in the same way toward things. This can diminish your sympathy for each other and make the relationship quite difficult.

Taking the second side of the eleventh house, that of friends outside the relationship, it can be said that when Saturn is operating positively, it indicates few outside friends, but those few will be firm and long-lasting. They may be older than either of you. But if Saturn's influence is not working out well, you may not have any outside friends, probably because of some rigidity in you that makes it impossible for you to share yourselves with others.

Composite Saturn in the Twelfth House

The twelfth house is one of the more difficult positions for composite Saturn. This placement implies that you find it difficult to deal with each other in an open and direct manner. Your responses to each other are automatic, as if you were acting out unconscious programs that you neither understand nor particularly like. You may often ask each other, "Now what made me do that to you?" You may also feel that as a whole the relationship is very cramping to your individual styles. You feel repressed and put down by the experience. In this case it would be best to avoid further contact.

However, if you decide that you have something of value together and would like to continue, here is what the two of you must do. First of all, recognize that many of the subversive tactics that you use against each other are not intentional. You seem to trigger in each other mechanical "programs" that run even when they are not appropriate to the situation. Therefore, you both must become very tolerant of these patterns—not only your partner's, but also your own. Blaming yourself all the time is no better than blaming the other person.

If you can learn to be tolerant of these patterns, you won't take their effects so seriously either. That, in turn, will help you learn to understand what lies behind them and how to deal with them. The first requirement is not to take so seriously the actions that hurt the relationship, because then you don't have to worry so much about protecting yourselves when you get into an analysis of your problems together. You will be able to concentrate all your energies on solving the problems. When you have done that, you are well on your way to making the relationship work. The important part is the initial commitment.

Composite Saturn Conjunct Composite Uranus

The conjunction of Saturn and Uranus in the composite chart indicates tension and conflict between you. One of you wants to be free and unfettered, and the other restricts that desire. This is an explosive situation and can lead to sudden outbreaks of temper when long-suppressed tensions come to the surface. Such bursts of energy can emerge suddenly and break up a relationship that has seemed to be running smoothly for some time. The result is surprising to those involved and to the people around them.

With this conjunction in your composite horoscope, it is a good idea not to hold back your feelings. Whenever tensions develop between you, discuss them. Don't hope that they will go away, because they won't. Problems that are not dealt with immediately descend into hidden depths, and later, when the pressure gets too great, they explode without warning.

This tendency to hold in your feelings can be very useful during short periods of tension or difficulty, however. At times it will seem as if the two of you can endure anything together. But when such a period is over, make sure that all the events and emotional consequences of that time are dealt with, or they will become part of an eventual blowup.

Composite Saturn Sextile Composite Uranus

The sextile of composite Saturn and Uranus is an aspect of endurance. The two principles of Saturn and Uranus, which in nature are quite opposed, are presented here in a creative balance. It gives your relationship qualities of endurance and patience and the ability to endure much stress. The two of you are not bothered by passing irritations, so you do not fly off the handle at every little difficulty that arises between you. Only the major problems occupy your attention. But patience can be carried too far. Tension may build up if you don't find some way to release it, and the blowups, when they finally come, are rather spectacular.

In the world around you, the two of you see a balance between the new, the innovative, and the unusual on one hand and the old reliable values of the past on the other. This viewpoint also results in a balanced way of thinking within your relationship. When you plan something together, you approach the problem in a practical, disciplined way that still allows you to grasp and apply new principles.

Although this aspect by itself does not make for a very powerful attraction between you, it does contribute to the stability of your relationship.

Composite Saturn Square Composite Uranus

The square of composite Saturn and Uranus is quite common in the charts of people born in the early 1950s. This aspect may account in part for the general instability of relationships in this generational group; it indicates severe tension that frequently leads to breakups and separation.

If this aspect is strong in your composite chart, you will find it difficult to handle the tensions that arise between you. Instead of dealing with each irritation as it arises, you allow tensions to build up to what can only be a breaking point.

Obviously you must learn to handle problems as they arise without letting them build up. You may think it will cause more trouble to handle them immediately because there are so many irritations. But, unfortunately, frequent petty irritations are one of the effects of this square. Nevertheless, the irritations become much worse if suppressed, for then they cannot be dealt with at all. When the situation is allowed to reach that point, all feeling is dead and there is little left to salvage. Do not let it go that far.

Composite Saturn Trine Composite Uranus

The trine of composite Saturn and Uranus does not create an especially free and open relationship. There is always some underlying tension and sense of restraint between you. Nevertheless, you can use this tension quite creatively, for it enables you to handle problems that most couples canot deal with. But this works only if there are long periods of letdown between the tense times. If there are not, the tension will eventually build up and explode, which will end the relationship once and for all.

This aspect favors planning and organizing your lives together. Uranus allows you to see new ways of doing things, while Saturn ensures that you will be careful and thorough. Similarly, your world views as a couple will be balanced between the old and the new, so that you experience the best in both worlds.

This aspect could be very useful if you have come together for the purpose of teaching others. All Saturn-Uranus combinations give some capacity for teaching, but the trine is the best. A teacher always has to strike a balance between conveying a discipline (Saturn) and changing and reforming his or her students (Uranus). The trine in your composite chart makes you complement each other, so that together you will have this ability, even if it is not so well-developed in each of you individually.

Composite Saturn Opposition Composite Uranus

The opposition of composite Saturn and Uranus can be quite difficult for a relationship. It implies a state of tension arising from the fact that one of you feels that the other puts a complete clamp on his or her style, while the restrictive partner experiences the first one as a disruptive force. Add to this your great difficulty in communicating with each other, so that pressures are not released, and you have an explosive situation. You will probably find it difficult even to relax with each other.

With this aspect, if your relationship does get off the ground, there is still the critical problem of tension building up rather than being let off gradually. This problem causes many such relationships to end suddenly and without warning. It is clearly a situation in which the only solution is to learn to let off steam gradually. Talk frequently about what is going on between you and try to be as honest as possible. Your principal aim should be to state the truth accurately, not to score points over each other. This way you will be able to let out the energy and release the tension before it gets critical. Or the relationship will not be very happy or long-lasting.

Composite Saturn Conjunct Composite Neptune

The conjunction of composite Saturn and Neptune can present some strange and difficult problems. This relationship is quite likely to challenge your accustomed ways of looking at the world. The challenge will not be wild and revolutionary, as is characteristic of Uranus; rather it will be a quiet, subtle change such that one day the two of you will find that you don't understand what is going on at all. You both will certainly be confused and may be fearful of what you don't understand. A strongly placed Saturn-Neptune conjunction is not favorable if you must work together in a situation that requires great clarity of mind and understanding in order to accomplish something.

There is a way to deal with the energies of this aspect in a relationship if you can learn to be extremely flexible. Saturn-Neptune signifies a breakdown of the ways in which you structure your perception of reality. If you can bring yourselves to relax and flow with its energies, this relationship can present you with a whole new way of structuring your world, which will greatly enhance your ability to deal with life. Therefore this encounter can be valuable, although it won't always be very pleasant. But you both will resist this aspect of your relationship very intensely, and you will be beset by fear, confusion, uncertainty, and especially self-doubt. You each may feel that your partner has a way of undermining your belief in yourself.

If that is true in your case, the situation is exposing something in you that is not strong enough. Instead of fleeing, try to understand what is happening. Even if you feel that you have suffered terrible damage through this relationship, you must recognize that you have a weakness that has to be dealt with. Try to learn what it is, so that you will not have to deal with it over and over again in the future.

The energy of this Saturn-Neptune combination will break down your old understandings of yourselves in a relationship, but in the long run it can also bring about a new and truer understanding.

Composite Saturn Sextile Composite Neptune

The sextile of composite Saturn and Neptune indicates that you will be able to maintain a balance between the ideal and the real in this relationship. If this is a personal relationship, for example, you will try to use what you know about yourselves and each other to progress and develop into what you would like to become. Very often the effect of a harmonious Saturn-Neptune combination such as this is that people will work toward the ideal by denying themselves in one way or another. This aspect is a symbol of asceticism. One way to understand this principle is to think of it as the idealization (Neptune) of discipline and austerity (Saturn). As a couple you are able to put up with having very little because you want very little.

The same tendency toward austerity makes it unlikely that this will be a sexual relationship, unless there are many other indications for it. The reason for this is not that there are blocks and repressions, as is usually the case with Saturn, but because Neptune denies the physical world and because this combination idealizes austerity. A couple with this aspect probably would not even want a sexual relationship.

Other kinds of relationships with this aspect will also be restrained and disciplined. That fact will not divide you, but may actually hold you together.

Composite Saturn Square Composite Neptune

If the square of Saturn and Neptune is strongly placed in the composite chart, there can be some difficulty, for this aspect tends to undermine confidence and to produce fear and insecurity. The effect of Neptune is to dissolve and weaken the solid physical basis of your world by making things seem uncertain and unclear. And this aspect has the same effect on a relationship also.

Sometimes there is a conflict between realism and idealism in your relationship. It may appear that the ideal you seek—how you should relate to or feel about each other, or some other ideal you want to work toward together—is totally blocked by circumstances in the real world. Often this belief can make both of you pessimistic or depressed. This aspect is not noted for producing a good, lighthearted sense of humor.

However, you must remember that the situation is seldom as bad as it appears with this aspect. Much of the apparently depressing circumstances are only an illusion, so you must circumvent the illusion and get at the true reality, which is usually not so bad. Don't accept conditions as they first appear in this relationship and don't give up seeking what you want. If you do, you will only undermine each other and weaken your ability to deal with the world. Obviously, that is not a desirable result.

Composite Saturn Trine Composite Neptune

The trine of composite Saturn and Neptune produces austerity of self-expression, self-denial, and even asceticism. With this aspect prominent in the chart, it is unlikely that the two of you have formed a relationship purely for pleasure. More likely you have come together with some higher purpose in mind, something involving discipline and working toward an ideal. You may even have come together to pursue a spiritual purpose. But even if the task is of a business or professional nature, the two of you will work very hard to attain your purpose and will indulge yourselves very little. Work and discipline themselves may be the ideal toward which you strive.

Obviously this style would not usually be found in a love relationship, except in an idealized platonic one. But the self-denial and discipline that are characteristic of this aspect will be a spontaneous self-expression, not an imposed condition that you are unwilling to put up with.

Composite Saturn Opposition Composite Neptune

The opposition of composite Saturn and Neptune suggests that the two of you have rather incompatible ideals and that you will constantly challenge each other's notions of reality. The danger is that you will systematically weaken each other's self-confidence to the point where both of you will be less capable of handling the world than you were before.

Negative Saturn-Neptune energies can lead to fear, depression, sadness, and a sense of futility, as well as to material want and deprivation. However, material deprivation usually results from the negative psychological energies generated by the aspect. You have to believe that something is possible before you will go after it.

You both must learn to recognize that you are probably making your relationship seem worse than it is. Be very careful not to make mountains out of molehills and exaggerate problems out of all proportion. This is one of the chief dangers of the aspect.

At the same time, it is necessary to play very straight with each other. Otherwise, every time you discover that your partner has deceived or lied to you, your relationship will become weaker and weaker until there is nothing left except suspicion.

Composite Saturn Conjunct Composite Pluto

The conjunction of Saturn and Pluto in your composite chart indicates that the two of you may have to face difficult times together and that you will have to struggle quite hard to keep going. But these difficulties are not so likely to occur within the relationship; more probably the two of you will experience difficulties with the outside world.

You may undergo periods of economic scarcity, for example, or times when everything seems to be working against you. However, this aspect also gives a tremendous resistance to adversity. Together you will have a kind of rugged persistence that people will envy. You will survive where others fail.

Although this aspect is not the easiest, it may actually strengthen a relationship because of the ruggedness it confers. At the same time, if the two of you have gone through a lot of trouble together, you may feel more strongly about staying together. One might say that you thrive on adversity. It is a challenge you are able to meet, and it builds you up.

Composite Saturn Sextile Composite Pluto

The sextile of composite Saturn and Pluto can give your relationship considerable survival power. By itself it does not indicate that the two of you are attracted to each other, but if you are, this aspect will help you deal with the hard times that can arise in any relationship. The effect of Saturn is to slow down and strengthen transformations, symbolized by Pluto. The result is that the relationship becomes more resistant to the negative effects of changes that may go on around you.

On the other hand, it must be pointed out that this aspect can also make a relationship more resistant to positive changes. All sextiles and trines inhibit changes to some extent, while one of the key ideas behind Saturn-Pluto is the changing of structure. Therefore the sextile's energies inhibit the normal expression of the planetary combination.

While the toughness and durability that this aspect gives your relationship are desirable, make sure that they do not become rigidity. Always keep yourselves open to necessary changes, or you will find that your relationship has become stultifying, nothing more than a mass of habitual responses to each other, with little real thought or feeling.

Composite Saturn Square Composite Pluto

The square of composite Saturn and Pluto creates difficulties. One of you will feel that you are struggling in chains forged by the other, that the relationship is restrictive, and that your natural growth is being inhibited. It is most likely that each of you will affect the other this way at different times. It will not be a one-way street.

The energies of the aspect may not be experienced directly, however. The Saturn-Pluto combination seems to have the effect of creating a shortage or lack of something that seems essential, so the two of you will not always have what you want, whether it is material comfort or psychological support. Something in the dynamics of your interaction brings this situation about. As a consequence, your freedom of movement is very much hindered, and you will blame each other for this problem.

Please realize, however, that the dynamics of your relationship is the problem, not the other person. In other words, both of you are contributing to the situation. Until you acknowledge this fact, you will not be able to straighten out any problems that you encounter.

Such a relationship can face quite unpleasant circumstances, most commonly in the form of increasing emotional coldness and remoteness between you. From there you may get to the point of resisting each other strongly and wanting to break free at all costs. If the relationship has anything going for it and you want to make it work, you must recognize how you have created this situation. How do you limit each other, not only by actions, but also by attitudes? Do you undermine each other in any way? Ask yourselves these questions, not to prove each other right or wrong but only to get at the truth.

Composite Saturn Trine Composite Pluto

The trine of composite Saturn and Pluto confers a certain toughness and rigidity upon a relationship that can be both good and bad. On the plus side, it makes the two of you able to handle some fairly difficult times without folding up. You can endure quite a bit of hardship, either from each other or from the outside world. You develop a view of the world and of your relationship that helps you understand why circumstances can be bad, and you resist the panic that sometimes destroys a relationship when times are tough.

On the other hand, it is possible to become rigid and unadaptable. No matter how great the pressure, you may be unable to bend at all and make the necessary adaptations that could enable your relationship to survive and produce happiness for both of you.

Try to avoid unconscious habits in dealing with each other. Your relationship, like any other, requires that you make changes from time to time. But you tend to resist these changes because of the habit patterns that you have built up unconsciously with each other. Learn to approach each situation as if you had never seen it before. Apply the same fresh and innovative tactics that you would have used the first time. You will probably see that this situation is quite different and that you had been imposing a similarity that was not actually there.

Composite Saturn Opposition Composite Pluto

If the opposition of composite Saturn and Pluto is strongly placed, it can create a great deal of tension between the two of you, which will be expressed as rather explosive outbursts of feeling and passion.

The problem is that the rigidity of Saturn encounters the irresistible transforming power of Pluto. An analogy can be found in the theory of continental drift, in which the continental land masses come together almost imperceptibly, but the accumulated pressure throws up mountains and produces earthquakes of terrifying violence. A relationship in which this aspect is strong is like that. Both of you are constantly changing, slowly but powerfully, but you operate in such a way that it is difficult to let the changes happen. The result is that they happen all at once in a cataclysmic way rather than expressing themselves gradually.

Whe an emotional eruption occurs, it is because one of you has lost all hope of being able to deal with the other and bring about any kind of constructive change. Finally, when the pressure gets too great, you blow up, not to change your partner but to let off the powerful feelings stored up inside you.

If either of you is rigid, you must learn not to be. Don't allow your beliefs and ideas to persist unchanged. Do not wait until the pressure is so great that you can't handle the matter easily.

Composite Saturn Conjunct Composite Ascendant

The conjunction of composite Saturn and Ascendant can have several very different effects, depending on other factors in the relationship.

On the positive level, it can signify a relationship that is bound together so strongly that almost nothing can break it up. This is not so much because there is a positive attraction between you as because you are intensely involved with each other in a way that seems fated or strongly predestined. Unfortunately, even if one of you wants to break out of this relationship, it might be difficult because of material circumstances, psychological needs, or other factors that seem beyond your control. This characteristic of the Saturn-Ascendant conjunction is helpful, if the rest of the relationship is basically sound, and not so good if the relationship is shaky.

If either of you experiences this relationship as a trap from which you would like to break free but cannot, you must examine why you are together. People sometimes stay involved with each other for reasons that have nothing to do with happiness. If you examine the relationship carefully, you may find that the two of you are getting something else from the situation. You may be reluctant to give this up, even though the relationship itself is unsatisfactory.

At another level, if the two of you do not have much interaction with each other, the conjunction of composite Saturn and Ascendant may be the final indication that you do not have enough in common to allow a viable relationship. Certainly, if you are interested in being lovers or marriage partners, you should make sure that other indications in the relationship are extremely positive to compensate for this aspect. Even under the best of circumstances, this aspect is likely to mean that emotional contact between you is limited.

Composite Saturn Sextile Composite Ascendant

The sextile of composite Saturn and Ascendant can have a positive, steadying effect upon a relationship, or it can make the relationship rather rigid. In either case, this aspect causes structures to become hardened and stabilized. Obviously this is fine for the good elements in a relationship, but not good for the less positive elements. There is a danger that the two of you could become so enmeshed in bad habits that you do not think about what you are doing. You may act unconsciously instead of stopping to consider what is really happening. A possible result is that many of your actions toward each other may be inappropriate to the circumstances, which will cause problems between you.

This aspect may curtail communication between you, but not in a way that is truly detrimental. What it will do is keep your communication focused on fundamentals. Instead of engaging in small talk with each other, you will talk mostly about the matters that you both consider important.

In this relationship your ideals are pragmatic. You both are anxious to deal with the truth; instead of indulging in idle speculation about what could be, you deal with what is. That includes each other, which means that this may not be the most romantic relationship, but at least you are willing to make do with what you have. For that reason, this relationship may be more enduring than those that are characterized by a romantic attitude.

These same attitudes also make this aspect a very positive one for a business relationship in which strong emotional interaction is secondary to clear and objective consideration of the facts that you are working with.

Composite Saturn Square Composite Ascendant

The square of composite Saturn to Ascendant can cause real problems in a relationship. It signifies that the two of you have a great deal of difficulty cooperating with each other and coordinating your purposes in life so that you can work together. In the composite chart, this aspect indicates alienation of one partner from the other.

Only if other elements of your relationship are very positive can you compensate for the negative effects of this aspect. It can make you both feel that your past experiences have made you into such completely different people that it is difficult to get together in the present. Your personal and inward experiences of life in general are so different that you will have great difficulty in understanding each other, which adds to the overall sense of differentness and alienation.

If this is a marriage or other relationship in which you share a home of some kind, that home is not likely to be a very rewarding place to be. Neither of you is willing to invest enough of your personal feelings and emotions into making it pleasant. This is a reflection on the material plane of the inward sense of barrenness that the two of you feel in this relationship.

Another factor can interfere with the smooth functioning of a relationship with this aspect. You may feel that external circumstances have placed such a burden of duty and responsibility on your relationship that you cannot relax and enjoy each other's company. There is always the feeling that something else must be done first.

Even in the best relationship, this aspect is likely to cause problems in mutual acceptance and understanding. If other areas of your relationship are not too good, you should ask yourselves very honestly what you want from this relationship and whether it is possible to attain it.

Composite Saturn Trine Composite Ascendant

The trine of composite Saturn and Ascendant will have a very stabilizing effect on a good relationship, but an inhibiting effect on one that is not so good. When Saturn's energies operate in a positive manner, as is often the case with the trine aspect, they promote stability and help keep the relationship on an even keel. This aspect prevents wide swings from extreme happiness to extreme sadness or from very positive to very negative feelings. But it does so at the cost of a certain spontaneity and exuberance. A Saturnine relationship, even a good one, is more sober than most, more concerned about practical realities and less about ideals and romantic fantasies.

On the positive side, the two of you are able to make each other function in a more regular manner. You give each other a sense of discipline. At its best, this aspect makes it possible for the two of you to be your honest selves with each other, but at the same time to exercise restraint. You are not inclined to act in a completely free and loose manner when you are together.

If the energy of this aspect operates negatively, however, then each of you may be a serious obstacle to the other's self-expression. Even worse, you may find yourselves locked into such rigid attitudes about each other that it is difficult to make changes in your relationship. At the same time, these energies may cause you both to become more rigid in your attitudes to the world around you.

Which effect you are likely to experience depends in part on your willingness to deal with each other openly and honestly.

Composite Saturn Opposition Composite Ascendant

The opposition of composite Saturn to Ascendant should be thought of as a conjunction of Saturn and composite Descendant. Because the Descendant is a very important point in the chart of a relationship, this is a very important aspect. Unfortunately, it is also a difficult aspect for most people to handle well. It implies that the two of you are unable to relate as a team. You both feel there are great barriers between you that make it difficult to relate to each other. This problem may derive from either of two sources.

It may be that external circumstances are making the relationship impossible. People around you may try to prevent you from getting together, perhaps because one of you is involved in another relationship that makes this one impossible. Or, especially if you are lovers, there may be a great age gap between you that makes your relationship difficult.

But it is also possible that the two of you simply do not have a basic affinity for each other. Saturn on the composite Descendant can be a sign of mutual alienation.

If other areas of the relationship are positive, you will probably encounter the first problem—persons or circumstances trying to block the relationship. But if your relationship is not going well in other ways, this aspect is a sign that it is not likely to be a very rewarding one, because you are not basically compatible. In any case, with this aspect, you must examine your relationship very carefully to see if you really want it enough to overcome the obstacles it presents.

Chapter Twelve

Uranus

The Meaning of Uranus in the Composite Chart

Uranus is the planet of the unconventional and the unusual, at least in its ordinary manifestations. It can also reveal alternate views of reality that will help you to learn and grow. Unfortunately, this usually happens by means of a surprising upset that seems to completely invalidate your previous beliefs about life. Uranus is often regarded as the planet of unpleasant surprises. The only way to deal with it positively is to maintain a very open attitude and to structure your life as little as possible. Some structure is necessary, of course. But Uranus demands that you maintain a very flexible attitude toward the world.

In a relationship it is important to let the areas most affected by Uranus be much freer than you might otherwise allow. The aspects to Uranus in the composite chart usually indicate the area of the relationship that you must release. Not that you will lose it, but you must let it take its own course, with a minimum of expectations. Venus-Uranus aspects, in particular, represent relationships that must not be restrained from following their own course.

The house position indicates where Uranus is most effective, and that area must be treated most gently. Any attempt to make a basically Uranian characteristic conform to rules or expectations will only cause disturbances; the energy of Uranus under pressure becomes rebellious, insisting on doing everything in exactly the opposite way from what people want.

Uranus is simply an energy that insists on being given free rein. Your ability to handle it depends upon how free you are.

Composite Uranus in the First House

With Uranus in the first house of the composite chart, your relationship will have a strong drive for freedom of expression. At the very least it will be a highly individualistic one.

It may be that this relationship will begin very suddenly. Or perhaps the two of you would not ordinarily be expected to come together. In either case, being together will have a revolutionary effect on both of you. It will reveal aspects of yourselves that you never even knew existed. By the same token, the lives of those around you will also be affected.

The danger of this placement is that you, or those around you, will try to make this relationship conform to established patterns of behavior. This usually triggers the negative side of Uranus, which results in instability and unconventionality for its own sake. Uranus means restlessness and not wanting to be trapped into predictable patterns. You both tend to be easily bored by predictable situations and then want to get out.

Only if the two of you are willing to approach this experience with a totally open mind, free of expectations, will you get the maximum benefit from it. That benefit will be a challenging experience that will enable you to grow and expand your consciousness for as long as the relationship lasts.

Composite Uranus in the Second House

Composite Uranus in the second house of the chart may indicate that the two of you will obtain your resources in an unusual manner, or that the resources themselves will be unusual. It may also mean that the material and financial aspects of the relationship will be unstable. The concrete manifestations of this energy depend largely on the kind of relationship it is.

For example, in a business or professional association, a second-house Uranus could simply mean that the two of you are involved in doing something in a new way, perhaps some new invention or technique, which produces income for you. In a personal relationship it can mean that the two of you have a very unconventional set of values, such that you view possessions very differently from other people. Specifically, you are likely to feel that possessions are an encumbrance to be avoided wherever possible, with the result that you will own very few things. Or it may indicate a desire to collect unusual objects that other people do not collect.

In any relationship, however, by far the most likely possibility is material and financial instability. This results from your tendency to regard material possessions and dealing with money as a nuisance. When you neglect your finances, they begin to go awry. In this case you must first recognize that you do not take care of money and material matters properly. Second, you must try to learn how to handle them so that you do not experience them as such a problem. With any planetary energy, you must recognize its effects and then learn how to flow with it.

Composite Uranus in the Third House

Uranus in the third house of the composite chart indicates a relationship that will revolutionize your basic ways of thinking about life. It must be remembered that the effects of Uranus, although always noticeable, are not always huge and cataclysmic; they may vary from very slight to very great. This relationship will change your thinking somehow. And the two of you may try to communicate to others your new ways of looking at the world and try to change their thinking.

As with any situation in which Uranus is prominent, you must avoid the tendency to make your relationship fit your expectations. If you try to do so, the unstable aspect of Uranus will come into play. Communication between you will become erratic and disruptive, and you will often make each other angry. After a while you might even find that you begin to make each other nervous whenever you are together, instead of being at ease as you should be, at least in a personal relationship. Of course, some relationships do exist primarily so that one person can challenge the consciousness of the other, but these are not often long-lived. Such a situation is not particularly desirable in a close personal relationship.

As always with Uranus, you must flow with the energy and let it take you wherever it goes. In this house, especially, it is unlikely that Uranus will take you somewhere you do not want or ought not to be.

Composite Uranus in the Fourth House

Uranus in the fourth house of the composite chart signifies a relationship that has an unusual home base. In a personal relationship, particularly a love relationship or marriage, this can mean that the home itself is unusual. Or there may be something unusual about the two of you living together. An unmarried couple living together might have this placement of Uranus, but only if they themselves regard the situation as unconventional or in defiance of morality. Other couples, for whom living together seems the most natural and obvious move, would be less likely to have the fourth-house composite Uranus. This placement means that you express your unconventionality through the home you share.

It may also be that your home life is unpredictable and unstable, that whenever you come together, you don't know what to expect. This situation can make the two of you very uneasy, to say the least, for the fourth house represents that aspect of your lives that is the basis for everything else. It is the reliable center from which you go out to face the world and to which you return to find rest. If there is no rest for you there, your relationship can be very unpleasant.

Before setting up housekeeping together, you must first determine which effect is operating in your case. If it is the second effect, perhaps you should reconsider. Your relationship can continue, but keep your homes separate.

In other kinds of relationships, this placement simply means that you continually challenge some inner aspect of each other. This can make for a valuable learning experience, or it can simply make you very uneasy with each other.

Composite Uranus in the Fifth House

When composite Uranus is in the fifth house, a relationship may have to take an unusual form in order to express itself fully. How this works out depends on the kind of relationship that you have.

If this is a love relationship or a marriage, you will probably find that you have to give each other a lot more freedom of movement than is customary in such cases. A love affair with this position may be better off if it does not become a marriage. You both value your freedom greatly and do not wish to be restrained by the obligations that a legal arrangement entails.

If you do decide to get married, you must give each other a great deal of freedom. For example, you must not let the marriage or the agreement between you become a barrier to other relationships. Yet the permission you give each other must be genuine. Otherwise your partner will sense that you don't really mean it and will begin to hide what he or she is doing. That, of course, will destroy the relationship even faster. It is not that this placement of Uranus requires that you have outside affairs, but that the relationship must not be felt as a barrier. Either of you is free to restrict yourself to this one relationship, but your partner cannot make you do it.

Other kinds of relationships will experience this placement of Uranus as a desire to have fun and express yourselves in unusual ways. You will seek out unusual forms of amusement and entertainment. For example, you might become interested in off-beat art forms together. Or it might be that when you are together you like to act a little crazy or wild or unconventional. This, of course, may apply to a love relationship or marriage as well.

Composite Uranus in the Sixth House

Composite Uranus in the sixth house is not the most congenial placement. The sixth house in a composite chart represents the duties and responsibilities of a relationship. Uranus, naturally rebellious, tends to rebel against all such impositions. The most obvious effect of this placement is that your obligations to each other or to other people are likely to be sources of disruption within the relationship. One or both of you will continually be in a state of rebellion against this aspect of your relationship.

It is also possible, however, that the two of you may carry out your responsibilities in some very unusual way. Instead of being impatient about doing what you must, you are impatient about doing it in some particular manner. In this case, it is a good idea for each of you to let your partner carry out the responsibilities in his or her own way, as long as the tasks get done.

This placement of Uranus is most helpful in a professional relationship that involves doing some scientific or technical work or in any relationship in which a new solution to a problem must be found. One meaning of this placement is work carried out in a new or unusual way. This principle also applies to a personal relationship, and you will encounter the best aspects of the sixth-house Uranus if you always seek out new and unusual solutions to any problems that you have with each other.

Composite Uranus in the Seventh House

Uranus in the seventh house of a composite chart means that together you will strike out into new paths, whether your relationship is professional, business, marriage, or friendship. This may refer to the structure of your relationship or to what you do with it.

In a marriage, a seventh-house Uranus can be a source of difficulty, unless the two of you have the courage to do things your own way and not worry about conventional notions of marriage. Uranus requires that you come to an accommodation with each other that is uniquely your own. If you try to act along purely traditional lines, you may create pressures that make your relationship very unstable. Most commonly, in fact, this placement in a marriage chart does indicate an unstable and short-lived marriage. This is also true of any other type of partnership with a seventh-house Uranus.

In any partnership with this placement, you must grant each other an unusual degree of freedom of action, especially in regard to other people. Attempts to restrict each other will only increase the pressures against your survival as a couple.

It is also a good idea for the two of you to work together toward something that is new, different, and unconventional, such as a movement for humanitarian or political reform, or something similar. But whatever you choose, be sure that you are doing it that way because you want to rather than because it is supposed to be done that way. The energy of Uranus does not easily permit doing something for the sake of convention.

Composite Uranus in the Eighth House

As is the case with all eighth-house placements, composite Uranus in this house affects two different areas of the relationship. In the first place, it affects your handling of the major transformations that must occur in any relationship from time to time. In the second place, it also affects the way you experience and handle the resources—finances, property, possessions—that you share.

In the first area, an eighth-house Uranus may signify that the two of you experience important changes as undesirable disruptions to be avoided at all costs. Such an attitude can only worsen the situation because it signifies the kind of mental rigidity that is so incompatible with Uranus. If you can be more flexible and approach changes with an open mind, you will be able to weather any difficulties that may arise. Even at best the changes are likely to be rather sudden and unpredictable.

The eighth house ultimately signals growth on the most profound level, growth that results when an old attitude dies and gives way to a new one. It is the house of death and regeneration of the self—not necessarily death in the literal sense, but the passing away of some element in your lives. The more rigidly you face these situations that challenge the very core of your relationship, the more likely it is that the relationship itself will die.

In the area of joint property and resources, this placement of Uranus, much like the second-house placement, can indicate that the two of you consider possessions to be a burden rather than an opportunity for growth. As a consequence, you may not pay enough attention to your material affairs, so that as a result they become a source of disruption. Either you must learn to deal with the material aspect of your lives, or you must find a way to minimize its power over you.

Composite Uranus in the Ninth House

Uranus in the ninth house of the composite chart indicates that this relationship will challenge your ways of looking at the world. The ninth house represents how the mind consciously views the world and makes decisions and judgments about it, based on a higher world-view and philosophy. In a composite chart, this house signifies the ability of the relationship to expand and enlarge your view of the world, both as a couple and as individuals.

Uranus in this house is both an opportunity and a challenge. The two of you may be in considerable disagreement about your views of life, which at first may be a constant source of trouble. You both will have to learn to understand each other completely and enlarge your views to encompass your partner's. This will allow you to have a true growth relationship. But if you cannot do this, intellectual, philosophical, and even spiritual disagreements will become the largest single source of disruption between you.

If you do learn to encompass each other's views of life, the two of you will probably arrive at a position that is quite different from the views of the people around you. You may be regarded as a pair of mavericks whose ideas don't quite fit with other people's. There isn't much you can do aobut that, but don't worry; it is not likely to become a real problem. You may even come to enjoy the role. It is rather interesting to see the effects of new ideas on others.

Composite Uranus in the Tenth House

With composite Uranus in the tenth house of the chart, the purpose of your relationship may be to challenge and revolutionize the views and even the lives of the people around you. Such a relationship may also revolutionize your own lives as well.

The tenth is the house of social status, overall life objectives (as they really are, not as you wish them to be, which is the function of the eleventh house), and your role in society. This applies to composite charts as well as to natal charts. Uranus here means that these areas may take an unusual direction or that they will be a possible source of instability and disruption.

This placement of Uranus can signify that the two of you simply like to do things in your own highly individualistic style. On the other hand, your view of life may be one that others consider literally revolutionary. In the latter case, beware of stirring up unnecessary opposition to your views. You may feel that it is important to arouse some opposition, but make sure that what you do stir up is intentional. Uranus in the tenth can also produce sudden changes in your own social status, such as an abrupt and disastrous fall from grace, which can result from letting your activities get out of control. One thing is certain, however; this relationship must be allowed to do its own thing.

Composite Uranus in the Eleventh House

Uranus in the eleventh house of the composite chart signifies that your guiding ideals are quite different from the usual ideals in a relationship of this kind. The eleventh house represents the ideals of a relationship (as opposed to its actual purposes, which come from the tenth house) and the kinds of friends that you have as a couple. You have your own reasons for being together, and you have chosen not to seek out the same things that others seek in life.

While most people marry for love, companionship, or sex, with this placement you might marry for mutual intellectual stimulation, or to work together for cause, or for some other unusual reason. This fact does not affect the viability of the relationship, no matter what type it is. If your motives are strong enough, they will serve the purpose just as well as more conventional motives.

You may also find that as a couple you are attracted to a different set of friends, people you would never have become involved with except for something that this relationship has opened up in you. This is a reflection of the fact that your relationship has brought you new expectations of life and made you more open to a variety of experiences.

Composite Uranus in the Twelfth House

Composite Uranus in the twelfth house creates situations that you will not understand until your consciousness has grown. The twelfth house relates to unconscious or barely conscious actions that the two of you commit, which eventually have very important consequences for you. The problem is that these consequences seem to have little connection with the actions that precipitated them. In fact the consequences usually seem to be creations of fate and beyond your control. But you can be sure that you have helped to bring them about, so it is very important to understand what is going on.

Uranus in the twelfth indicates that the two of you send out disruptive energies. You do little things to others that may not be obvious to you or to them. You make people angry, or you may make them feel that the two of you are an irritating disruption. It is hard to pin the problem to specific instances and causes, but the energies build up until something breaks. The result is that you are severely affected by outside disruptions that seem to have no apparent connection with the two of you.

It may be that you are caught in some difficult situation that you feel quite resentful about but can't admit. You try to give the appearance of going along with the situation, but you are continually sending out signals to others of resentment and the desire to rebel. This attracts troublesome disruptions in ways that may be subtle but are not necessarily occult. Do not try to hide the elements of your lives that you would like to alter, change, or rebel against. Express the energies somehow.

Composite Uranus Square Composite Neptune

The square of composite Uranus and Neptune occurs in the charts of the children of the early 1950s, who as young adults brought the drug culture to its climax, before it subsided. The problem signified by drugs and the drug culture is the problem of the nature of reality. One of the key phrases for Uranus-Neptune is revolutionary idealism, which is not content to merely exist but tries to impose itself upon the world and become part of the way you live.

Your relationship may have a radical feeling of disorientation. Ideally, the two of you should know yourselves and each other, but instead you feel totally lost about almost everything, including yourselves. This aspect will make it more difficult for you to find yourselves, unless you can learn to be hard-headed realists.

The only problem with your ideals is that even if realized, they might serve no useful purpose. You may be using these ideals as devices for escaping a reality that is not truly adverse but that you will not deal with. Perhaps you are afraid that the truth is too strong for you and that if forced to face it you will lose something that is very important to you. That, however, is more fear than truth. If you can learn to live together in the real world, you will be better able to make it all work.

Composite Uranus Trine Composite Neptune

Uranus trine Neptune occurs very frequently in the charts of people born in the late 1930s and early 1940s. Like many such aspects, the Uranus-Neptune trine expressed itself much more clearly when the generation born with it grew up than at the time it occurred. Its symbolic meaning is alternate states of consciousness. It was this age group that first became very much involved with LSD and the other psychedelic drugs and with the general issue of consciousness expansion.

In a relationship in which this aspect is prominently placed, the two of you will probably seek to explore new kinds of consciousness in the way you relate to each other. You may be interested in spiritual growth, mysticism, the occult, or other such phenomena.

Your relationship is likely to be unusually idealistic, especially since many of you have Neptune in Libra, the sign of relationships. You may experience it as a way of transcending the ordinary. In that case, watch out that you don't put too much of a strain on the relationship by demanding that your partner be more than human. You will not find divinity in someone else or in a relationship. At best you will find it in yourselves. Look for it there and then use each other to help bring it out.

Composite Uranus Opposition Composite Neptune

The opposition of Uranus and Neptune occurs only in the composite charts of people born early in the twentieth century.

This aspect signifies that either your ideals or your illusions will bring about changes and upsets in your relationship. It can indicate that one or both of you is unwilling to put up with what you consider "dull reality." You will try to make radical changes in the relationship, which will be difficult to adapt to. This aspect is a clear indication of impatient idealism.

Sometimes this aspect may signify ideological conflicts within a relationship, that is, great disagreements between you about fundamental philosophical beliefs. In this case you both adhere stubbornly to your own point of view and find it difficult to reach a compromise. You must develop a greater sympathy for each other's position, so that even if you do not agree, you can understand why your partner has his or her particular beliefs. At least you can learn to disagree amicably.

In some cases this aspect can indicate severe psychological disturbances within a relationship, particularly if it ties in with the composite Moon or Mercury. A key phrase for this opposition is "altered states of consciousness," such as with drug problems, psychological disorders, or alcoholism. Such a state will affect your relationship negatively.

Composite Uranus Sextile Composite Pluto

Uranus sextile Pluto occurs very frequently in the natal and composite charts of those born in the early 1940s. Usually, this aspect in the composite chart will not affect this relationship especially.

The symbolism of Uranus sextile Pluto is revolutionary change, but the sextile is not a very violent configuration. It suggests that your relationship has the capacity to evolve and grow as you face new conditions. It also implies that the two of you will in fact have to face new conditions. But you will probably regard this as a challenge, because you prefer change to the status quo.

Your outlook together and your way of dealing with the world around you is very strongly affected by your desire to examine every situation closely and come up with new ways of doing things. You are not satisfied with the usual methods of handling problems that arise between you. Most likely, if this is a love affair or a marriage, you will have an outside therapist help you discover what is disturbing your relationship. You will actually benefit from such encounters through personal growth and expanded awareness.

Composite Uranus Square Composite Pluto

The square of composite Uranus and Pluto is quite common in the charts of people born in the early 1930s. This was one of the aspects that signified the Great Depression; in fact, it represents the energy that made that period so revolutionary. During the 1930s, fascism made great inroads in Europe, and even in the U.S., many people sought radical solutions to the economic problems of the time. The sweeping, revolutionary changes of President Franklin Roosevelt's New Deal were also characteristic of the Uranus-Pluto square.

In a composite chart, this aspect indicates that there are times of great change in your relationship. The Uranus-Pluto square was transited in the horoscopes of individuals and of relationships in 1973 and 1974. During this period the characteristic energy was felt by many couples as a necessity either to radically change the basis of their relationship or to break up.

Wherever this aspect falls in the composite chart is an area in which the two of you must display considerable flexibility and willingness to adapt. If you try to resist the changes that must come in your relationship, you will experience an upheaval that will make it very difficult for your relationship to survive. On the other hand, if you can adapt and accept the challenges, your relationship will be revitalized and renewed. It will be like a completely new relationship. Pluto means death to the old order, but it also means the creative birth of the new. You must learn to look forward to this change.

Composite Uranus Conjunct Composite Ascendant

The conjunction of composite Uranus and Ascendant signifies a relationship that will probably have a strong impact on your lives. The nature of that impact can vary tremendously, depending in large part on your own attitudes.

First of all, this relationship will certainly expose you to a radically new kind of experience. It will not be the gentle consciousness-raising of Jupiter, but the jarring action of Uranus, the planet that challenges all your basic precepts about what life is and how it should be lived. Your reaction to Uranian energies is determined by how rigid you both are. The more flexible you are toward change and new experiences, the more constructive Uranus is likely to be. If the two of you are rather rigid, its effects can be devastating.

A relationship with this aspect will cause great changes in your lives. It may be that the two of you would not ordinarily be expected to get together, perhaps because of some difference in your backgrounds. Or it may be that one of you is always challenging the other. Sometimes this aspect means that you have come together precisely because the relationship does challenge your usual modes of thinking. It becomes a kind of rebellion against the world, which raises a problem.

This aspect often signifies instability in a relationship, simply because consciously or unconsciously you have come together to challenge or upset your usual patterns of life. This is fine until you try to settle down into some regular pattern together. Then the same restlessness that brought about your relationship may serve to break it up.

A relationship with this aspect in the composite chart must always stay loose and unstructured. Unless you allow it to follow its own unique course, it will not prove to be very stable or lasting.

Composite Uranus Sextile Composite Ascendant

The sextile of composite Uranus and Ascendant signifies a relationship that will be unique in many ways. It will cause the two of you to think about life in new ways that you would never have thought of until you met each other. You will not experience this as a disruptive change, however. Instead, it will be like a fresh breeze blowing through your minds and your lives, clearing away all your old and outworn attitudes and ideas.

One result of this change is that you will see elements of the world around you that you have never seen before, and this will enable you to enlarge your capacity to deal with life in appropriate ways. The sextile of Uranus and the composite Ascendant is quite disastrous to old habits in a relationship, but you can do very well without those old habits.

One likely change will be in the company you keep. Both of you will want increasingly to be around people who embody the new ways you have found of dealing with life.

The only point you must keep in mind is that any action of Uranus makes it difficult to hold on to old and cherished, but largely unconscious attachments, things that you want to retain although they have no real purpose in your lives. Even in a sextile aspect, Uranus is likely to produce circumstances that make it impossible to hold on to them. If you can let go gracefully, you will experience the effects of this aspect as totally refreshing and stimulating. If letting go is hard, the two of you may find this relationship disruptive and upsetting, although not as harsh as the square.

Composite Uranus Square Composite Ascendant

The square of composite Uranus to Ascendant can be quite a disruptive aspect in a composite chart. It signifies a relationship that is unstable because it offers constant challenges that may be difficult for the two of you to handle. First of all, it can mean that your directions in life are so radically different that you can't reconcile them easily. Unfortunately, you won't be able to deal with this problem just by letting matters be. You each have a tendency to goad the other, either consciously or unconsciously, and to challenge each other's ego. You each seem to regard the other as a representative of an established order that you have to rebel against.

In an otherwise good chart, the issue of rebellion may mean that you have come together in defiance of someone else. If you are lovers, for example, you may be rebelling against parents. Such a relationship exists simply as a form of rebellion against established standards. This can be an excellent binding force between you, until you have finished rebelling. As long as the disruptive energy of Uranus is focused outward, you will not have any great problems between you. But the day will come when you have to deal with each other, at which point you are likely to have the problems described in the first paragraph.

The only way to work with Uranus is to be very open to elements that are outside of your usual way of looking at things, and this includes elements of each other. If the two of you can broaden your views of the world and accept new challenges, you should be able to handle the energy of this aspect.

Composite Uranus Trine Composite Ascendant

The trine of composite Uranus to Ascendant signifies a relationship that will be very stimulating to you both. It will help you establish a new orientation to the world around you. Perhaps you were drawn to each other by a feeling of delicious outrageousness in the fact of your getting together. With each other, you will find freedom to express yourselves in new and different ways that you would never have dared before. But it all feels good, and you need not worry about negative consequences.

This relationship requires both of you to be flexible in your attitudes. If you cannot enjoy anything outside of an established routine, this is not likely to be a very happy relationship. In that case you will find it upsetting, but if you pass it by, you will be wasting a valuable opportunity to enlarge your own consciousness.

Assuming that you both are mentally flexible, as a couple you will be attracted to new ways of thinking that you might not have considered before; these attract you precisely because of their stimulating nature. In this relationship you absolutely cannot tolerate boredom, but that is not likely to be a problem. Uranus rules both real electricity and things that feel "electric" in nature. "Electricity" will permeate this relationship, giving it an excitement that will make it all worthwhile for both of you.

Composite Uranus Opposition Composite Ascendant

The opposition of the composite Uranus and Ascendant should be thought of as a conjunction between Uranus and the composite Descendant, which is a very significant point for understanding a relationship. Uranus on the composite Descendant signifies that it will be very difficult to settle this relationship into any accustomed and conventional patterns. For this reason it is often a sign of an unstable relationship, one that has many serious ups and downs and may even break up and come together again repeatedly. If the two of you are thinking of a marriage or some other legal arrangement, you would be well advised to give the matter a great deal of consideration. Trying to fit a relationship like this into any kind of legally set pattern is likely to trigger its most unstable aspects.

This relationship will work well as long as it revolutionizes your lives, which it will at first, and as long as it is exciting. After the initial excitement, however, you may have problems, because any kind of routine is anathema to this relationship. If this is a marriage, the two of you must operate with as few rules as possible. It may even be necessary to allow outside relationships with others as a matter of course. At any rate, you must not prohibit that possibility. If one of you begins to feel confined by this relationship, your troubles will begin. You cannot impose rules upon each other, only on yourselves.

One other problem that may arise with this aspect is that the two of you may be challenged by people outside the relationship. This may happen because you have unknowingly challenged them in some way, or you may be quite aware of how you did it. Others may try to disrupt this relationship and break it up, but if their power does not become too great, it may even be a binding force between you. Of course, circumstances could reach the point that it becomes impossible for you to stay together.

With this aspect in the composite chart, the two of you need to have many good and binding factors in your relationship, if it is to survive for any length of time.

Chapter Thirteen

Neptune

The Meaning of Neptune in the Composite Chart

Neptune in the composite chart is an energy that most people find quite difficult to handle. It has two quite separate areas of meaning that are ultimately connected, although they do not seem related on the surface.

First of all, Neptune is related to disappointment, delusion, deceit, falsehood, and the gradual disappearance of things. Yet it also represents whatever you idealize, legitimately and otherwise—that which is spiritual and mystical, which is actually at the root of love in its most spiritual sense, even more than Venus. It is the two-sidedness of Neptune that is so difficult to deal with.

To a considerable extent, all true love is based on your idealization of some aspect of the other person. That is one side of Neptune. But you must also keep in mind the reality of the situation and not make that person into something he or she is not. The nature of Neptune is such that you often go too far and turn the other person into a myth; when you discover the truth, bitter disappointment sets in. Yet if the Neptune energy were not working to some extent, you would not have been attracted to that person in the first place.

In a relationship, some things cannot be spelled out in words. It is necessary for two people to have some inner understanding of each other, or you will never be able to communicate very well. Neptune rules this kind of sensitivity within a relationship also. But again, its twofold nature can cause you to overdo your sensitivity, to the point where you make up things that aren't there or exaggerate the significance of what is.

How can you keep a balance? The answer lies in an aspect of Neptune that provides the key to really understanding it. Neptune is a totally selfless energy, not readily harnessed to the demands of the human ego. If you have a strong ego-wish that something be a certain way, Neptune's involvement becomes dangerous. The more your ego needs to enforce a situation, the more Neptune will delude you about it. Your own wishes seem to create a barrier to your seeing clearly, because you are too involved in the situation. Neptune often makes the two of you think that what you want is already so, even when it isn't.

However, if you can learn to accept the situation as it is, Neptune will help you to learn even more. If you can hold your ideals and still be able to deal with reality, Neptune may even help you realize your ideals.

Neptune in the chart tells about those areas of the relationship that are idealized, maybe dangerously so. It tells about the depth of spiritual communication and about the extent to which all communication is disrupted by your illusions about each other.

Composite Neptune in the First House

With composite Neptune in the first house of a chart, there is a great danger that the two of you don't understand what this relationship is all about. You each may have quite widely different views of your relationship, with neither of you aware of the difference. Or you may have a fairly clear idea about the direction you should take as a couple, but you have difficulty understanding where you are at a particular time.

Typical of the problems that Neptune induces is a situation that can occur in a love relationship. One of you thinks that everything is beautiful and ideal, and the world may agree, for a first-house Neptune can deceive others as well as yourselves. But you will discover that something is radically wrong between you when you wake up one morning to find that the other person is gone, having been unhappy for months.

Another common Neptune pattern that applies here, although it is even more characteristic of the seventh house, is that one of you sacrifices yourself to "save" the other from some problem. Or you both may offer yourselves in service to the world. This is usually the rankest form of self-delusion, because one or both of you is using this pattern as a device for working out your own hangups. People do not "save" each other in this manner.

Unfortunately there are endless possible sources of self-delusion. But a first-house Neptune does signify that you must work for a realistic relationship and not let your ideals overwhelm your ability to see the truth. Yet at the same time you must not surrender your ideals.

Composite Neptune in the Second House

With Neptune in the second house of the composite chart, there is likely to be some confusion between you about what you hold to be important, for the second is the house of whatever one values, most commonly but not exclusively your material resources. With Neptune here, it may simply be unclear to either of you just what you do value. You may not even know, in which case you must find out, because if you don't know what you consider important, you will find out only when someone takes it away.

But Neptune in the second house may also signify a great confusion about managing your money and possessions. The two of you may have serious misconceptions or be totally ignorant of how to deal with what you own. Yet because of Neptune's double nature, you may also share an uncanny sense of where to find money and have the ability to sniff it out in very unlikely places. With this placement, it is very important for the two of you to examine all matters ruled by the second house to determine whether you are experiencing the first or the second effect.

One of two situations will apply to you. In the first, material possessions are not very important to the two of you, in which case you should have no problems with them. On the other hand, if they are important, they should not be to such an extent, and then you probably will have trouble with them. Neptune does not deny things in general so much as it denies things to which you are too attached.

Composite Neptune in the Third House

Neptune in the third house of the composite chart is usually experienced as confusing to the mind, for in its lower manifestations, Neptune is a planet of confusion. The third is the house of the mind functioning on a day-to-day level, routinely, without much consciousness of itself.

In a relationship, Neptune in the third house can create very severe difficulties in communication between you, at least verbally. You have difficulty putting into words what you want to say. Strangely enough, though, Neptune may actually improve your nonverbal, intuitive communication, while it is fouling up verbal communication. You may in fact have a very good intuitive understanding of this relationship, even when you cannot talk about it.

Beware of subtle feelings of inferiority preventing either of you from saying what you want. You have every right to speak to each other and make yourselves understood.

Because the third house is the house of immediate environment, Neptune here also has the effect of confusing your relationship to the people around you. They may do things that the two of you do not clearly understand, or they may appear to deceive you. In a marriage or love relationship, relatives may be particularly troublesome this way. The path to take is to learn to communicate with everyone, even though that may be difficult.

Composite Neptune in the Fourth House

The fourth house is one of the most ambiguous placements for composite Neptune. If yours is a relationship that could have some recognizable home, it is likely to be an ideal that the two of you will work very hard to attain. You daydream about it together, saying, "How nice it would be if we had a home of our own," or "A home like this," or phrases of that sort. Yet at the same time, you tend to totally ignore what is actually going on in your home. Frequently, what is happening is important and you should know about it, but you are too wrapped up in your private fantasy world.

Sometimes the fourth-house Neptune indicates that although your personal lives together have become quite difficult, neither of you is paying any attention to that fact.

As always with Neptune, it is neither possible nor desirable to give up your ideals. What is necessary is to learn to recognize reality and to allow your ideals and reality to coexist without conflict in your world. At its highest, a fourth-house Neptune can signify that spiritual ideals are at the very basis of this relationship. If this is the case, most of the problems described above will not be as difficult for you.

Composite Neptune in the Fifth House

Neptune in the fifth house of a composite chart will have the strongest effect on a personal relationship, especially a love affair or marriage. In these instances, at its best it denotes a particularly idealized and refined kind of love. The nonphysical tendencies of Neptune may even have such a great influence that the relationship will be platonic. This happens when Neptune is working out well.

However, more commonly, one of you romanticizes your relationship much too much. Everything seems to you to be perfect, ideal, and beautiful, when actually there are serious problems, which are being covered over by a romantic fog. Such a relationship can be very beautiful while it lasts, but the end usually comes in a crash of disappointment when the truth comes out, and the ideal lover is seen to be at best an ordinary man or woman and at worst a lout.

Neptune can create the fact as well as the illusion of a highly spiritual relationship, particularly the sort in which one of you views the other as a savior. While this view may be justified in some instances, the problem is that the two of you are not relating as equals, as you should in order to grow from your encounter. Or the Neptune energy may take the reverse tack, with one of you spending your time caring for the other because of some severe problem that he or she has. Here again you are not relating as equals.

As is usual with Neptune, you must learn to live with reality as well as with your ideals. At the same time you must be very certain that you are really assisting each other and not working out your own hangups by seeming to help your partner. Help given in that spirit is no help at all and only serves to perpetuate your problems.

Composite Neptune in the Sixth House

Composite Neptune in the sixth house indicates that the two of you may have a very high ideal of service to others, or else you may be unclear about what you are supposed to do as a couple. The sixth is the house of responsibilities, duties, and work, and Neptune makes these a possible source of confusion. Sometimes a sixth-house Neptune can indicate that the relationship has troubles of obscure origin. In many ways, however, this house placement is not bad, because, like Neptune, it demands putting something else before your own wishes.

Work, or just plain getting things done, becomes kind of a philosophical ideal for a couple with this placement. But remember that every relationship must provide to some extent for the individuals' legitimate demands for self-expression. Not everything can be done for some "higher" cause. Whether or not you acknowledge them as such, your own needs are legitimate and must be met.

If the two of you become too wrapped up in the ideal of service, either to each other or to others, it can lead to a very subtle form of resentment, in which one or both of you plays the martyr. Thus, every time you do something for your partner, you make him or her pay for it in ways that are not very subtle but are difficult to deal with. If you are sincere about your ideal of service, fine, but give yourselves room to get what you need in the relationship also.

Composite Neptune in the Seventh House

With Neptune in the seventh house of the composite chart, the two of you will have to be very careful that you understand the true nature of this relationship, particularly if it is a partnership, such as a marriage or a business partnership. This placement can make such a relationship seem quite different from what it is in reality.

Neptune tends to subvert one of the most important aspects of the seventh house, namely, one-to-one relationships between equals. With Neptune in this house, regardless of the type of relationship, you often get the "savior-victim" pattern, as one astrologer refers to it. One of you looks for someone to rescue you from your problems, while the other looks for someone to save. In reality you both are in equally bad shape, because neither of you can relate on an equal, face-to-face level.

Typical of this syndrome is the "selfless" wife caring for her indigent, alcoholic husband, apparently giving no thought to herself. You can be sure that both are really getting what they want from this situation, because neither has to take the responsibility of handling a normal relationship, which is what they truly need.

Neptune in the seventh house can also simply indicate a relationship in which each of you is dealing with the other not as a real person, but as an ideal image derived from inside yourself rather than from the actual experience of the other person. Such a relationship is bound to end in a major disappointment when one discovers that the other is not the ideal that was sought.

Yet a seventh-house Neptune can indicate a relationship that really does have powerful spiritual bonds, in which the two of you have a deep intuitive understanding of each other. But this requires understanding and accepting the truth about yourselves and each other.

Composite Neptune in the Eighth House

Neptune in the eighth house of a composite chart signifies that a major source of confusion and uncertainty in your relationship may be the material resources that you hold jointly or that concern both of you. Neptune's energy is nonmaterial in nature, so the area of the chart affected by Neptune will have difficulty with material things. Because the eighth is the house of joint resources, this effect is felt particularly strongly here.

Obviously, this will affect a business or professional association most, but the financial dealings of any relationship except the most casual friendship will be affected. All areas involving business and financial transactions should be regarded with some care. Neptune is the planet of deception and fraud, and these are the dangers you may encounter in your financial dealings.

However, Neptune has two sides here, just as it does in the other houses. It can also indicate tremendous intuitive awareness about financial and material resources. And it is very hard to tell when Neptune will have either of these two effects. The only solution is to be very careful until you know what Neptune is doing. Even if the relationship is generally working out well for both of you, be prepared for an occasional unpleasant surprise.

The eighth is also the house of major transformations that can occur within a relationship. Neptune here can indicate that hidden and unseen factors in the world around you are causing changes that are difficult to understand. You will have to be very clear in your thinking in order to examine such factors.

Composite Neptune in the Ninth House

Neptune in the ninth house of the composite chart signifies that this relationship is enormously concerned with ideals. The ninth is the house of higher mentality—the mind as it views the world, conscious of doing so. This house relates to your overall philosophy of life and the mental structure through which you interpret the world. Neptune here gives this whole area a mystical and religious flavor, or at least a fondness for delving into psychic or spiritual matters. In a composite chart this placement could signify that the two of you are very much concerned with such matters in this relationship.

It is also possible that the ninth house signifies that your ways of thinking about the world are confused by this relationship. There is a danger that you could be looking at the world either through rose-colored glasses or, quite the reverse, from a needlessly pessimistic point of view. Either way, the ninth house indicates that the two of you are dealing with the world in a way that is not entirely realistic, and therefore leaves you open to disappointment. It is all right to be idealistic, but do not confuse your ideals with the facts.

Composite Neptune in the Tenth House

Neptune in the tenth house of the composite chart can be a source of difficulty, for it indicates great confusion about exactly what this relationship is and how it fits into the world at large. One manifestation of a tenth-house Neptune is that the two of you may be affected by all sorts of things that others are totally unaware of. On the surface your relationship may appear perfectly proper, but this appearance conceals situations that would make people think quite differently about you, if they knew. Do not get caught in the trap of a relationship that is all illusory appearance with no substance behind it.

The tenth-house Neptune can also indicate that the two of you do not have any clear sense of where your relationship is going or what its purpose is. In an individual chart, this is the house of one's profession. Similarly, in a composite chart, the tenth tells something about what purpose a relationship serves for you. Neptune makes it hard to perceive that purpose clearly.

On the other hand it is also possible that this placement indicates the actual purpose of your relationship. Neptune is the planet of ego-transcendence, the process of going beyond your own narrowly conceived ends. It helps make you more concerned about your needs in a greater metaphysical context. In the tenth house of the composite chart, Neptune may signify a relationship in which each of you must learn to deny your own desires in favor of another's, as a way of satisfying your greater needs. It can also signify that you are heavily involved on a professional level with metaphysical or spiritual activities.

Composite Neptune in the Eleventh House

Neptune in the eleventh house of the composite chart indicates an unusually idealistic relationship. The eleventh is the house of hopes and wishes, and with Neptune, the planet of ideals, it makes an extremely idealistic combination. Be careful that your expectations of this relationship are not excessive. Try to relate to your partner for what he or she really is, not for what you imagine or dream.

As in the other houses that concern relationships, Neptune here can transform a relationship that normally would have been sexual into a platonic affair. This is because of Neptune's nonphysical nature. You both may feel that physical love is not pure enough for the kind of idealism you share.

As the house of friendship, the eleventh can also signify the kinds of friends that you attract through being together. Neptune indicates that your friends are likely to be people who are in some way Neptunian. They may be very artistic or sensitive or involved in occult or psychic matters. Or they may simply be unreliable or dishonest. They could even represent both these extremes. Wherever Neptune falls in the chart is the area you have to be most clear about and understand what is really happening, because you are most likely to delude yourselves in that area.

Composite Neptune in the Twelfth House

The twelfth is Neptune's natural house, according to the traditions of astrology. Therefore this placement in the composite chart is likely to be relatively untroublesome. Both Neptune and the twelfth house stand for the need to go beyond oneself and deal with a higher-order universe. At its best, a twelfth-house Neptune indicates that both of you are able to give to each other and to the relationship what is needed to make matters work out in the best way. At the critical moments, when it really counts, you each can disregard your ego's demands and do what must be done without having to protect your own emotional investment. You both are willing and able to sacrifice to the common good when it is necessary.

Oddly enough, however, this can also be a fault, if you carry it too far. The negative side of this principle is the martyr attitude, a peculiar kind of passive aggressiveness. The partner with this attitude always yields to the other's demands, while at the same time making him or her feel as guilty as possible for taking advantage of a weakness. This can be quite a sincere attitude, in that one of you really believes that you are unworthy of a good break from your partner, and therefore you don't stand up for your rights.

Remember that however selfless you think you are, both of you must get something valid from this relationship, or it won't be any good for either of you. Eventually, unacknowledged, hidden aggressions will come out into the open and begin to foul up your relationship.

Composite Neptune Conjunct Composite Ascendant

The conjunction of composite Neptune with Ascendant has a twofold significance. One or the other of its manifestations will emerge in the course of your relationship. But in either case, a strongly placed Neptune such as this introduces the element of idealism. The question is, what kind of idealism and how does it affect your ability to see the truth?

At its highest, this aspect indicates that there is a strong spiritual bond between you. An invisible thread links the two of you together, so that without having to say very much, you each can feel what the other is thinking. You would be willing to do almost anything for each other. You feel as if you have been truly united into one being, which is ultimately the highest form of love.

In such an idealistic relationship, however, the emphasis is on a spiritual bond. In a relationship that might otherwise be sexual, this aspect may give you such a strong concern for the spiritual that you do not wish to "contaminate" it with physical contact, or at least that is how it appears to you. Therefore, this aspect can be an indication of a platonic relationship.

Unfortunately, such an ideal bond is not usually realized. More commonly this aspect indicates a relationship in which there is an unusual amount of illusion and self-deception. The beautiful selflessness of the ideal is corrupted into self-martyrdom, which is often used as a means of controlling the other.

Usually the problem is that one of the partners is not relating to the other as a real human being. Instead, you create a mental ideal, which you force the other person to fit, whether or not it is appropriate. But when the other person's real identity emerges, you will experience great disappointment. This theme is repeated again and again, wherever Neptune is strong. You must stop searching for an ideal and be willing to appreciate your partner as he or she actually is. Only then can you get the best out of the relationship. And by so doing you may be able to experience the higher manifestation of this aspect.

Composite Neptune Sextile Composite Ascendant

The sextile of composite Neptune and Ascendant emphasizes the idealistic and sensitive sides of this relationship. The two of you have a great deal more sensitivity to each other's needs than most couples do, and you work well together on an intuitive level. Much of the communication that two people usually have to spell out for each other is obvious to the two of you without words. This saves a lot of time in establishing the basis of the relationship. Just be careful that your idealism about each other does not become unrealistic. You must appreciate the reality of what you are to each other and not dwell in some illusion.

If this is potentially a sexual relationship, this aspect may make you friends rather than lovers. It can be a sign of a platonic relationship, partly because you both feel that the spiritual bond between you would be tainted if you came together physically. It may be that you are afraid of the emotional upsets and entanglements that would arise from a sexual relationship. But this is not because of a desire for freedom; it is that you do not want to disturb your "beautiful friendship" with the kind of concerns that sex introduces.

At the same time, the experience of this relationship may make you both feel more idealistic about the world in general. This aspect can be a sign of seeing the world "through rose-colored glasses." Here again, you must be careful not to let your idealism overwhelm your sense of reality. You may tend to gloss over the flaws in your immediate surroundings, which in the long run could prove quite detrimental to your relationship.

If you can keep your feet on the ground without losing the sense of the beautiful that Neptune can bring, you should not have too much trouble with this aspect, and you should experience its good qualities as well.

Composite Neptune Square Composite Ascendant

The square of composite Neptune to Ascendant can be quite a difficult aspect. It means that the two of you are going to have trouble finding out exactly what this relationship is all about. And for some reason you may not feel very confident that it will last. There is a deep sense of insecurity in a relationship such as this—insecurity about yourselves and each other.

If you are living together, you may find that your home life embodies this insecurity. You can never quite figure out what is going on in your most intimate surroundings, and even if you do, you are never sure that you aren't kidding yourselves.

In a relationship that does not include living together, you may have a great deal of trouble deciding exactly what your mutual objectives are. Where do you want to go, both as individuals and as a couple? This problem can be compounded by exaggerated ideals about what you ought to be doing together.

If your relationship is otherwise sound, the worst attributes of this aspect can be avoided. After the confusion is gone and you have learned to experience tranquility with each other, you will be able to build a deep spiritual bond between you. Such a bond arises from the ability to sense what is going on inside each other. But you will have to work out many problems before you can do that.

Composite Neptune Trine Composite Ascendant

The trine of composite Neptune and Ascendant indicates a relationship in which idealistic and spiritual elements are very strong.

If you are a man and woman, this aspect may be a sign of a platonic relationship. Here, as in other Neptune-Ascendant combinations, the nonphysical is often emphasized at the expense of the physical. Neptune has a very strong world-denying quality. Even if your relationship is not platonic, there will still be a strong spiritual emphasis.

A related manifestation, but one that applies to any type of relationship, is that one of you may feel very strongly that the other has been sent to you as a kind of spiritual guide. It is quite likely that this is true, but you must understand that the guidance will go in both directions. It is not a one-way teacher-disciple relationship, but a mutual teaching situation. Also, this relationship may stimulate interest in occult and metaphysical studies.

In a love relationship there is often a strong tendency toward excessive romanticism. You both may idealize the relationship and each other to a degree beyond all reason. Be very careful of this, and make sure that you are relating to your real partner and not to some illusion you have created.

In a marriage, this aspect sometimes signifies that you may have a problem with one of your children, usually allergies or a similar long-term, mild debility. It may not be very serious, but you should watch for it.

In general, this aspect can make a relationship quite beautiful, although not totally realistic. Strive to emphasize the beautiful without being carried away by your own idealism.

Composite Neptune Opposition Composite Ascendant

The opposition of composite Neptune and Ascendant is really a conjunction of Neptune and the composite Descendant, which is a very important point for understanding a relationship.

This aspect can have a number of effects, most of which are quite difficult to deal with. First of all, it implies that something is preventing this from being a true relationship between equals. It is very often the case that one of you has entered the relationship with the idea of sacrificing yourself in order to "help" the other. Quotation marks are used, because the "help" is usually designed to ensure that the "helped" partner remains dependent on the "helper." There is a very subtle kind of egotism operating here under the disguise of self-sacrifice.

Sometimes this symbolism takes the form of one of the persons being an alcoholic or having some other type of psychological disorder, which requires much attention and so-called sacrifice from the other.

At other times the effect of this aspect is simply to make a relationship very unrealistic. There is a danger that the two of you are not relating to each other but to some ideal image you have created in your minds. Instead of dealing with your real personalities, you impose this image on each other.

There is also another possible manifestation of this aspect. It may be that you are quite realistic about each other, but not terribly realistic as a couple about others outside of your relationship whom you must deal with. This is particularly so with people you consult for advice, such as lawyers, doctors, or counselors. For some reason, the advice these people give you is misleading rather than helpful. Be quite careful when working with such people, and do not take their advice uncritically. You may also experience difficulties with people who oppose your relationship, not openly, but by secretive acts.

With this aspect in the chart, it is very important that neither of you indulge in fantasies about matters that must be dealt with realistically.

Chapter Fourteen
Pluto

The Meaning of Pluto in the Composite Chart

Pluto is the planet of death and regeneration. In a composite chart it represents those energies that cause a relationship to go through periods of heavy change. When Pluto is operative, something goes out of existence and a new order comes into being. Its action is absolutely essential to prevent the stagnation that occurs when an old way of life has outlived its purpose. The old must be cleared away to make room for the new state of being that will follow. When dealing with Pluto, you must let go of whatever is going through the Plutonian crisis. If you try to hold on to something that is properly dead, you will not succeed in saving it. You will only make the situation worse.

Pluto operates with such tremendous power that it may be divorced from its "death and regeneration" aspect and be experienced purely as power. The power results from the inevitability of Pluto's transforming quality. The transformations ruled by Pluto are those that arise from the very nature of what is transformed. Its effect is as much an integral part of an entity as an object's weight, size, and color. Every living thing contains the set of circumstances that will eventually bring about all its fundamental changes, including its death. The power of Pluto comes from within.

In a relationship, Pluto is very often experienced as power conflicts between the two of you. In a sexual relationship it also gives special power and impact to your emotions and makes every happening very dramatic and important. This heaviness is one of the more difficult attributes of the planet, because it can warp your perspective completely.

The house position of Pluto indicates the area of the relationship in which there is most likely to be a conflict of power, either between the two of you or with the outside world. It also indicates which area of the relationship is most likely to be transformed through your being together and, as a result, which area is most likely to produce crises.

The aspects to Pluto indicate whether this energy will be experienced as difficult or easy and what other energy patterns it will be linked with.

Composite Pluto in the First House

Pluto in the first house of a composite chart indicates that this relationship will try to project itself onto the world with some degree of power, that it exists with the intention of making changes in the surrounding world. It will also have a great impact on the two of you.

It may be that you want to bring about some kind of reform, or it may simply be that you want to have the power to affect your environment strongly. In either case, be very careful how you use the power that this relationship will call up from within you. When Pluto's energies get too strong, they tend to provoke strong antagonism in others, who will turn against you and try to bring down your efforts.

This energy can also be something that transforms both of you. Pluto rules major psychological transformations, those that are related to psychotherapy. A relationship with this placement often brings about major changes in you, much like those induced in therapy. In other words, this relationship is likely to have a very powerful effect on both of you. The only way that this placement can cause a serious problem in the long run is if you try to resist the effects of Pluto. Go along with whatever is happening and do not try to fight it. If you learn to flow with the energy, your relationship will work out as it should.

Composite Pluto in the Second House

With composite Pluto in the second house, the two of you may find that acquiring property becomes a strong and overriding passion. It is as if you unconsciously regard the material world as the source of all power. You feel that you must control it in order to keep control over your own lives. However, too great a concern with acquiring property and possessions can become a factor that controls your life, thus causing you to lose the very control you were seeking.

But this placement does not always work out on the material plane. It can indicate that this relationship enforces a strong sense of values in both of you. Or, if you cannot agree on your values, they will be a source of conflict. Whether or not you agree, this relationship is quite likely to change your sense of values. This fact in itself may cause conflict between you, if you cannot develop the flexibility needed to accommodate each other's value systems.

Property or material resources may become a factor in this relationship in another way. They may be a decisive factor in restricting your movement or your development as a couple. Or property and possessions may become a controlling issue in your lives. This problem ultimately stems from the excessive concern with your value systems that has been discussed. You must learn to give material resources precisely the importance they deserve, and no more. Pluto in the second house often makes these matters too important.

Composite Pluto in the Third House

Composite Pluto in the third house indicates that this relationship will have a profound effect upon the thinking of both of you. In turn, the two of you are likely to have an impact on the thinking of other people around you. Pluto in the third indicates deep, profound thought whose purpose is to understand the forces that lie behind events.

In more concrete terms, you are likely to spend a considerable amount of time discussing the relationship itself and trying to analyze what makes it tick. You will also look more deeply into yourselves to find out what makes you act as you do in a relationship. The end result of this introspection could be a considerable increase in your understanding of each other as well as yourselves.

The danger lies in the other side of the third-house Pluto, a side whose effects should be minimized or avoided altogether. Because the third is a house of communication, Pluto here may indicate that one or both of you will try to mold the other's mind and thinking according to your own beliefs. Most people do this to some extent, but the danger here is that your efforts to convince your partner will become an all-pervading concern, to the point that the other may feel that he or she is being brainwashed and that the only solution is to flee from the situation. Obviously this can be very dangerous to the relationship.

It is also possible that the two of you will turn the energy outward and make a career of influencing others to adopt your point of view. If you do so with subtlety, this is all right, but watch out for a backlash from others.

Composite Pluto in the Fourth House

The fourth house can be a very important and critical position for Pluto in a composite chart. It indicates that powerful forces are at work in the innermost depths of this relationship. The actual effects of this can vary considerably. For instance, the fourth house rules the past. Therefore you may find that past circumstances have a stronger than usual conditioning effect on the course of your relationship.

The fourth house also rules the deepest levels of the unconscious mind, so the two of you may act out very deep, unconsciously motivated patterns that change the course of your relationship. It is very important to establish whether this is happening. If you can ascertain that some of your problems are being caused by your individual mental patterns rather than by external events, then you can begin to deal with the problems.

In a love relationship or marriage, one or more of your parents may have an unusual degree of influence on the relationship. Unfortunately one cannot tell from Pluto's house position alone whether that influence will be good or bad.

The fourth house also rules the home, and in a relationship that has a clearly recognizable home, very powerful forces may be experienced there. The problem is that home should be a place where you can get away from pressure, but with Pluto in the fourth house, home could be the place where pressure is most intense.

Whatever the effect of the fourth-house Pluto, it does provide for resolution of its problems, because it gives you the desire and the ability to get at the depths of your own being. Just don't carry it so far that you begin to lose all perspective about life.

Composite Pluto in the Fifth House

Composite Pluto in the fifth house has its most intense expression in a personal relationship or love affair that involves deep feelings. The fifth is the house of self-expression, the house of your own being. Pluto here indicates that in this relationship it is unusually important for both of you to be able to express yourselves fully. You each have a powerful drive for self-expression.

In a love affair this placement can signify extremely powerful emotions that make you feel that this relationship is extraordinary. However, it must be pointed out that by itself Pluto does not specify which feelings are so strong. If your love is strong, Pluto in the fifth will intensify that, but if the forces of discord are strong, Pluto will intensify them also. Whatever the dominant emotions are, they will be experienced strongly.

In a sexual relationship, physical sex will assume a greater than usual importance and will be experienced as an escape from the everyday world. But that is a fairly heavy burden to place upon sex, and unless the relationship is working on a physical level, you are likely to have severe difficulties. Pluto in the fifth house does not indicate a platonic relationship.

The relationship itself may be viewed, at least subconsciously, as a vehicle for self-regeneration, for making a new person out of yourself. This too places a heavy burden on a relationship, but it may very well fulfill that purpose.

Composite Pluto in the Sixth House

Pluto in the sixth house of the composite chart gives importance to duties and responsibilities, to work that must be done. In a relationship, this work may be what the two of you must do in order to maintain the relationship.

The actual effect of this placement varies. On the one hand, it can give the two of you a strong desire to get things done. It provides a kind of ambition, not to get ahead, but rather to keep busy. In a personal relationship you may feel that you must work constantly to keep the relationship moving, that it will grow and develop only through constant effort.

But there may also be a reverse effect, in which the continued necessity to get things done strangles the relationship, and duty gets in the way of joyful self-expression. The two of you may feel you always have to try very hard to make anything happen; there is a continual sense of effort and struggle.

Which of these two effects comes about depends largely on your individual attitudes toward responsibility. If you make the effort to fulfill each other's needs, your relationship will grow. It will also confront its greatest challenges, but they are the basis of growth in a relationship.

Composite Pluto in the Seventh House

Composite Pluto in the seventh house can have two quite opposite effects. On the one hand it can signify that the two of you work very hard to create a viable relationship. You will make any necessary changes in yourselves in order to make it work. And at the same time you both are aware that this is a team effort, and neither of you takes on an unfair share of the burden.

You recognize that this relationship is having a great impact on both of you, and you experience it as a way of gaining a new, regenerated life. This can be expected if your relationship is otherwise quite good.

If there is a great deal of stress, however, a quite different effect will emerge. In this case each of you will continually try to dominate the other: in other words, a power struggle. If one of you wins this struggle, the other will feel extremely stifled, which will probably lead to further trouble. The "loser" may accept fate and continue in the relationship with a disgruntled, grudging acceptance, taking every opportunity to make the other's life miserable. On the other hand, he or she might just disappear rather than risk a losing confrontation. If neither of you wins, the battle simply goes on and on.

Most couples experience a mixture of good and bad effects from a seventh-house Pluto. If you wish to keep this relationship going, continue working together for growth and development. And try to lower the pressure.

Composite Pluto in the Eighth House

The eighth house is Pluto's natural home among the houses, but the effect of this is simply to make its action, for good or bad, more intense. A relationship with an eighth-house Pluto will have many major changes and periods of transformation. It gives an intensity to whatever emotional involvement you have with each other.

In a relationship with this placement, your innermost psychological drives will be brought out into the open and examined. This process may not always be pleasant, but nevertheless it is good to have it happen from time to time. If you allow it to happen you will learn a great deal about yourselves, and that can only be good. In many ways this relationship is a mirror in which you can see your own soul reflected. Remember that, when you are tempted to blame each other for your problems.

A sexual relationship with Pluto in the eighth house will be particularly intense. Sex will be more than simply sex, it will also be a pathway to self-transcendence. That is, you can use sex as a vehicle to carry you away from the ordinary concerns of reality into an experience beyond, an experience everyone should ultimately have in order to make their lives meaningful. In such a relationship physical sex has a very strong metaphysical and philosophical importance that extends far beyond the physical nature of the act.

However, Pluto is an energy that is not easily expressed in words, and you probably won't think too much about the importance of your sexual relationship in philosophical terms. You will simply feel that sex has a greater significance to the two of you than to most couples.

In other relationships, the eighth-house Pluto may create a curious bond that seems to hold you together even when you do not want it to. You may feel that you are trapped in this relationship, although that is not really the case. It is more likely that both of you are deriving an obscure satisfaction from what you do to each other and have actually built up a dependency between you on this basis. If you are honest with yourselves, you will see what is happening and will be able to deal with it. It is not fate that has created this relationship, it is the two of you, with your acknowledged and unacknowledged needs.

Composite Pluto in the Ninth House

Pluto in the ninth house of a composite chart signifies that the two of you will affect each other's way of looking at the world in a very fundamental manner. And you will have the capability of affecting those around you in the same way.

Pluto in the ninth house represents an energy that wants to "convince" others of its point of view. "Convince" is in quotation marks because it may seem to those being convinced that "bludgeoned" is a better word. You will have a strong effect on each other, and together you will have a great impact on other people. There is no need to make a special effort to do this, beyond what happens naturally; in fact, it is not a good idea.

The energy of Pluto should never be harnessed to your ego. You should not try to use this energy to show people that you are right, simply to reinforce your ego. Most people want to know the truth in order to be right, not to understand and gain wisdom for themselves. But when you use the energy of Pluto for this purpose, which is very likely in the ninth house, others are provoked to try to prove you wrong. And they will try very hard, even at the risk of really hurting you.

In a relationship, you run a great risk of doing this to each other or to those around you. This can make for a very difficult situation, because necessary communication is replaced by contests of "rightness" between you. The things that must be said are not.

Kept under reasonable control, the ninth-house Pluto can mean that the two of you have an uncannily deep perception into the basic psychological nature of your relationship. You can use this perception to make needed changes in your relationship and to adapt to the changing world around you.

Composite Pluto in the Tenth House

Pluto in the tenth house of a composite chart signifies that there is a very powerful energy in this relationship that is strongly oriented to attaining some objective. The nature of the objective that you seek will depend upon the nature of the relationship, but in every case it will have to do with making changes in the world around you.

A tenth-house Pluto means that the relationship will somehow heighten your ambitions as a couple. Other people will feel that the two of you are very powerful, even if separately you do not impress them that way. At the same time, this relationship will alter and transform your life direction and heighten your desire to achieve your objectives.

If the two of you handle the energies of this position well, it is a good indication that together you can achieve something of note. Perhaps you will gain power in business or politics, or perhaps you will simply become influential among the people around you. Or you may feel the effects most strongly between you, as this experience helps you to discover what you really want to do with your lives and to start doing something about it.

But there is some danger if the energy is not handled well. Pluto in the tenth house can be destructive, and its effect is to utterly ruin your reputations, and possibly some more fundamental aspect of your lives. Usually this happens because you have been ruthless in some way, either toward others or with each other. Pluto here can signify that you let no one stand in your way as you strive to get where you want to go. But when you encounter a stronger person or a situation that you cannot control, havoc breaks loose.

The only way to deal with this is to control your ruthlessness. Keep in mind other people's needs and wants as the two of you pursue the goals and objectives you have set for yourselves. And treat each other with the same consideration.

Composite Pluto in the Eleventh House

Composite Pluto in the eleventh house brings to a relationship ideals and hopes that you will feel very strongly about and work very hard for. You both feel that you have not come together casually and that this association has great importance for your lives. You have a very strong emotional involvement with your ideals and if necessary will fight to maintain them against all comers. By the same token you will work hard together to accomplish what you want.

This kind of intensity attracts others who are similarly inclined. And since the eleventh is also the house of friends, this placement of Pluto signifies that your friends either are very emotionally intense people, or they possess some kind of power, or both. The power can be anything from an intense aura of power that radiates from them to actual power on the material plane, as in business or government. Pluto is by nature somewhat secretive, and the friends that the two of you attract are not likely to be people who are known to the world at large, but rather those who wield power from behind the scenes.

An eleventh-house Pluto may also signify that the two of you are involved in large-scale humanitarian movements that seek to transform and regenerate the world, such as reform and revolutionary movements, movements of mass consciousness, and so forth.

Composite Pluto in the Twelfth House

Composite Pluto in the twelfth house signifies that this relationship will expose all kinds of previously hidden psychological characteristics, which will necessitate a strong inner psychological transformation in both of you. Fortunately, this position also signifies that you will be very interested in working with each other on this level. While you may have great resistance to some things in this relationship, you won't resist the idea of exposing these characteristics in the first place. Inward transformation is one of the objectives of this relationship, and you both know it.

Whatever comes up between you should be dealt with immediately, because Pluto's energies can smolder for a long time if not dealt with right away. And when they do smolder, they break out at last with such a bitter fury and fiery intensity that it is difficult for a relationship to survive.

Another effect of this position is a kind of "leaking out" of energy, so that the two of you unknowingly radiate an intense and powerful energy. But others react to this and often become afraid, because they do not know what the energy signifies. This situation often causes people to work against you behind your back.

The twelfth is traditionally the house of secret enemies, usually generated in the way described above. Your actions and manner of acting somehow trigger a response in others that makes them work against you. To deal with this it is necessary to be straightforward in your dealings with others and make clear to them exactly what you intend to do in any situation.

Composite Pluto Conjunct Composite Ascendant

The conjunction of composite Pluto and Ascendant is a sign of a profound relationship. Powerful forces are at work here, which can manifest themselves either in a very positive way, a very negative way, or in some combination of positive and negative. Pluto, the symbol of death and regeneration, works with great power and force. Consequently, you can expect that this relationship will call up energies within you both that you probably never knew existed.

At its most positive, this relationship will bring out forces in each of you that will completely transform your lives and set you on a totally new path. You will experience this relationship with an intensity that will affect every area of your life. Often, if the two of you are involved in a heavily Plutonian relationship, you will feel a tremendous fascination for each other that pushes aside all other considerations.

Sometimes the fascination is felt as a sinister force leading you down an evil path, and often that sense of evil is the source of the fascination. Whether or not the relationship really leads down an evil path depends on other factors in the relationship. In itself Pluto is not any more evil than the other planets, but its energies are so strong that they can overcome ethical considerations. Hence the "evil" of Pluto's fascinations.

There is a negative side of Pluto that you may experience, particularly if this is not a very sound relationship in other ways. It can signify intense power struggles between the two of you, in which one partner feels an irresistible power emanating from the other, which deprives the first one of freedom of will. Such a relationship may be destroyed by the efforts of one partner to break away from the spell of the other. Under these circumstances there is often great bitterness associated with a breakup.

Obviously the energy in this relationship is powerful. Unless you use this energy wisely, it could create great difficulties for both of you. Yet it is also a great opportunity to experience a relationship that can change your whole life.

Composite Pluto Sextile Composite Ascendant

The sextile of composite Pluto and Ascendant indicates that this relationship will cause you both to analyze yourselves in depth and to analyze the nature of your relationship. Taking very little for granted, you constantly seek ways to change and improve yourselves as individuals and as a couple. But the analysis that you undergo will not be a superficial intellectual exercise. It will go on in your hearts as well as your minds. And the changes that take place in both of you will affect all levels of your being.

This will not be a negative process. Elements of your personalities will pass away, but the transformation will be experienced as good and necessary, following naturally in the course of events. This is transformation through evolution rather than revolution. It will be very deep, very powerful, and very useful to both of you.

One consequence of this aspect is that your hopes for life will probably be altered. Your earlier goals were based on what you were then. Because this relationship changes you, it will change what you seek as well.

When the two of you talk, you discuss your serious concerns, not light subjects. Others may consider you excessively serious, but this is because you recognize the importance of what is happening in this relationship, and you do not want to waste time with trivia. And this is right, at least for the two of you. This relationship will bring about much growth in both your lives.

Composite Pluto Square Composite Ascendant

The square of composite Pluto and Ascendant indicates the danger of a serious ego conflict between the two of you at all levels of interaction. It is not merely that you are different from each other and have different aims. If that were the case, you could simply ignore each other. But unfortunately, you have an irresistible desire to interfere in each other's lives. One of you will attempt to dominate the other, or perhaps both of you will try to be the dominant one. The problem here is to learn to leave each other alone and let each other be.

If this contest between you continues, one of you will at length emerge as the loser, who can "win" only by breaking away. Then the fight for independence becomes another of the many struggles that mark this relationship. The energies become so fierce that when the two of you break up, all that is left is bitterness and mutual recrimination.

Fortunately, there is another side to this aspect, which you should strive to develop. It can also indicate that you transform each other inwardly and outwardly, but in a positive way. The key is to just let it happen. You cannot undertake this as a project; transformation of your partner cannot be an egoistic goal. While you may naturally be concerned for each other, you must not make an ego issue of your partner's development. You must just allow the process to unfold, as it surely will.

When Pluto's energies are used for selfish and egoistic purposes, they tend to become malevolent. Pluto must be allowed to remain a force of nature and not harnessed for purely personal motives.

Composite Pluto Trine Composite Ascendant

The trine of composite Pluto and Ascendant indicates a very intense but constructive relationship. Whatever feelings you have for each other you express strongly. Because you do not keep your problems bottled up, a lot of pressure is released that would damage the relationship if held in. If you are lovers, you express your love with depth and feeling, for this is not a light-hearted affair.

Your emotional involvement with each other is intense. Consequently, when things go wrong between you, the energies that are released are also very intense. You go to extremes in expressing yourselves, and you may be inclined to overdramatize. If you do, however, you will find that what ought to be rather trivial concerns get blown up out of all proportion.

The two of you experience love as a way of transcending the everyday world, which is the reason for your great intensity. To you, love is a life-or-death issue.

Whatever your reasons for being together, you will constantly examine the overall importance of this relationship. You will be very concerned to understand what it is all about and how it fits into your lives. But you will not be satisfied with an intellectual understanding alone. You will want to feel it and comprehend it with your body and soul. This aspect stimulates an interest in the mysteries of life, and you will see your relationship as one of those mysteries that must be comprehended.

Composite Pluto Opposition Composite Ascendant

The opposition of composite Pluto and Ascendant should be thought of as a conjunction of Pluto and the composite Descendant, which is a very important place in the composite chart.

Pluto on the composite Descendant can have very different effects, depending on how the relationship works as a whole. In any case, this will be a very intense relationship, whether it is good or bad. You will not take each other at all lightly. If you love each other, you will love passionately. If you hate each other, you will hate with just as much passion. But you may have difficulty in regarding each other with detachment.

At its worst, this aspect denotes an endless power struggle between the two of you, with neither one able to let the other be. You might spend all your time trying to dominate each other and at the same time avoid domination. Such a relationship can develop into a situation of unparalleled bitterness.

Sometimes the energy of Pluto will turn outward, in which case you will be caught in power struggles with others. Either they will not let you two be what you are, or you will not permit them to be what they are. Sometimes this aspect indicates that very powerful enemies are working against your relationship.

No matter whether you are trying to dominate other people or each other, the cause is the same. This relationship arouses energies in the two of you that will not allow matters to stay as they are. What you have to learn is that the changes you seek must come about through natural evolution, not through your urging. It is your own egoistic involvement that makes the energies of Pluto difficult. Even if you do not consciously work at it, the Pluto energies will operate, but they will work out better if your ego is not so heavily involved.

What you can have in this relationship, if you learn to let matters be, is a tremendously significant encounter that will revolutionize your lives and put you on a whole new path.

Chapter Fifteen

Moon's Nodes

*

The Meaning of the Moon's Nodes in the Composite Chart

The nodes of the Moon have long been a source of controversy among astrologers. A variety of delineations has been suggested, but there has been little agreement. In Western astrology, at least, the result of speculation about the nodes has been that the north node is vaguely "good," while the south node is vaguely "bad." Some astrologers have gone further and spoken of the nodes as relating to karmic patterns, but they have not been very clear about what that means.

But one man has been an exception to this trend. He is Alfred Witte of Germany, the founder of the Uranian (or Hamburg) school of astrology, whose work has been confirmed by Reinhold Ebertin and the Cosmobiologists. Their approach has been to minimize the distinctions between the north node and the south node, treating them together as an axis about which planetary patterns form. Collectively, the two nodes of the Moon rule unions, associations, coming together, groups, and connections. The nodes, therefore, have a great deal to do with relationships of all types. If this theory is correct, it is obviously important to the subject discussed in this book, and in my own experience it does seem to be the correct interpretation. But I would not say that this delineation for the nodes is true to the exclusion of all others, because nothing in it precludes other delineations. But it is certainly one of the most important ways of interpreting the meaning of the nodes and should be taken into consideration.

Personally, I feel that there is some distinction to be made between the north and the south nodes, but that this distinction becomes clear only when a planet is conjoined with one of the nodes and opposed to the other. Otherwise, the planet is equally involved with both nodes, and it is impossible to distinguish between them. However, if there is such a conjunction with one of the nodes, the north node seems to have more influence on forming unions, groups, and associations, while the south node has more influence on dissolving them.

Because the two nodes are always opposed to each other, the following are the only possible combinations with planets:

1. A planet may be conjunct the north or the south node. It is necessary to distinguish which node the planet is conjunct to.

2. A planet may be in a trine-sextile relationship with the two nodes. In this case it is immaterial which node the planet is trine or sextile to.

3. A planet may square the two nodes. Of course, to be square one node is to be square the other.

The following pages give delineations for these different combinations. Because the nodes are not planets, they are not energies in the same way that planets are. They are more like houses, in that they denote a place or circumstance in which a planetary energy manifests itself. Therefore the energies that are combined in the node aspects are fairly simple. As a consequence, the delineations for the nodes in this chapter are not quite as extended as the delineations for the planets. Also, the effects of the nodes in the houses are not very clear as yet, and anything said here would be quite hypothetical. Therefore, no delineations are given in this text for the house positions of the nodes, although that may be changed in a future edition of the text.

The aspects to the nodes of the Moon can be very significant because they have so much to do with the formation of relationships. However, they are not considered to be as strong as the planetary aspects, and in themselves they are not likely to make or break a relationship. They simply add more detail to a picture that has already been spelled out in broad outline by the planets in the houses and their aspects. The most important aspects involving the nodes are those in which a planet is conjunct the north node or south node. The trine-sextile and the square are significantly less intense.

Although this is not spelled out in all cases, it is always true that the energy of the node aspects can be felt either between the two persons involved or between them and the outside world. Some of the delineations stress effects that occur between two people, while others stress what happens between them and the outside world. But remember that it can usually go either way.

One more factor should be mentioned. In all the currently existing ephemerides, the position of the node is that of the *mean* node, that is, the node of the Moon as it would be if the Moon's orbit were not seriously perturbed by the gravitational attractions of the Sun and the Moon. However, in reality the orbit is perturbed, and the true or perturbed node may differ by as much as 1°45′ from the mean node. In approximate work this difference is not great enough to get concerned over, and in composite charts it is usually sufficiently close. However, in precise work involving directions and transits, I have found the true node to be more accurate than the mean node. The charts given in this book contain the true node, calculated by a computer from the elements of the Moon and corrected by a standard formula involving the positions of the Sun, Moon, and mean node relative to each other. The tables, which are very simple to use, requiring nothing more than addition and subtraction, are found in Carl W. Stahl's *Beginner's Manual of Sidereal Astrology, Book I,* as are the original formulas upon which the tables are based. There is nothing inherently "siderealist" about the true node of the Moon. It is simply that the siderealists were the first to become aware of the issue, through the work of Cyril Fagan, the great Irish astrologer and founder of the Western school of sidereal astrology.

Sun-Node Aspects

All Sun-node aspects indicate a relationship that brings about many important connections with other persons. In other words, relationships with others will be unusually important in maintaining the relationship between you.

Sun conjunct north node opposition south node. The two of you will have many significant encounters with others, particularly men of some social importance. These encounters will further your relationship and give it additional strength.

Sun trine-sextile the nodes. This aspect means very much the same as the north node conjunction, but it is not quite so strong an indication.

Sun square the nodes. This aspect raises the possibility that the two of you may have ego conflicts with others or that you may wish to withdraw from others, which could lead to difficulties in your own relationship. Any Sun-node contact means that other people are important to your relationship, so you should try to minimize the conflicts that do arise. Regardless of your intentions, your relationship will depend heavily on others.

Sun conjunct south node opposition north node. You may find that some prominent people, or possibly men in general, are opposed to the survival of this relationship. They will not necessarily be effective in breaking you up, however, unless the relationship is unstable in other ways.

Moon-Node Aspects

Moon-node aspects in general signify the importance of soul-unions and emotionally based unions, either between the two of you or outside your relationship. They may also indicate that women outside the relationship are very important to its survival.

Moon conjunct north node opposition south node. This aspect signifies that this is a union based on feelings and that you both share a strong sense of soul-union. Also you may have strong emotional bonds with other people, particularly women, who in turn reinforce this relationship.

Moon trine-sextile the nodes. This aspect has very much the same meaning as the above, but it is not quite so strong in its effects.

Moon square the nodes. This aspect also indicates a very strong emotional union. However, here there is a strong danger that your extreme subjectivity will make it difficult to clearly understand this relationship. It may signify that you relate to each other almost entirely through your emotions, but not very harmoniously.

Moon conjunct south node opposition north node. Much like the square, this aspect signifies that emotional discord will tend to divide the two of you. It is also possible that women will work against this relationship, but if it is otherwise sound, this should not be a great problem.

Mercury-Node Aspects

These aspects generally signify that mental and intellectual affinity between you is very important in establishing this relationship. Although communication is always important in a relationship, it is unusually so with these aspects. Relationships with others will also be strongly influenced by intellectual considerations. If we say that the Moon-node aspects signify soul-unions, then the Mercury-node aspects signify mental and intellectual unions.

Mercury conjunct north node opposition south node. The need for communication and shared intellectual experiences is very great in this relationship. Mental affinity may have been a decisive factor in bringing you together. You will also have an unusual number of intellectual associations with people outside the relationship.

Mercury trine-sextile the nodes. This aspect means very much the same as the above but is less strong in its effects.

Mercury square the nodes. This aspect also signifies the need for intellectual and mental affinity between you. But it also indicates that lack of agreement may cause some problems in this relationship.

Mercury conjunct south node opposition north node. With this aspect, it is necessary to work on communicating very clearly with each other. Otherwise, remarks that slip out unconsciously could make your relationship difficult.

Venus-Node Aspects

All these aspects signify a love union, and none is especially difficult. Friendships with this aspect will be very loving even though not sexually based.

Venus conjunct north node opposition south node. This is a very strong indication of a love union or deep friendship. The two of you have a strong sense that you complement each other in a very positive way, and you seek to build up that quality to make your relationship work even better.

Venus trine-sextile the nodes. This is very much like the north node conjunction but not quite so strong in its effects.

Venus square the nodes. This is not a difficult square. It simply means that similar past experiences or future life plans give you a feeling of affinity and are a strong bond between you. Often you do not consciously understand what these elements contribute to your relationship.

Venus conjunct south node opposition north node. The forces that have brought you together are mostly unconscious, but that is not likely to lessen the benefits of the Venus-node combination. This is still a positive aspect.

Mars-Node Aspects

These aspects signify that the two of you should make a common effort toward a goal. The key phrase here is "work-union." A Mars-node aspect can also indicate a relationship in which ego forces are unusually disruptive, either between yourselves or between the two of you and others.

Mars conjunct north node opposition south node. This aspect is the strongest indication of a work relationship as described above. Its significance is not limited to professional relationships, but in a personal relationship with this aspect, the two of you should work together for some very concerete goal. Sharing tasks will bind you together.

Mars trine-sextile the nodes. This aspect has very much the same meaning but is less compelling in its effects. The two of you are able to work well together, but it is less necessary that you do so.

Mars square the nodes. It is very important that the two of you make a special effort to work together. If you do not do so, you will be likely to quarrel because of certain discordances between you that have to be worked out consciously.

Mars conjunct south node opposition north node. Of all the Mars-node aspects this one is most likely to create discord, because the two of you do not clearly understand how your egos interact. You must try to consciously understand what is happening between you in order to minimize the divisive effects of this aspect. Also be careful not to stir up opposition from others, for this could be detrimental to your relationship.

Jupiter-Node Aspects

These aspects are usually quite beneficial, indicating a pleasant and positive relationship that enables both of you to grow through the experience of knowing each other. Negative effects of certain of these aspects are noted where relevant.

Jupiter conjunct north node opposition south node. This aspect indicates that the feelings between you are very positive and that your relations with others are also good. You help each other, you help other people, and they help you. The two of you are very happy together, and you have a strong feeling of friendship, whether you are lovers, friends, or involved in any other way.

Jupiter trine-sextile the nodes. This aspect has much the same significance as the above, but it is not quite so strong in its effects.

Jupiter square the nodes. Usually this aspect works quite positively.

However, if there are other indications of strong ego conflict between you, it can mean that one of you will try to dominate the other or adopt an attitude of superiority.

Jupiter conjunct south node opposition north node. The effects of this aspect are like those of the square. In addition, there is a danger that you will also have ego conflicts with persons outside your relationship. If the relationship is otherwise sound, however, this aspect as well as the square will have positive rather than negative results.

Saturn-Node Aspects

Most of these aspects are rather difficult to deal with. Saturn emphasizes the principle of separation, which is already inherent in the meaning of the south node. Therefore, most of these aspects are separative in nature.

Saturn conjunct north node opposition south node. This is an extremely separative aspect. In addition, it can create a situation in which one of you tries to control the direction of the relationship instead of simply letting it take its own course. This effort to control can make the other partner feel smothered and consequently try to break free, resulting in separation.

Saturn trine-sextile the nodes. This is the least difficult of these aspects. It can stabilize the relationship and make its course more predictable. But this result is at the cost of spontaneous self-expression. Even at its best, this aspect signifies that the two of you are too concerned about keeping your relationship under control and being careful with each other.

Saturn square the nodes. The square is very similar in its effects to the conjunctions with the north and south nodes. Ego conflicts may prove to be divisive.

Saturn conjunct south node opposition north node. The effects of this are much like those of the north node conjunction. However, since the south node is the point of separation, this aspect is somewhat more divisive.

Uranus-Node Aspects

These aspects usually indicate sudden unions or relationships that are unusual, peculiar, erratic in their course, or otherwise exceptional. A relationship with this aspect may come about very suddenly and then disappear just as quickly. It is difficult to settle into any kind of routine in such a relationship.

Uranus conjunct north node opposition south node. This aspect indicates a relationship that may have a very jarring or unsettling effect upon the two of you. The relationship itself may be a radical departure from past experiences or it may be a totally unexpected occurrence. Often it is this very quality of unusualness that has brought you together in the first place. Both of you sense an excitement that has been missing in past relationships, so you enter into this one for the novelty of it and the changes it can bring about in your lives.

Uranus trine-sextile the nodes. This is the easiest of these aspects to contend with, but even so it does imply that you both want a lot of excitement from this relationship. You are willing to let it take its own course and express itself as it will.

Uranus square the nodes. This aspect can be very disruptive. Its effects are similar to those of the north node conjunction, but it is even more likely to produce an unstable relationship with many ups and downs. It can also signify that you find it difficult to coordinate your lives and work toward the same objectives.

Uranus conjunct south node opposition north node. The effects of this aspect are very similar to those of the north node conjunction, but it is even more likely to be disruptive. When the initial excitement of the relationship wears off, you will find it difficult to deal with each other. Consequently you may create conflicts just to keep feelings stirred up between you and to keep from being bored.

Neptune-Node Aspects

The nature of these aspects is particularly ambiguous (just as Neptune is in most aspects with other points in the chart). They can signify an intensely spiritual union, a union based completely on illusion, or various combinations of the two extremes. Disillusionment is a very serious danger of these aspects, and it can cause you to withdraw from each other psychologically without actually breaking off the relationship.

Neptune conjunct north node opposition south node. This aspect can bring about any of the ambiguous situations described above. Be extremely careful to sort out the facts from the illusions in this relationship, and do not make any permanent commitment until you are sure of the facts based on long experience with each other.

Neptune trine-sextile the nodes. This is the most easily handled of the

Neptune-node aspects, but even here you must avoid overidealizing each other. You must learn to deal with and accept each other as real people.

Neptune square the nodes. This aspect is bound to create quite a bit of confusion in a relationship. It makes your objectives very unclear, so that much of the time you do not know quite what you are doing. It also introduces unconscious actions into the relationship so that you will act unconstructively toward each other without understanding why you do.

Neptune conjunct south node opposition north node. The effects of this aspect are very similar to those of the north node conjunction, but it is possibly a bit more severe. You must try to detach yourselves and be very realistic in dealing with each other.

Pluto-Node Aspects

These aspects indicate a very heavy sense of power in a relationship, power that can transform and transfigure your lives. At their best, these aspects can reform and rejuvenate you, leaving you in a very different place from where you started out. On the other hand, they can represent a relationship in which one of you dominates the other destructively.

Pluto conjunct north node opposition south node. This aspect exemplifies most strongly the energies described above. In an otherwise healthy relationship, the effects of this aspect are likely to be quite positive. But they will be negative in a relationship that is not so well favored.

Pluto trine-sextile the nodes. This aspect has a milder effect than the north node conjunction. It designates a relationship that will transform you both, but you are less likely to encounter the negative domination pattern described above.

Pluto square the nodes. The energies described in the introductory paragraph are present with this aspect, but the harsher effects are quite strong. It indicates that your aims in life differ, which is a source of conflict, because both of you try to force your objectives upon each other.

Pluto conjunct south node opposition north node. The struggle to dominate each other in various ways is strongest with this aspect. Your manipulative efforts are likely to be very destructive and can only lead to the breakup of the relationship. So you must learn to be more tolerant of each other. In any case, this relationship will have a strong effect on both of you. Be careful of people outside the relationship who may try to manipulate you.

Ascendant-Node Aspects

Certain comments can be made about all these aspects in general, for their effects do not differ from each other very much. They all denote an unusually strong interaction between the two of you and your surroundings. Connections with others are very important to both of you. At their best, these aspects signify gregarious behavior; at worst, an inability to be independent and on your own.

Of these aspects, the trine-sextile is the weakest in its effects. The square is not particularly difficult, and there is virtually no difference between the north node conjunction and the south node conjunction. That is because like the nodes, the Ascendant is also a two-ended axis, consisting of Ascendant and Descendant.

Index

Planets in Aspect:
Understanding Your
Inner Dynamics
Robert Pelletier.
Explores aspects–the
planetary relationships that
describe our individual
energy patterns–and shows
how we can integrate them
into our lives. Every major
aspect is covered.
Size: 6 1/2" x 9 1/4"
363 pp.   paperbound
ISBN: 0-914918-20-6
$19.95

Planets in Youth:
Patterns of Early
Development
Robert Hand
A major astrological
thinker looks at children
and childhood. All
important horoscope
factors are delineated.
Size: 6 1/2" x 9 1/4"
paperbound 372 pp.
ISBN: 0-914918-26-5
$24.95

**Planets in Houses:
Experiencing Your
Environment**
Robert Pelletier.
Delineates the meaning of
each planet according to its
house position. Also interpreted is the relationship of
the occupied house to the
other houses.
Size: 6 1/2" x 9 1/4"
paperbound   372 pp.
ISBN: 0-914918-27-3
$19.95

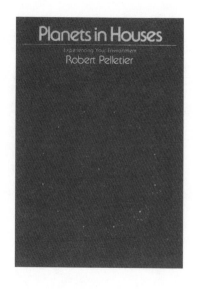

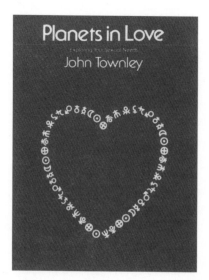

**Planets in Love:
Exploring Your Emo-
tional
and Sexual Needs**
John Townley.
An intimate astrological
analysis of sex and love,
with 550 interpretations of
each planet in every sign,
house, and major aspect.
Size: 6 1/2" x 9 1/4"
372 pp.   paperbound
ISBN: 0-914918-21-4
$19.95

Planets in Signs
Skye Alexander.
The complete picture of the Sun,
the Moon and planets through
the twelve signs of the zodiac.
Includes elements and modali-
ties, and the meaning of dominance or weakness of one of
these important energies. Examples of famous people are included for illustration. A complete and in-depth study of the
planets operation through the
astrological signs.
Size: 6 1/2" x 9 1/4"
paperbound   272 pp.
ISBN: 0-914918-79-6
$18.95

Planets in Transit:
Life Cycles for Living
Robert Hand.
Delineations of the Sun, Moon,
and each planet transiting each
natal house and forming each
aspect to the natal Sun, Moon,
planets, Ascendant, and
Midheaven.
Size: 6 1/2" x 9 1/4"
532 pp.   paperbound
ISBN: 0-914918-24-9
$24.95

Other Books from the Whitford Astrological Library

Planets in Synastry: Astrological Patterns of Relationships. E.W. Neville. Synastry examines the interaction of two astrological charts, answering relationship questions often asked of the astrologer. The art of synastry is a basic skill needed to practice astrology at any but the most casual level. (paperbound)
Size: 6 1/4" x 9 1/4"   276 pp.
ISBN: 0-924608-01-3 $16.95

Astrology Inside Out
Bruce Nevin.
This original rethinking of astrology uses visualization and meditation exercises to help beginners and experienced astrologers strengthen their intuitive grasp of astrological patterning.
Size: 6 1/2" x 9 1/4"
300 pp.   paperbound
ISBN: 0-914918-19-2
$18.95

Astrology, Nutrition and Health Robert Carl Jansky.
Demonstrates in non-technical language how astrology can help the reader understand the components of metabolism and health.
Size: 6 1/2" x 9 1/4"
180 pp.   paperbound
ISBN: 0-914918-08-7
$14.95

Astrology & Past Lives
Mary Devlin.
This unique and original book is the first to examine birth charts for previous incarnations. Devlin shows you how to interpret past-life charts and compare them to your present one.
Size: 6 1/2" x 9 1/4"
287 pp.   paperbound
ISBN: 0-914918-71-0
$ 19.95

Astrology & Relationships
Mary Devlin.
More people consult astrologers about relationship problems than any other single issue. The author of *Astrology & Past Lives* helps you understand your relationships from a variety of astrological perspectives. First, she considers the relationship needs of the individual, as revealed by the natal chart. Next, she analyzes parent/child relationships–where it all begins. Finally, she examines love, romance, sex, marriage, and friendship in depth. Devlin includes synastry delineations, case histories, and past-life interpretations in this thorough study of interpersonal relationships.
Size: 6 1/2" x 9 1/4"
288 pp.   paperbound
ISBN: 0-914918-77-X
$19.95

Birth Pattern Psychology
Tamise Van Pelt.
Utilizing a synthesis of major personality theories, Van Pelt establishes a context in which to understand human communication and behavior. Illustrated.
Size: 6 1/2" x 9 1/4"
351 pp.   paperbound
ISBN: 0-914918-33-8
$14.95

Compendium of Astrology
Rose Lineman and Jan Popelka.
The *Compendium* contains the basic information needed to build a horoscope. A detailed reference text for practicing astrologers and students.
Size: 8" x 9 1/4"
304 pp.   paperbound
ISBN: 0-914918-43-5
$24.95

Essays on Astrology
Robert Hand.
Essays on Astrology is an invaluable reference book. Provides fresh insight into the latest thinking of this very significant astrologer.
Size: 6 1/2" x 9 1/4"
176 pp.   paperbound
ISBN: 0-914918-42-7
$19.95

Essential Dignities
J. Lee Lehman, Ph.D.
In this exciting new book, Dr. Lehman recovers an important ancient aspect of astrology which has become misunderstood and diluted: rulerships. By attempting to simplify astrology, contemporary sources have completely obscured the essential differences between planet, sign, and house. While the novice may benefit from this simplification, much of the old logic of the rulership system is covered up. What was nearly lost is given new power and the potential for understanding. A wealth of information is presented in a clear and concise way with many accurate charts.
Size: 6 1/4" x 9 1/4"
256 pp.   paperbound
ISBN: 0-924608-03-X
$14.95

Horary Astrology Rediscovered
Olivia Barclay.
Exploring a branch of astrology that is concerned with answering questions pertaining to life and life events. Ms. Barclay's book is a captivating and beautifully written survey of horary astrology and its relationship with other forms of the science. More than 25 charts and graphs illustrate planetary rulerships, planetary movements, fortitudes and debilities of planets, and answers to questions. *A* fascinating look at this little-studied branch of astrology.
Size: 6 1/4" x 9 1/4"
340 pp.   paperbound
ISBN:0-914918-99-0
$24.95

Horoscope Symbols
Robert Hand.
Explains the basics with insight, wisdom and perspective. Explores midpoints, harmonics, retrograde planets and more. (Whitford)
Size: 6 1/2"x 9 1/4"
385 pp.   paperbound
ISBN: 0-914918-16-8
$24.95

A Look at Tomorrow Today
Leonard Cataldo and Robert Pelletier.
In this compelling and fascinating study readers are invited to find and utilize the vast riches within.   They will discover that they are constituents of one of the twelve zodiacal signs, what that means, and how it influences his life and behavior.
Size: 6 1/4" x 9 1/4"
500 pp.   paperbound
ISBN:0-914918-94-X
$18.95

Marriage Made in Heaven:
An Astrological Guide to Relationships
Alexandra Mark, Ph.D.
Beginning with the construction of a solar chart and birth time chart, this concise, easy-to-read, book takes the reader through the complexities of love and marriage. For the novice astrologer or the experienced, Dr. Mark brings new insight and understanding to how our relationships are influenced by the heavens.
Size: 6" x 9"
256 pages   paperbound
ISBN: 0-914918-90-7 $14.95

Our Stars of Destiny
Faith Javane.
This study focuses on one specific advance in Esoteric Astrology--the introduction and study of the Pentacle (Star of Destiny) and the Pentacle Aspects of the Horoscope. These tools, both old and new, will aid the reader through the symbols they reveal in the Quest for Higher Consciousness.
Size: 6" x 9"
256 pages   paperbound
ISBN: 0-9149189-92-3
$14.95

Quintiles and Tredeciles
Dusty Bunker.
Explores the little-known 72-degree and 108-degree aspects and explains their cosmic significance in the individual chart. The numerological and astrological relevance of quintiles and tredeciles unfolds in four chapters and a wealth of diagrams and charts. Historical details on the meanings of numbers--taken from numerology; sacred geometry; masonic, religious, and Egyptian symbology; and astrology--transport the reader to times when numbers were an "extreme reduction of philosophic thought."

Size 6 1/4" x 9 1/4"
182 pp.   paperbound
ISBN: 0-914918-69-6
$12.95

The Ultimate Asteroid Book
J. Lee Lehman, Ph.D.
The most complete book to date on asteroids. More than seventy of these fascinating heavenly bodies are covered in this book by one of the world's foremost authorities on asteroids. Lehman groups the asteroids according to their areas of influence--business, power, intellect, sex, escapism, and more--and shows you how to interpret their positions to fine-tune your understanding of the birth chart. Lehman also looks at the asteroids from a mythological and historical perspective.
Size: 6 1/4" x 9 1/4"
352 pp.   paperbound
ISBN: 0-914918-78-8
$18.95

World Ephemeris: 20th Century, Midnight Edition.
World Ephemeris: 20th Century, Noon Edition
The *World Ephemeris for the 20th Century* by Para Research is the first computer-calculated and computer-typeset ephemeris with letter quality printing. Sun's position accurate to one second of arc; planetary positions given to one minute of arc. Please specify edition desired.
Size: 8" x 9 1/4"
524 pp.   paperbound
ISBN: 0-914918-60-5 (Midnight edition)
$29.95
ISBN: 0-914918-61-3 (Noon edition)
$29.95